A Shadow on Summer

Born in 1932, the son of a Dublin bricklayer, Christy Brown was the victim of the athenoid variety of cerebral palsy. With the help of his family and Dr Robert Collis, he overcame his physical disability and won immediate fame with his best-selling novel about life in Dublin, *Down All The Days*. He was also the author of a second novel *A Shadow on Summer* and two volumes of poems, *Come Softly To My Wake* and *Background Music*. He died in 1981.

CHRISTY BROWN

A Shadow on Summer

Minerva

A Minerva Paperback
A SHADOW ON SUMMER

First published in Great Britain 1974
by Martin Secker & Warburg Ltd
This Minerva edition published 1990
by Mandarin Paperbacks
Michelin House, 81 Fulham Road, London SW3 6RB

Minerva is an imprint of the Octopus Publishing Group

Copyright © Christy Brown 1974

A CIP catalogue record for this title
is available from the British Library
ISBN 0 7493 9181 2

Printed and bound in Great Britain
by Cox and Wyman Ltd, Reading, Berks

For Mab
deliverer of all my dreams
taking me ever towards morning

I

Eyes for once closed upon his new world, he lay unquietly toasting in the sand, in his thin flannel trousers and gossamer-thin vest, testimony to his still dominant feelings of self-exposure, toasting himself unmercifully in the broad bewildered noon, his rather anaemic, traditionally indoor skin almost crinkling in the heat which seemed to bounce off the sand and quiver, hovering almost visibly, in the air. He lay in a sort of expectant ecstatic stillness, as if clutched in the talons of some marvellous malevolent monster, a little bit terrified, a little bit elated at the thought that he might be devoured, eaten up, annihilated, while he did nothing, absolutely nothing, to stop it, to survive, to resist. The thought thrilled him; he flung himself at the image that he was slowly and wilfully burning himself to death while the waves gave their soft faraway cry and the gulls wrote asterisks down the brilliant air and the happy sound of children filled the earth.

His eyelids felt heavy, moist, glued. He was all one consuming savage burning glorious ache, his body a crooked song desperately wanting, demanding to be heard, harpooned to the sand beneath him, a thin white flame wilting, vanishing, burning within a larger merciless flame, until soon he imagined there would only remain a small frail heap of ashes where he had lain.

He forced himself against his will to open his eyes. He had to escape momentarily from that inner little cosmos threatening to engulf him once more. The sky stretched above him, eternity reflected, a broad painted blue canopy of endless dimensions. A few fragile clouds sailed like tiny galleons in that sea. Against the sun-dimmed horizon the varicoloured sails of boats bobbed languidly up and down, some trailing intricate wakes behind them like so many white shining snakes tracing their separate destinies. A few feet away a rather obese man was snoring like some oncoming ever-distant train, face obscured under a newspaper, pudgy fingers entwined upon an Everest of a belly, knuckly hairy legs spread wide, and beside him his obvious little ferret of a wife, knitting endlessly, a mountain of pillows behind her, anonymous behind enormous dark sunglasses, clucking to herself from time to time like a grossly self-satisfied broody hen, thin spidery limbs seducing the sun unabashed. And children, always the children, glorifying the day, making a hymn of it, splashing in the lisping surf, taking the great harm out of the world, laughing as only children can in the rare ecstasy of that time, making sandcastles, destroying them, building new ones, racing joyously to meet the ceaseless wave, crying in their freedom, squaring up to each other, causing sweet chaos in the sand, their very rowdiness lending an odd peace to the day, water glistening down their small articulate limbs, happy and victorious, playing with life and sure of winning.

He closed his eyes against the burning day, listening to the soft lisp of the sea, an ever-present background music filling the whole land and sky, advancing, receding, rising, falling, a slow imperturbable rhythm, harpstrings gently strung, gently stroked, passing like peaceful shadows over his mind, gentle ghosts of sounds pleasing him, light wisps of soft air passing over him, tender and sensuous as the fingers of a lover, intimate to the point of pain, yet scarcely touching, infinitely untouchable. He felt himself sink into the sand, deeper, ever deeper, felt the sand closing in upon him, upon his mind, upon his now languid limbs, like veils of heavy burning satin, entombing him, shutting out all other intrusions, until even these faint and febrile tinklings of the world around him grew still, and his thoughts grew still as shadows in the depths of a cool Sunday stream.

Yet there remained always the dark implacable hawk of foreboding: how would tomorrow go, what would it bring, how would it change the map of his life?

The children were building sandcastles, and he lay in the sun trembling at tomorrow, at the uncharted geography of the future, bemused and bewildered by all that had brought him to this beach, in this beautiful improbable present, against all odds, wildly out of the context of all that had gone before in his life. Could a book and a friendly letter have brought it all about? He remembered now snatches of conversation, the expression of expectancy on his friend's face.

'You must go, Riley,' said Martin, quite earnestly, in that slow intense way of his, gripping his glass of gin and tonic with equal earnestness in those rather Chopinesque fingers that seemed to have been exclusively created to play magical rhythms upon the ribs of some delectable woman rather than work on an ordinary typewriter. 'God knows it won't be easy, the physical side of things, your bloody handicap, braces and all—stop grinning like an idiot—I'm deadly serious—'

'A feather in your cap?' said Riley rather sourly, wishing almost instantly he had not said it.

Martin smiled a magnanimous smile. 'Yes, if you like—an extra large feather in my cap.' He drank swiftly, impatiently, as if the act were an interruption in itself. 'Don't be so bloody coy. I'll be there, I'll come with you. It isn't every day Jay Simon invites one of his authors over as his guest. He's hard as nails—charming of course, but hard as nails. He'd sell his grandmother if he thought she'd make a good price—'

'Yes,' said Riley gloomily, glancing rather wearily at the handsome legs of the passing waitress, hunched in his chair, not as yet quite ready to tackle his severely watered-down whiskey. 'Yes. And I'm not his grandmother.'

Martin grinned in a suddenly boyish way which blended rather charmingly with the silver gloss of his hair and his over-fiftyish countenance prematurely crevassed by half a lifetime of snap decision-making and laborious self-questioning in the meticulous pursuit of his trade. 'Exactly. Neither are you his godchild. You are your own man, Riley, and you always will be. But you can't become famous and hope to remain anonymous. This book of yours has taken the world—'

'Balls,' said Riley quietly, at last tasting his whiskey.

Martin grinned more broadly, delightedly. 'Exactly. Your book has taken the world by its balls. Riley McCombe is no longer another anonymous cripple doomed to go through life wearing bloody braces. The world wants to know Riley McCombe, all about him, his life, his family, what made him

3

what he is, what made him write that book. You're no longer private property shut up in a room sweating your balls out over an antiquated typewriter and struggling to go to the pisshouse in the middle of the night without disturbing the rest of the household. You are a writer now—'

'Jesus,' said Riley.

'A writer about to become a greater one,' insisted Martin with the same unswerving and absolute air of conviction. 'Think what you like of me, but I'm a damned good editor, and think what you like of Jay Simon—he's a damned shrewd publisher. And you'll be with my best friends—Laurie and Don Emerson are among the best people I know—they've read your book and want to have you as their guest while you're there, so all the usual horror of hotel existence is cancelled—'

'But I don't know these people,' said Riley, in a mood for argument. 'They're just names to me—Jay Simon's probably a big fat oily-faced self-made man occupying a glass building somewhere in Manhattan who puts olives in his gin, and the Emersons are no doubt tremendously respectable middle-class Americans with two cars in the garage and a couple of well-scrubbed blonde kids who would deafen me with their hi-fis and their knowledge of the world. Maybe,' he added glumly, 'maybe a hotel would be best after all. They cater for all kinds in hotels.'

Martin sighed patiently. 'God, you're difficult,' he said. 'And I suspect deliberately dense. Jay's not so bad. A smooth dealer, but charming. You'll like him, despite the olives— which incidentally he doesn't take. And as for Laurie and Don—they're good people, kind people, ordinary, decent, thoughtful, who had to work hard to have the two cars in the garage and plan a reasonable kind of future for their kids. I've known them for years, Riley. They want you as their guest. It's no act of charity. If you like you can stay the whole summer. You could finish this second book there. Laurie's a good critic—she could help you a lot—'

Riley took a good swipe at his whiskey and inwardly groaned.

Martin sensed his alarm and smiled. 'No, it won't be like that, I assure you,' said Martin. 'It won't be like that at all.'

Martin beckoned the waitress with his finger . . .

4

The surf came back, the ship-laden sky at noon, the sand. There was only silence now, loud as a thunderclap in his breast, deep as the blood running through his veins, singing along the canals of his body, holding no menace of memory, no midnight awakening of fear, no dream, no desire. If he had any conscious thoughts at all it was to wonder vaguely and rather wistfully if he were dead, if this indeed were death, stretched upon this strand at this rather improbable hour of his life. Yet it was no more a thought than a sigh is a spoken utterance, and did not intrude or trouble him at all except in the remotest peninsulas of his senses, far from the hard comprehension of it all. Nothing had power to trouble him now, because he was now faceless, without identity except that which he hugged zealously to himself, a grain of sand buried under an ocean of sand. He was invulnerable now because he was nothing, infinitely less and immensely more than nothing, precisely because he did not know even that . . .

All over again the insidious invasion began, he felt the heat going out of the day, felt with all too familiar dread the day turning cruelly bright, terrifying, dark and blind. Like rats scampering in the dark his thoughts ran riot, encroaching upon him, torturing him, over-running the brittle barricades he had laboriously erected between himself, in this new time torn from time, in this new place beyond the grey discerning sea, and torn and scattered remnants of that other world from which he had separated.

A world at once proud and pitiful, reckless and weak and wilfully strong, a world of mad demented dreams and strange wonderful realities in which he drew breath and had his unique being, yet a world he had come now, if briefly, to look upon almost with the eyes of some surprised and saddened stranger, with the cool deceptive vision of distance, regarding it as something odd, curious, painful, tender, almost as something alien to him, not of his blood, a charade, a circus of deadly intent. Yet the invidious invasion began again, haunting him all again, taunting him, never letting go, a dark hand shutting out the sun, a slowly advancing army of relentless ghosts pursuing him across time, space, water.

Creatures half of his own making, belonging to that loud-hearted narrow islanded world he had fled from for this brief

5

heartbeat of time, denizens equally of his love and his despair, thronging through his mind now, each face blazing under its separate banner, things real and imagined, real beyond all imagining, more violently imagined beyond the bruised stuff of any reality. Faces like distorted stars above him, seen through a cloud, reproachful, vexed, laughing, regretful, sad, mad, mocking, tender, faces and voices he knew as well as the functions of his own body, faces and voices he loved and feared, feared out of love and half-loved out of fear with tender frightening intimacy. Hands reached out to him, timeless in their gestures, kind, threatening, taunting, tantalising, tortuously inadequate and inarticulate, touching him out of love, sorrow, rage. Ghosts long lived with, as real as a slap across the cheek, of his own mould, flesh, brain, spirit, remote from him as the stars, remote from all he imagined himself as being, yet closer and as dear and dreadful to him as the green and painful earth that opened up its pores to him season by season, after rain and after sunshine, clinging to him remorselessly as the sweat and smell of his own body.

The sun struck across him cruelly, a burning whip stinging his flesh, and he could no longer even flirt with the fantasy of death. He was still all an ache, but the pain throbbed in his mind now, no longer sweet, no longer pleasurable, no longer remotely splendid, but dark and swarming, vinegar in his desert, salt in his unclosed wounds, biting viciously into the very marrow of him. Too soon he had came back to the things he had foolishly imagined he had left behind him on the far side of the world; there was no escape from that knowledge.

'Riley,' said the voice.

A whisper, a soft unhurried sound falling as a leaf into the dark clamour of his mind, so near it seemed almost to come from inside his skin.

'Riley.'

Once more it came, more anxiously, more concerned, dropping softly; still he did not open his eyes. He lay alert, back from the dead, savouring the sound of her voice, hearing it hum like music along his veins; slowly the terrible tenseness that had gripped and held him locked in a rigid stark coil of muscle and sinew left him, like steam evaporating. The shrill high-tension humming ceased inside him, a fine gradual

6

lassitude pervaded him, a slow pulse of peace ran through him, deep, luxuriant, mobile, delicate, poised on a feather-edge, refined to a tremulous ascension of sense and sensation. He opened his eyes to the sun, to the broad beneficent day above him, to the face he was to know with such pain and beauty all the days of his life.

'Relax,' she said, very gently, stretched beside him in the sand, her green swimsuit glistening with water, swim-cap neat and tight upon her head. 'You were away again. You're always going away and leaving me. It isn't very polite, sir!'

And then, after a pause: 'It was the book, wasn't it?' she said into the silence that had grown between them. 'The book and the fear of tomorrow. It was that, wasn't it, Riley?'

The wail of the gulls sounded nearer now, clearer, careering high in the air, out over the sea, the melancholy surf breaking upon the defiant shore, whirling and swirling in a strange languid aerial ballet, swooping low from time to time as if to pluck sustenance from the great universe beneath them, black asterisks against the sky. He heard the sea plainly now, lullabying him, speaking gently to his mind; the waves rolled slowly in, friendly creatures, splashing with slow rhythm upon the toothy offshore rocks. And the children thrashed in the surf amid shouts and hoots and loud hurrahs, calling out to each other, yelling, splashing, chasing each other, diving, ducking, laughing, drenched and happy, running, leaping, romping uproariously, leaving trails of small wet footprints in the sand, out-jumping one another for the sun.

Everything now had the clarity of broken glass; he saw, heard, felt and tasted everything with instant, intent awareness, the tiniest granule of sand, the criss-cross embroidery of its very texture. Small puffs of cloud drifted up lazily from the fragile horizon, sailing dreamily across the limitless sky. Sails dipped and bobbed in the distance, tiny many-coloured triangles, a thin spidery tracery of masts and rigging breaking the skyline. He felt a movement. She knelt beside him in the sand, staring at him with that single-minded intentness that thrilled even as it frightened him a little, so utterly oblivious it seemed to make her to everything outside of him, her face at once grave and remote, alive and restless with an agility and intelligence that gave lithe vibrant meaning to her most ordinary words and gestures.

It was a neat face, small, fine-boned, high-cheeked, mobile, alert, yet reposed, pensive, lit at all times by the quick black-green brilliance of the eyes: eyes that seemed to take in and absorb everything at once, and yet concentrate utterly upon a single object or person to the total exclusion of everything else, as if that object or person or moment were all that mattered or existed for her at that point and encounter in time. And her eyes would find him out in some unwary, unprepared moment, sending his thoughts swirling in disarray, like a flock of birds that something had alarmed and sent flying in all directions. Often he imagined he felt the gentle humour, the gentle mockery almost, of her eyes upon him, as if she were trying to puzzle him out, as if daring him to come out into the open where she could really see him, as if by use and means of her eyes alone she could slip inside his skin and know all there was to be known and understood about him. He did not consciously withdraw or hold back from her; he could not, if he tried with all his might, yet he was afraid, afraid of all the open and un-charted spaces where her concern might wound him, so unsure was he of all that he was now feeling, knowing, going through, as if unwilling to emerge and encounter all that might live behind her slow smile, behind the shadow of her eyes. He felt rather like a prisoner, reluctant and more than a little afraid to leave his cell because it was the one place in the world he could claim really to know, because it was his world where he hoarded zealously to himself his own small knowledge of himself. Yet if indeed she mocked him it was with the gentle sureness born of absolute concern and conviction in him as a person, in her faith and awareness of him standing alone in his own truth, though he might lie down in darkness.

'It was the book, wasn't it?' said Laurie, kneeling between him and the sun. 'The book, and tomorrow. Wasn't it, Riley?'

'Yes,' he said. 'Yes, it was.'

'Are you afraid, Riley?'

'My God, yes.'

'I knew you would be,' she said, settling once more into the sand beside him, stretching out, closing her eyes. 'But you had to write as you did,' she said, crossing one arm idly across her

8

midriff, drawing one knee up slightly, spreading her toes in the sand. 'You can't afford to regret it now. And you do regret it a little, don't you?'

'I'm sorry I had to write it,' he said.

'There was no other way,' said Laurie. 'It sounds a tremendous cliché, I know, but you were writing about life—'

'Ah, yes,' he said, throwing back his head and looking at the sky, watching the gulls circling and interlacing against the intense blue.

'You must never be afraid to write about life,' Laurie said. 'You must never be afraid of that.'

'I won't,' he lied, knowing he would never be more afraid of anything else.

'It took courage to write as you did,' she said.

He saw the little hollow at the base of her throat, the clean line of her jaw, the sleek sheen of her hair rising from her temples. Her words unnerved him; he felt uneasy, almost angry. He did not know about courage, he did not feel very brave or daring or reckless, he did not know about such things. He had not crossed sky and ocean to be told he was brave because he had written what he had to write, say what he had to say, because it had all been there inside him, waiting to get out some day, somehow. Some people were like volcanoes: they might remain silent, dormant, unstirring for years, almost as if they had died but were somehow continuing to pretend and to delude themselves and everyone else that they were alive by some trick of fantasy or miracle. And then one day they blew up, they exploded, erupted, burst and roared into raw violent life, spewing forth all the rage, wonder, love and lust that had lain unvoiced and unsuspected in them all the time. It frightened him to think that he might be like that. Volcanoes on erupting destroyed all in their path; he did not want to destroy, he had witnessed too much of that, he had seen too many things destroyed, too many lives twisted and broken simply because they happened to lie in the path of sudden mindless violence that came pouring out of people who were themselves trapped and baited by this violence, lost and helpless in its grip, breaking and bruising others along with themselves, violence all the more frightening because it did not have a voice, taking hold of people by the throat,

9

shaking them like animals, breaking them like sticks of straw. Now he had captured that violence, had cornered it and given it a voice and made it articulate; but the raw core of it was still there, tumbling below the flashing and facile words, shaking and thrashing inside him. And he was afraid; afraid of what he might have triggered off and set free inside himself. He was afraid, and he wanted her to know it.

He realised she was watching him intently, and had been for some time, and though she was smiling her eyes were deep, dark and still.

'I know,' she said, very quietly, as if every thought he had been thinking and feeling were mirrored in turn for her in his eyes. 'You will hurt many people with this book, people you would not want to hurt for all the world. We hate hurting others. That's the sane rational loving side of human beings. But we do it just the same—we hurt others, every moment we draw breath, sometimes on purpose, which is hateful, and sometimes because it cannot be helped, which is sad but only less tragic. It hurts like hell, just the same,' said Laurie, 'but perhaps the one who gets hurt most of all is yourself. That's why I said you were brave, why it took courage, the sheer guts of writing it.'

He felt the truth of her words, felt her sure uncanny knowledge of him. He wanted to build, create something out of all the waste and squalor, to build something out of all the chaos and violence and the mindless waste of lives that he had known; but he might well be building upon quicksand, he might well be creating a greater wilderness, in danger of losing the clarity of the vision that had been his since he first saw beyond the grime of asphalt and tar and daringly glimpsed a clearer piece of sky beyond the acrid burning smokescreen of the pithead. He was in danger of lashing out blindly and destroying with the artillery of words those things and those good souls who had been the wind and the rain and the sun and the very earth to him through all the light and dark of his sapling years. He looked away from her, from the truth that was in her face, straight up at the sun, wishing that it would blind him.

Midge came splashing up the beach, showering sand everywhere, her hair a wet golden aureole, blue eyes dancing with the joy of living, making awkward splay-footed marks on the sand, throwing herself down between the two of them, scattering water all around like silver beads prodigally flung from her pink wet skin. Midge the many-rainbowed, many-daffodilled child of light awaking in him the awe and beauty of first snow and so many undiscovered things of joy unknown now or unremembered from the past.

Laurie looked down into the laughing face of her child, and he saw there the fierce pride and love beyond words, sweeping out, tender, wild, and wistful. She embraced her daughter, with the wide sea, and the sky stepping in tune above them, enveloping them . . . mother and child as so often seen above his bed in that other world. He felt a stab of solitary envy at such perfect possession and belonging; he wondered how he came to be there, looking on, an intruder almost, and he remembered when he had once been a child too, looking into a bright shop-window full of magic and delight, and he had felt such a piercing pain and longing for all that forbidden bounty that his throat had swelled with rage and his tears stung under the lash of falling snow.

'I'm going for a quick swim,' said Laurie, rising, brushing sand from her legs and hips and pushing stray wisps of hair under her swim-cap. 'After that we can grab a bite to eat back at the house and maybe go for a drive later—would you like that?' she asked him, smiling.

'Fine,' he said.

She left him then and went down to the water's edge hand in hand with Midge. The other children and people had somehow disappeared and it seemed he had almost the entire beach to himself. He was once more alone with his fears and thoughts of tomorrow trapping him, wondering what that day might bring, what new quests, what new directions would open up for him, what new shape his life would take after tomorrow and for all foreseeable tomorrows after that. He thought what a dark, lovely, unknown and frightening thing tomorrow was in the life of any human being, waiting to enchant or entomb, to fulfil or to destroy, a friendly stranger waiting to greet one and show one the way, or a great predatory beast intent only upon devouring, carnage rendering one blind and maimed and lost to all hope. Would tomorrow turn out to be enemy or friend? Rescuer or assassin, lover or implacable adversary?

He felt his guts knot together with fear and tremulous anticipation. He sat up, his body almost molten with perspiration, looking for Laurie, for evidence of her existence; but she was nowhere in sight, out beyond the waves making love to the sea, and save for the gulls and their lonely crying he felt he was the last and only creature left on earth, facing tomorrow alone.

'It's beautiful here, isn't it?' said Laurie, sighing contentedly and lying back against the car seat, her face soft and reposed with peace, savouring each facet of the scenery as though gazing lovingly upon the contours of a familiar well-loved room that held her most secret and cherished possessions. 'Just beautiful. I feel so lost here, so happily lost. I often come here alone just to sit and gaze across the lake. My nerves sometimes need it.'

It was the afternoon of the same day; after lunch Laurie had asked Midge if she would like to come along for the drive, but, being wise, she had declined the tedium of adult company and gone off to the beach once more to frolic with her friends and kindred spirits in the sun and spray unhindered by adult discipline and the curious mores and paradoxes of that strange species. So she and Riley now had the rest of the day to themselves, parked by the side of a large lake with thick terraces of trees sloping down almost to its edge and mirrored brilliantly in the waters. The sky was immense, deep and unbelievably blue with few clouds at all to break its serenity save some fluffy wisps floating about like delicate filigree, insubstantial as breath upon a window-pane. An old dilapidated long-discarded rowing-boat was tethered at the end of the crumbling wooden pier, gleaming in the long afternoon sunset like ancient bronze. Everything lay in an Eden-like stillness; not the merest murmur of a breeze stirred the glassy surface of the lake or touched the branches and leaves of the trees etched vividly and perfectly against the sky.

One part of him was glad and gave thanks that they were alone and spared the happy but disruptive intrusion of Midge and her friends with their incredible energies and ceaseless flow of chatter and curiosity; another more perceptive if less resilient part of him trembled in involuntary trepidation and uncertainty, shrinking back from the challenge her presence seemed to present to him when they were alone together, turning into confusion everything that once was clear and comprehensible to him in that once neat, brittle, intensely private little world where before only his own trimly packaged emotions mattered and had relevance. He resented perversely his growing dependence upon her; where before he had only himself to abhor or admire, praise or condemn, accept or reject, flaunt or hide, there was now her exquisite intrusion into that painful secret world, an intrusion he had yet to understand and accept and fit into the rugged contours of his mind. He longed to look at her from a distance, to have the safety of distance between them, in order to think her out, to think about her separately, with calm detached rationality, sorely tempted to toy with the delusion of his own resources of self-containment and the grand myth of clinical impartiality. Yet not for a moment could he now imagine himself as being further from her than the barely perceptible shadow of her eyelash on her cheek.

'This other book you're writing,' she said after a lengthy pause, putting on the pair of rather owl-like spectacles and immediately assuming that professorial classroom attitude that both annoyed and amused him. 'I read the chapters you gave me last night,' she continued, reaching forward to open the glove compartment and extracting a large unwieldy stack of thin foolscap paper, long legal-sized pages closely typed, stained here and there with the imprinted rings of mugs of tea or glasses of beer drunk through many a long night and in the dark of many a cold or feverish dawn above the whirr and purr of the old-fashioned creaking black-bodied typewriter in a one-eyed hovel of a backyard room. Laurie rustled the pages gingerly, selecting the sections she wanted and spreading them out upon her lap and on the seat between them.

'There are some things I don't understand, some things that escape me. They might be crystal-clear to you, but a writer, a good writer, should make things clear to his reader as well—you shouldn't have to interpret or analyse things for your audience—it should be implicit, it should all come out in the writing. Far too often you seem to be writing merely for yourself, for your own eye and ear alone—'

'That's the only way I can write—the only way for me,' he

broke in quickly, having the sudden sick feeling that she misunderstood all that he was so laboriously, so heart-achingly
trying to say.

She looked at him then, and though her look was kind and
patient he quailed under her studied detachment and the
distance that the austere formidable spectacles seemed to cast
between them.

'I know,' said Laurie patiently, sifting more pages. 'That
might well be, and it's quite all right, as long as you let the
reader in on what's going on, what you're thinking and feeling
and saying—he shouldn't be expected to struggle Spartan-like
through a welter of words and images in order to arrive at the
mere gist of what you are saying—that's asking too much, and
anyway it's just downright bad writing.'

Her hand felt ineffably soft and cool where it lay briefly
upon his; then she began gathering up the pages of manuscript
and replaced them in the glove compartment bound with a
string of elastic. 'End of pep talk for one day,' she said gaily,
starting up the engine. She gave another long sigh, taking
leave of the red onslaught of sunset shimmering above the lake.
'That's enough for now. I hate to leave all this,' she said, 'but
duty—and a hungry family—call.'

She skilfully manoeuvred the car around and headed back
towards the long twisting lane through the trees that led back
on to the road. He looked back, seeing the intricate maze of
imprints the car tyres had made in the sand, and thought
wryly how these markings resembled the twists and turns of
his own life leading now to this strange moment carved out of
some dear improbable nowhere, awaking in him all the old
inklings and tinklings of the immense wonder and inconquer-
able mystery of even the most mundane mortal existence. They
took the coast road home; he saw the white caps of waves
plunging upon rocks, a slow faraway rhythm barely carried
on the breeze, saw the vague horizon dimly knifing earth and
sky, sheer-dropping cliffs tossing jagged demonic shapes into
the ocean, the wild rushing of his heart outpacing the seething
waves. He began to recognise certain familiar features of the
countryside; the old wooden houses with great red barns, some
dating back to colonial times, overgrown gardens full of deep
shade, redolent of memories throwing their gaunt shrunken

shapes across the faded façades of the houses, quiet half-glimpsed streams meandering eternally under old red covered bridges, that had so captivated and flared his curiosity the first time he saw one. The earth and sky dyed in the broad fiery arson of evening were all one throbbing pulse and Laurie's words echoed in his heart.

Suddenly he wanted only to get back to his typewriter, to be reunited with it, to converse with it, to pound upon it with as much passion and frenzy as a love-crazed man might pummel the flesh of the woman he loved, seeking an answer or an ending to his existence. Absurdly now he longed for that typewriter as an alcoholic might crave for that first terrible all-saving drink; he longed to inflict the violent intensity of all he was feeling upon the inanimate yet alive extension of himself, the typewriter, to pour himself into that garrulous contraption of iron and metal and sink himself in it. He longed to get back to where he could be uniquely himself; outraging the night with his audacity, thinking things out to his pain and ecstasy, laughing and crying quietly inside himself, without trumpets, without ceremony, daydreaming and nightdreaming it to perfection, feeling the pulse of the typewriter under his touch, obedient to his will as no woman would ever be. The world of sky and sea, surf and cliff, wind and the smell of the wind, the world of Laurie and, incredibly, absurdly, Laurie herself, grew threadbare, thin and insubstantial, and the only real world was a cock-eyed room with no view of sea or sky, from which he had come across the Atlantic, a room of retarded vision, swarming with smelly backyards crawling with decadent life, with a typewriter in it waiting for his touch, waiting to splutter and erupt into quick tender bruising vivid life. He felt an itching to be back at that mad frenetic thing, that madman's trade, in that deranged sphere of consciousness, discoursing, arguing, quarrelling with himself over an honest rapidly diminishing drink, the morning threatening to break too soon, the clock a mad cricket in the background tolling out the hours and he beyond the knowing of it, his limbs pleasantly aching from effort crouched in that gargoyle position in the chair, his mind mercilessly alert and questioning even when he had at pre-dawn finally switched off the light and climbed wearily between the cool sheets, hearing the slight complaining creaks in the timber beams overhead and tiredly seeing over the edge of his bed the blue glint of moonlight on the typewriter, reminding him there was still wonder left in the world and much work and searching to do.

'Where are you now?'

It was Laurie's voice bringing him back from the far side of the ocean. He looked at her intent profile, concerned, a bit bemused by him, the sunset touching her hair; and he longed that one day she might understand his world, and his reasons for living in it.

It was later than they thought, and arriving home the house was strangely quiet. Laurie drove the car into the garage and helped him negotiate the steps that led from there into the huge kitchen with its shelves stacked with cookery books, condiments, spices, gleaming utensils dangling from silver hooks, ladles, gargantuan pots and pans, walnut presses, glittering sink and oven, the innumerable paraphernalia of a kitchen at once modern and charmingly antique, festooned with bright odd drawings and posters extolling the virtues of various seaside resorts. Cricket, the large golden-fleeced retriever dog, twitched an ear in somnolent acknowledgment of their presence when they entered the spoiled brute's unquestioned domain, after which it promptly and wisely returned to the canine limbo from whence it had been disturbed no doubt by the sound of Riley's clogging, dragging steps.

'I wonder where the kids are?' said Laurie as she went about getting the evening supper ready, tying a neat little check apron round her. 'It's suspiciously quiet round here.'

As she started to light the oven and put the already prepared meat loaf in, Don suddenly appeared in the doorway, coming from the living-room, in slippers and yawning, holding a newspaper limply in his hand. Laurie seemed surprised.

'You're early, aren't you?' she said, opening the door of the oven.

'Am I? Don't think so,' said Don, coming in, throwing the paper aimlessly on a chair, taking off his thick lenses and rubbing his eyes. 'How did it go today, Riley—manage to do any work? Well, never mind—I imagine you're all keyed up about tomorrow. I know I'd be if I were in your shoes. Let's all relax and have us a drink. Hey, woman, you know who I am?'

said Don, going over to Laurie at the sink and putting his strong arms around her waist, nuzzling her neck.

'Yes, honey, I know who you are,' said Laurie, smiling, half-heartedly pushing him away. 'Now quit fooling and fix us all that drink. Supper is at least an hour away. Where are those kids of ours, Don?'

'Need you ask?' said Don, mixing the drinks. 'Just listen.' From a top-storey bedroom there came the raucous sound of some current recording idol blessedly diminished by distance. Don, expert cocktail conjurer, duly concocted a brew and passed it around; Riley hurriedly sampled his, and was grateful for the swift warm response it provoked. He leaned back less tensely in his chair, the stuff warming him, dimming the sharp edges of his envy, enabling him to look on with a certain benevolence as Don and Laurie joked and kidded each other and exchanged certain funnily licentious limericks above the appetising odours of supper. Riley's glass was refilled; he gazed down at the fluffy golden body of Cricket stretched out upon the brown linoleum floor, its soft heavy-laden ears twitching from time to time, recapturing some dream of canine conquest from its long-dead doggy youth, once the youthful guardian and frolicsome darling of the household, now its venerable antique, its tolerated nuisance and antiquated relic, un-witting barometer of time's passage. Riley gently toed the sleeping animal, wondering what dreams still sluggishly crept inside that cranny cranium, snowy scraps of winters past and cold breath static in the air, eternally pulling toboggans and the gay laughing galaxy of pink-cheeked children behind, and roaming proud among the snap-dragons in its hardly re-membered lustihood smelling all new the desire of heavy bitch-heat among the tall grasses of the sunburned seasons. Dog unwitting, doomed to this senile scrap of faded fur and brittle bone upon the floor.

That evening supper was unusually quiet; Midge seemed subdued, and though he glanced over at her often hoping for the glad zany alliance of eye and mischief-making smile that had cemented their friendship from the very beginning, the child studiously avoided him and, almost immediately after supper, asked to be excused. Laurie, worried, took the child in her arms, crooning endearments, hushing, shushing, pampering, but Midge stayed stiff, sullen, unresponsive, and at bedtime kissed nobody goodnight, which everyone thought was strange.

In his room at last with the typewriter, Riley inserted a sheet of paper in the carriage, paused, leaned back, and could not understand why he was not happy, safe in his world again. Then a child's sullen face appeared to him again across the supper table, blue eyes downcast amid a tumble of yellow hair.

Riley looked down into the deathly-still garden, feeling the cold snap of the moon high above in the clear New England sky.

II

He awoke slowly, feeling the sun on his face and shining through his lids; everything about him was warm and soft and luxuriant, and for a while he imagined he was still lying down on the beach. Then he heard the warbling of a bird, tentative, unsure, but defiant, quite near, and he opened his eyes. The undrawn curtains let in the full brilliant flood of the sun, filling the room, above the front lawn, facing down the avenue towards the beach. With gradual pleasurable familiarity the outline of the room and the objects in it assumed their quiet unobtrusive proportions: the large chair by his bedside, comfortable, old-fashioned, in which he would sit for long unnumbered nocturnal hours crouched over the typewriter; the squat dark-brown bookcase in the right-hand corner of the window, filled with new and old companions, liberally embellished with the pen-knifed initials of the two children over the dozen or so years of their existence; the small flower-faded armchair facing the window, rocking on its spidery legs; the flower print hanging above his bed, stark, exquisite in its Oriental simplicity. It was a room he had come to know well, and at night when he had switched off the main light and left the bedside lamp burning, he would sometimes look up, pausing in the perennial pursuit of words, and catch his own gaunt hawk-faced reflection staring back at him in the black pane of window, and he would start a little, in absurd fright, as if encountering the demon face of a stranger met suddenly at that deep dreaming hour.

He listened to the warbling outside his window, joined presently by other songsters until there was almost a chorus going, making a happy turmoil in the air. Suddenly he thought he detected a single discordant jarring note, and for no reason to which logic could be ascribed he remembered what day it was, and felt again the nervous elation and dread of what that day might hold, and for a while he almost tried to will himself back to sleep. He shut his eyes again tightly, but the sunlight almost hurt now, and petulantly he threw aside the blankets.

With the usual slow methodical movements, as if he had consciously to think everything out, as indeed for the most part he had, he began to put on his clothes, his fingers fumbling with buttons and zips and other conventional torments, working himself up into the usual mild state of near-hysteria before he was satisfied that he was more or less fully dressed. Luckily in the prevailing heat clothes were secondary to the primary purpose of remaining cool. Dressed at last, he picked up his crutches; feeling the hard familiar shape of them, fitting snugly into the hollow of his armpits, he was free and confident and sure of himself, his crutches two life-long friends always there to support and hold him up, however grievous a fall he might take. He went over to the window, feeling quick gliding elation as he half-raised himself with every stride, and looked out. Spread out below on the lawn, slumbering under a dog-wood tree, he saw Cricket, finding cool shelter from the already rising heat of the day; abandoned against a fence leaned Midge's red and white bicycle, the rear wheel still spinning, as if she had just left it there the moment before to seek the broader freedom of the beach. Craning forward, he could just see the red station-wagon directly underneath his window outside the front porch, the sun bouncing in shimmering waves off its roof. He looked up; the sky was almost denuded of clouds, save near the horizon where a few almost invisible white puffs lay, scarcely moving. Away in the blue vastness of the Sound a solitary sailing skiff bobbed distantly, its triangular red sails showing up like a varnished cuticle against the sky. It was beautiful, a day almost too painfully perfect; he heard again, if only in his heart, that one discordant note of birdsong, and wondered.

There was a soft tap on his door. 'Riley?' said her voice, and the brief shadow passed. 'Riley, are you awake?'

He swivelled around, straightening his shoulders, 'Of course,' he answered with bravado.

Laurie entered, smiling. 'What do you mean—"Of course"!' she said. 'Most mornings I'd need to come upstairs beating a drum! But I forgot,' she added, quietly. 'Not this morning—eh?'

'No,' he said. 'Not this morning.'

'Are you scared, Riley?'

'Scared as hell. You know that.'

'Yes, I know that. I'd be scared too.'

'You, Laurie? I can't see you being scared of anything.'

She did not answer for a moment, her eyes remote, looking beyond him as she leaned against the door. 'We are all scared of something, Riley,' she said softly, her voice a little tired. 'The past, the present or the future. Some of us just manage to hide it better than others. But it's too early in the day to be philosophical,' she said, brightening. 'Come down and get a good breakfast into you to sustain you for the rigours of the day. The kids are down at the beach since cock-crow and Don's in the garage tinkering with the old Buick, so you'll have to settle for looking at my ugly dial over the bacon and eggs—all right?'

'Can't think of a nicer ugly dial I'd rather look at,' he said with a grin as she held the door wide for him.

'God, you do say the nicest things!'

She went ahead of him. 'Mind those damn stairs now,' she cautioned, descending slowly backwards, holding on to both rails, a step or two below him. 'We really will have to fix up a bed for you down here—I've horrible visions of you hurtling head-first down that flight of stairs one of these days and ending up in a gory mess at the bottom—'

'It's all—a matter—of blind faith—' he said, gasping a little with the strain, negotiating the stairs, balancing his weight carefully on the crutches. It was not a new house, and the staircases were all rather steep and winding.

'You and your blind faith!' Laurie said, laughing with obvious relief when they reached the hallway. 'With all your new riches maybe you should invest in a pair of wings—'

The kitchen looked out on to the wide lawn at the back of the house; through the window he saw the twin garages and the long greenhouse in which Don the inveterate amateur grew his unpredictable tomatoes with untiring zeal and tenacity. They sat down opposite each other at the kitchen table, the room redolent with the smell of bacon and eggs and fresh coffee. She had on a simple crisp white blouse and dark skirt and a pair of loose sneakers on her feet; somehow he thought she smelt of cool lavender.

'There's so much I want to talk about with you, Riley,' she said, musing, playing absently with some breadcrumbs on the chequered tablecloth. 'Your first book—we all know you're going to make a great deal of money out of it. But about this second book. I keep making all sorts of little notes about it in one of Midge's school jotters. I'd like to go over these with you —I mean, when all this silly ballyhoo is over, this party the Simons are giving in your honour—would you like that?'

She sounded so earnest, so anxious for his approval and acceptance of her offer of assistance; she reminded him of a young girl eager to help in some grand project. He could not bear to sit there and confront the clear glow of willingness, warmth and interest in her eyes, and hastily took refuge in his coffee.

'Yes, of course,' he said, too loudly. 'I'd like that very much—anything that would help me with the book.'

'I've been thinking about it so much,' she went on. 'About the plot, the characterisation, the sequence of chapters, the points of crisis and conflict . . . I think about it at all hours of the day and night, almost as if—' She stopped. 'God, do I sound gushing, Riley?'

'Not a bit of it,' he answered instantly. 'That's what I need— enthusiasm, a good audience.'

'After today is over there'll be the whole summer to talk about it and map its course chapter by chapter,' said Laurie, twiddling idly with the rings on her finger, elbows on table. 'Just as soon as today is past . . .' Her eyes focused on him again as she seemed to return to the present. 'I wonder what he'll be like—this Jay Simon character? I have a mental image of him which is perhaps unfair. Have you one too, Riley?'

'Not really—no,' he replied. 'I'm not very good at mental images.'

Laurie laughed, making a mock face. 'Oh, get along with you!'

'I mean, not of actual people, anyway,' he amended lamely.

'Martin seems to like him quite a lot,' she said, rubbing the side of her nose with her index finger thoughtfully. 'And Martin Ruislip is nobody's fool. Under that cool unruffled polite exterior there's a hard glitter of shrewdness that no amount of flattery can touch or delude—'

'You like Martin?' said Riley, not really posing a question so much as presupposing an affirmative answer.

'Oh yes, I like him,' said Laurie, as if surprised that he should have the slightest doubt. 'We both do, myself and Don, for a good number of years now. He's fun in a dry sort of way— so prim and proper, such a stickler for etiquette, so terribly English—oh yes, we like him a lot. He's one of the really good editors left. You're lucky to have him, Riley, both as editor and friend—'

'Yes, I am,' he said, a bit angry, perversely wishing she would not keep harping on it so much, as though it were a kind of ritual with her that every time the subject of his book and writing came up even momentarily the name of Martin Ruislip had perforce to be mentioned; and even as he thought this he felt tremendously guilty.

'I'm just not so sure about Jay Simon,' went on Laurie, twining her fingers together and again looking very professorial. 'He sounds much too young to be so successful—' She stopped and laughed outright. 'Yes—I know that sounds grossly unfair and narrow-minded! I'm such a prude, really—my Puritan background and sheltered upbringing, as Don is always saying, and it wouldn't be so bad if he wasn't so right!'

'What is it I'm always saying?' asked Don, just that moment coming in through the back door, rubbing his hands in a greasy rag, smears of oil across his face and arms, wearing overalls and a somewhat bedraggled sunhat perched on his large arrogant intelligent head, smiling his usual laconic smile.

'I was just saying to Riley how you always end up an argument by calling me a prude,' said Laurie. 'There's coffee.'

'I'll have a beer, I think,' said Don, opening the fridge. 'And you are a prude, dear, though a real pretty one, thank God.'

There came the swift shrill song of a bird directly outside the window, and he looked out, catching the blue flash on the bird's

23

wing as it rose and went its way over the trees. His coffee tasted a little acrid now, with a smoky taste to it that did nothing to clear his throat, and he looked rather longingly as the sun struck the can of beer in Don's hand.

'All set for the big day, Riley?' said Don, lounging against the fridge, one hand in overall pocket, eyes blue and welcoming behind the thick lenses.

'No,' said Riley, a bit morosely. 'Not really.'

'I'd be terrified myself,' said Don. 'Still, it isn't every day the world acclaims a genius.'

'Oh, Don,' said Laurie, clearing the table. 'Don't rub it in.'

'I'm doing nothing of the kind, woman,' said Don, easily swigging another gulp. 'Why be modest? Riley's not a modest man. Why should he be? He has nothing to be modest about.'

'God, you can be awful at times,' said Laurie, rather furiously working at the sink, back to both of them.

Don laughed quietly. 'Oh, come now, Laurie,' he said. 'Do you know, Riley, a lesser man would be jealous, hearing his wife extolling the fine intellect and unlimited potential of another man when all I want to do is go quietly to sleep—'

There was a sudden crash as a plate went slipping through Laurie's fingers to the floor, landing at her feet. The garden outside was silent as if it had never known the sound of a bird. Quietly Don knelt down and gathered up the broken remnants of delf, putting them into the yellow pedal-bin under the sink.

'You're rapidly developing butterfingers, honey,' he said, straightening up, kissing her lightly on the cheek, fingers fondling her shoulder. 'Better let Daddy take over. You go and get yourself all glamoured up for Riley's big day.'

'I don't know what happened to me—' began Laurie, passing a hand over her eyes.

'Relax,' said Don, picking up the dishcloth. 'A good thing it wasn't one of your mother's good bone-china antiques. Get ready, dear. We should be ready to leave in about an hour.'

'Will do,' said Laurie, and left the room.

'Funny creatures, women,' said Don, drying dishes as if he really enjoyed the whole thing. 'Irrational creatures, but fascinating. A man could study them for a lifetime, and never get to know them. That's what's so fascinating about them, I suppose.'

24

'Yes, I suppose so,' said Riley. 'I wish I could help—'

'What?' asked Don.

'With the washing up.'

Don grinned, and Riley felt somehow helpless in the broad geniality of that grin. 'Save your energies for the typewriter, friend,' said Don. 'Aesthetically far more rewarding, financially far more profitable.' Don was silent for a moment or two as he studiously dried dishes. 'We both admire you tremendously, you know,' he said, in a different kind of voice.

Riley, not knowing what to say, decided to remain silent.

'I know you'll be hearing a lot of the same kind of talk from now on,' Don continued, assigning each cup and saucer, knife and spoon to its allotted and accustomed place as he dried each of them in turn, calm and efficient in this as in everything else. 'We admire you for a number of reasons,' he went on, in the flat tone of voice that was invariably his and which seldom varied, even in his most exuberant moods. 'The obvious one we share with perhaps most people—the one you yourself are probably bored with hearing, but it's true all the same. The way in which you made people not only accept but almost forget that you're a cripple—'

'Almost forget,' said Riley.

'Yes—almost forget,' said Don smiling, seeming to appreciate the point. 'I've little or no previous experience of writers—on the bookshelves, yes, but not as house-guests,' said Don, drying off the last of the breakfast things, looking around at him and smiling, and Riley experienced then a certain taut constriction in the chest, seeing the open-hearted amity in the man's large craggy sea-loved vulnerable face, at once tentative and boyishly eager for approval and acceptance. 'I'm not being fulsome—not my nature to be fulsome—' Don was saying, drying his big roughened yet sensitive hands on a piece of kitchen-roll and rubbing them along the sides of his time-used weather-beaten jeans. 'But we're damn proud to have you among us as our guest—no, that's not the word—as our friend. I only hope you're happy here and can work here— Laurie has had that old typewriter upstairs since God knows when—'

'It's perfect,' said Riley, remembering and loving every rickety jarring jangle of the keys, the capital letters that consistently came out as half capitals only and the carriage return that sometimes got jammed in the middle of a sentence and the peculiar whining sound that issued from its mysterious innards like that of a constantly reproving friend only just suffering one's unwanted enquiries into his private intestinal world of unmentionable woe. 'It's perfect,' repeated Riley.

Don paused, turned, looked across at Riley, and the blue eyes that were perennially dilated behind the lenses were unusually sharp and incisive. 'Laurie's a good woman,' he said, quite calmly, absently picking up his almost empty beer can and rolling it thoughtfully in both hands. 'Often mistaken, like most women. Well-meaning, of course, which—' Don smiled, 'can be bloody irritating at times. Listen to her, Riley, and try not to be irritated. No—' he said, raising his hand as Riley made some feeble effort to protest. 'Let's not be polite, for God's sake. She'll probably get on your nerves at times, so that you may feel like telling her to mind her own damn business. You must always feel free to do just that, Riley. I'll get conveniently lost at such times. I'll always let you two argue it out between you, because,' said Don, as he finished off the last of his beer on that blazing Saturday morning in the coolness of the kitchen, 'this is what I think you want. Am I right?'

Riley looked down at the checkered tablecloth and without thinking his hand strayed to his crutches leaning in the corner next to where he sat, his fingers touching the rough wood of them. Something white and fleeting caught his eye, and looking out the window he caught sight of Midge running across the garden, yellow tendrils skying wild behind her, chased with absurd loud-barking exultancy by Cricket, both of them out for devilment, running into the green shadow of the trees at the far end of the garden, child and dog, dog and child, both at that moment children alike, frolicking in the freedom of the early sun, one with the trees and the loud-hearted birds, the ever-present music of the sea nearby. They were in his sight, hearing, senses, in his heart, yet going ever away from him, taking with them Midge's wild lovely promise, leaving lost sad echoes in his heart, tolling out the hours, minutes, moments of his joy.

Laurie appeared in the doorway of the kitchen, smiling. 'I'm ready,' she said.

He would remember afterwards the long car drive through the lush rolling countryside, the deep thick woodland sweeping down on either side, the wide smooth freeways spinning endlessly into the distance like ribbons eternally unfurling, the painful blue brilliance of the sky, the rush of wind past the open window cool through the thin stuff of his shirt. All this he would afterwards remember clearly. But whenever that lost fateful day returned to him what came instantly and dramatically to his recollection was no recurring image of scenery; what instantly and insistently came to mind was that first totally unexpected appearance of Jericho Pines, hitting him with full frontal visual assault straight between the eyes, emerging with startling suddenness from behind a forest of trees that cast a green subtle gloom through woodland where the only sound was the purr of the car engine, where the pleasant pervading noon-day twilight was broken by occasional shafts of sunlight striking diagonally across their path; then suddenly there it stood before them, white and gleaming, slumbering like some enormous complacent lion, masses of clinging ivy green and shining climbing to the eaves, a brilliant splashing collage of colour, a spacious colonnaded façade, splendid marble columns rising like the noble limbs of a colossus, countless windows leaded and diamonded glinting like serpentine eyes, and wide lawns sloping leisurely down to dark recesses of forest falling far away beyond the eye. Thus for the first time Jericho Pines rose before his vision, Jericho Pines where he could not then have remotely imagined his life was to begin anew and the long lost wild anthem of his days was to be sounded for the first time, unheard as yet above the trumpeting and fanfare already gathering in his mind and heart.

It was like nothing he had ever seen, and eager to share it with them he turned to Laurie and Don, but their faces were quite ordinary, composed, a little resigned almost. He did not know why he felt sad and suddenly uncertain, as a child might feel when the joy and surprise he finds in something is accepted easily and nonchalantly by others.

'Quite a spread,' was all that Don said as he slowed to

a stop in front of the main entrance, and stopped the engine.

'I expect a footman to come running out any minute,' said Laurie.

'Footmen never run, honey,' corrected Don. 'Well, we're here, and I suppose we'd better get out. Let me get your crutches, Riley."

They started across the gravel path between the lawn and the broad stone steps, Laurie and Don on each side of him, just barely supporting him in case he should stumble on the rough surface; then the doors at the top were suddenly thrown wide and he looked up to see a small squat broad-shouldered man coming down the steps with surprising agility, a wide smile on his round tanned face, a smile full of gleaming teeth, short arms outspread in an all-encompassing gesture of welcome and pleasure, striding towards them. He caught a glimpse of a woman standing quietly on the top step, just catching the flashing white gleam of her dress before the advancing man reached them and stood before him, arms still outstretched, roly-poly countenance still swathed in that delighted brilliant smile.

'My dear friend, Riley!' exclaimed the man, clasping him around both shoulders and pulling him impulsively against him; instantly he caught the sharp fresh tang of after-shave. 'Welcome to my country, Riley, and double welcome to Jericho Pines! I've been looking forward to this moment for so long—at times I almost despaired of ever meeting you in the flesh, but, thank God, here we are at last, face to face—'

'Jay, dear,' said a quiet feminine voice from behind.

Jay stopped, grinned wider and shrugged his shoulders in mock self-deprecation, stepping aside. 'You are quite right, my dear,' he said, taking the woman by the elbow, bringing her forward. 'I guess I did get carried away!' He turned to Laurie and Don, profoundly apologetic, bowing slightly from the waist. 'Do excuse my appalling bad manners—I know you must be Riley's indispensable friends, the Emersons, Don and Laurie, am I right?'

'Quite right,' said Don. 'Glad to know you.'

'Hello everyone,' said the woman, who was about forty, petite, handsome, poised, with long dark hair caught up in a neat bun. 'I'm Sue Simon, and this highly voluble male creature here,' she said, smiling, putting her hand lightly on Jay's shoulder, 'is, as you may have surmised, my husband. You're all very welcome indeed.'

'Why, thank you so much,' said Laurie.

'I suggest we all go inside out of this heat,' said Sue, shading her eyes. 'Jay, dear, do lead the way. I'm sure poor Riley is positively cooking and imploring us silently for a long cool drink.'

'I wouldn't say no,' said Riley, armpits beginning to ache with the pressure of the crutches.

'This way,' said Jay. 'Can you manage the steps, Riley, or shall we use a side door? There's one just round that corner over there—'

'Oh, he can manage almost everything with just a little help,' Laurie said, a note of pride in her voice.

They ascended the steps without much difficulty, and found themselves in the front hall of the house, almost cathedral-like in its spaciousness, with stained-glass rectangular windows pouring down slender streams of subdued light. Riley was somewhat blinded by the quick change from sunlight to this pleasant gradual shade, and he could discern only faint images of paintings along the walls and the cool marble sheen of pillars and statues and busts mounted upon slim pedestals in deep recesses. Jay Simon went ahead of them, keeping up meanwhile an almost continuous commentary of which Riley could decipher only snatches as he tried consciously to steer a straight and disaster-free course over the smooth polished wood surface of the floor. Jay showed them into a large circular room that had a kind of glass dome high up in the ceiling; it was much brighter here, but still pleasantly cool, with plants flowering everywhere out of huge ornate pots and vines in bloom creeping upwards along the walls from the floor. He glimpsed the shapes of some people seated on a large curving half-moon couch around a glass-topped circular table on which a seemingly endless number and variety of bottles were stacked, but the strain and effort of so much walking had just about exhausted him, and he sank gratefully into a corner of the couch, relishing the sense of relief as he eased the crutches away from under his burning armpits and for a few moments closed his eyes.

'Poor Riley,' said Don quietly, sitting next to him on the

arm of the couch. 'We're fiends to tire you like this so early.'

'I'll be all right after a few minutes,' began Riley, adding with wry and comical fervour, 'and a few drinks.'

Jay came towards them carrying a tray full of drinks in tall glasses which he placed on the table before them. 'I think most of the alcoholic concoctions known to mankind you'll find here—'

'In fact some of them are quite unknown,' said Sue Simon, sitting nearby on an embroidered ottoman, several of which were strewn casually about the room, both hands clasped around one upturned knee. 'Jay is a frustrated creative connoisseur of titillating beverages—being a publisher comes a very poor second.'

'I think you will find this one particularly refreshing, Riley,' said Jay, handing him a long glass that had an amber glow to it and bits of pale green filigree floating on top. 'Though it might be too tame for your robust Celtic taste!'

'He'll try it anyway,' said Don humorously, sipping his own drink. 'Anything for a good cause, eh, Riley?'

'Never say die,' he said, lifting the glass to his mouth and swallowing almost half of it at once. He felt nothing except a slight cessation of his thirst. He saw that Jay was watching him closely, and he said with a grin: 'Don't ask me—I haven't tasted it yet!'

'So this is your Irishman, is it, Jay?' A man's deep voice spoke from somewhere along the couch, preceded by a startling wracking nicotine cough that seemed to echo to the very ceiling.

'Jake, you incorrigible reprobate,' laughed Jay, beckoning with languid flamboyance. 'Get up off your ass and come and be suitably ushered into the presence.'

After a pause a tall man, looking like a rather discredited down-and-out Messiah in a faded plaid jacket and greasy trousers, stood before him bowing elegantly from the hips, a bearded face that was at once carnal and angelic, an absurd out-of-season rose blossoming in his buttonhole, his entire presence somehow exuding a strange combination of ink, tobacco, and beer. His eyes were deep sunken brown pools of melancholy and defeat, humorous lines hovered nervously around his sensitive mouth under his stroking pensive fingers.

'Riley, this is Jake Pellmann, a refugee from Broadway,' Jay introduced. 'Don't take offence if he sounds outrageous—he is, but Jake insists it's a part of his rich Judaean charm.'

Jay moved invisibly away and Don discreetly arose and joined Laurie on the far side of the vast table, leaving him islanded with this mysterious marooned stranger, standing there looking somehow apologetic and doomed, twirling his glass dreamily in his hand. The conversation began to grow around them, at first hollow echoes in that huge beehive of a room, then gradually thickening and condensing to a steady burr and buzz.

'I hear you've got the disease too,' said Jake Pellmann gloomily. 'The pen-and-ink complaint, or have you graduated to IBM?'

'A very ancient version,' said Riley, 'and not even my own.'

Jake suddenly grinned. 'Drink up,' he said, finishing off his own. 'I'll find us another.' He left, and came back almost instantly carrying two well-filled glasses, to sit down on his hunkers facing Riley, handing him a glass. 'Brandy,' Jake intoned, 'the drink of strong and suffering souls.' He drank deeply, eyes partly closed, face intent, as if concentrating fiercely and communing with some inner primordial deity. Then he blinked, sighed, and caressed his glass in both hands. 'I write,' announced Jake, contemplating space. 'Oh yes,' he continued, as if unburdening himself of some great unpardonable sin, dipping his spaniel-like nose to sniff fastidiously at the unseasonable bloom in his buttonhole. 'I write. Just as I urinate, defecate, masturbate, and all too rarely fornicate.' He looked Riley over with eyes that were suddenly cold, clinical, professional, treating him as if he were a stage prop or as a character yet to be created and fully developed in a play yet to be written. 'I read that book of yours. You're uptight, like most of us. About ourselves, about God, about the price of booze, about our governments. Hell—' Jake drank down his drink with sudden savagery, his stringy gullet jerking jauntily with each swallow. 'Hell, we're all uptight. Writing about it is what matters—that's where the guts and the cowardice come in.'

He spoke gently, with almost gentle sleepiness, swaying slightly back and forward, eyes semi-closed, heavy-lidded, the

31

nostrils of his long snout-like nose quivering about his button-hole bloom, his long sensuous fingers caressing the brandy glass.

'Broadway—' Jake seemed to shudder and wake up, and he emptied his drink swiftly. 'That's hell, man—hell. A man goes into Broadway with a soul, and comes out of it with a credit card and fuck-all else. Believe me. And I'm made. Real made. Every line I write is worth a bottle of purest cognac.' Jake stirred his drink and sighed. 'Purest cognac.'

Some long-digested newspaper headline, article or review now dimly resurrected in Riley's mind intimated that he should have heard of Jake Pellmann, now talking in a kind of sad monotonous undertone that was actually more of an inner monologue about his own famous plays, speaking about the characters in those plays as about real people, calling them by their first names, as if they were at that moment sitting next to him, or facing him across the table, or were about to enter the room. Pellmann looked less like purest cognac than cheap seedy red wine; everything about him seemed tawdry, well-worn, borrowed. He might well have been a straggler from some medieval down-at-heel tattered bazaar full of sharp-nosed hawk-faced nomads haggling ferociously over destinies instead of faded silk prints and cinnamon-scented wares. Riley noticed a big blunt-nosed pencil protruding like the snout of an emerging submarine from behind the blossom nestling in the buttonhole, poised as if for instant warfare, jabbing the eye of the unwary beholder, seeming to glow mystically, as though it were the mythical giant phallic symbol of all strident masculinity. And as if reading his thoughts from behind those half-closed lids, yet with total and child-like absentmindedness, Jake's fingers crept slowly upwards to the pencil, fingering it dreamily, sensuously, his face lost in a Buddha-like bliss, looking vulnerable, yet impenetrable.

'Words, words,' Jake was intoning softly. 'Words are bloody worms nibbling away inside your brain. The sweet demented farce of it all. . . . They think writers are happiest when they're writing—Jesus, if only they knew! I'm telling you,' Jake opened his eyes wide and looked at him with a face alive with conviction, 'a writer is just an animated vegetable, a universal mouthpiece.' Jake shut one eye and glared at him with the other. 'I sit before my bloody pre-war portable typewriter, that damn screaming bitch of a machine, and say the most awful chicken-brained things to myself—that's what I do. Jesus, can you imagine!' Jake violently grunted, as if fiercely exasperated with himself. 'I can think of a thousand other things I'd rather do than write,' he continued after a while, composed and remote again, as if a minor storm had passed. 'I'd rather do things that demand real genius. You know, big challenging things—like baking casseroles, or duck-shooting, or hairdressing, or mixing zing cocktails, or hanging pictures. Major efforts like that, you know. But writing's strictly for the mentally retarded, the loquacious cabbage, the poor lost blasted Peter Pans of this awful world . . . Jesus, is this a wake or something?'

Jake stirred restlessly, rising abruptly with perfect precision and standing once more upright, proper and correct, smiling a bit sheepishly, scrawny beard going grey and brandy-amber, baggy Chaplinesque trousers sagging forlornly from the hips and draping around the ankles. 'In this life again, shall we meet, you and I? I don't know and don't dare guess.' He bent forward slightly and made an elaborate apostolic gesture of blessing over Riley, Gregorian in its authenticity. 'Go forth, my son, and multiply the earth.' Jake turned away and moved mournfully through the now rapidly gathering crowd, intoning sonorously: 'A drink, a drink, my kingdom for a drink. . .'

Riley, momentarily alone as though he were back on the deserted beach, picked up his brandy and drank, almost oblivious of what he was doing. He felt cocooned inside his own tight shell, invincible, all-seeing, a many-eyed demon of no little perception, looking as from a great distance at the foolish caperings and gesturings and empty mouthings of those thronging about him, standing their stilted stance, posing their preposterous poses, eyeing their neighbour most scrupulously for the least fault or blemish amid the clinkle of cocktail glasses, the popping of champagne corks and the rustle of satin afternoons and velvet evenings. And Jake Pellmann? Who the hell was Jake Pellmann? Had it all been a dream, part of a fantasy, a stanza of some long-forgotten abortion of a poem he might have written back in the other time, the old world? Yet that world-abused life-weary face had been for a time as real as the wooden crutches now lying under his feet on this enormous snake of a couch in this enormous egg-shell ovary of a room with all its millions of garrulous talking cells. . .

The talk was getting louder, more animated, interspersed by the high laughing thin-edged ripple of female voices, the deeper more intimate male tones of derision and amusement; people sat on the floor or stood about in separate little groups, listening, gesticulating, holding their glasses idly, protectively, meditatively, heads tilted intently, the observed well aware of the observers, loquacious, lachrymose, agitated, quiet, the nervous hedge-hopping chirpy sparrows jumping from one buzzing group to another, the more or less silent watchful hawks not missing a word, movement, gesture, detached and alert.

In a kind of panic he looked for Laurie, and saw her in a circle of people on the far side of the room, beside what he now perceived to be a French window opening on to green spaces of lawn, oblivious of him, nodding her head from time to time in the flow and interflow of conversation. And Don, that big large-hearted man, always by her side, taking obvious pleasure in the conversation, in surroundings far removed from the suburban evenness and predictable placidity of his own, listening with keen-eyed pleasure to the people around him, most of them young or in their early thirties, starting careers, or embroiled in careers that had, hopefully, wistfully, reached a tricky pass, living in a world which none of them were naive or trusting or foolish or perhaps strong enough to believe to be either new or particularly brave. And yet, looking at the un-mapped faces of these same young people, Riley saw in them a terrible desire to be both new and brave, and he felt an alliance with them which something in him told him would be brief and therefore all the more precious while it lasted. He guessed even then that he would move on away from that kind of well-rounded passionate belief in the future and in the future of the intellect to something that was to be uniquely and bleakly his own, away from all the lush promise of summer to his own familiar winter landscape where alone his gaze was perceptive and undeluded, finding in the bare skeletal bones of that landscape the germ of all his hopes.

'Hello,' said a voice out of nowhere. 'I'm Abbie Lang.'

He did not at once look up, he did not at once associate the shabby sneaker-clad feet directly before him with the rather husky voice that had just spoken to him. It seemed to him he stared at her feet for an awfully long time, there on the carpet in front of him, before he lifted his head and met her face. She was smiling down at him, a little puzzled, a little amused.

'As I said,' she said. 'I'm Abbie Lang. I'm afraid I'm one of these terrible professional creatures, here to take pictures of you—with your permission, of course. That's why I'm wearing these weird bloody things, you see.'

He looked at her more fully then, a bit amazed. Around her neck there dangled half a dozen or more cameras of various shapes and sizes, like a chain of mysterious medallions, all caught together on a black leather string and all, as he now observed, gathered around a rather beautifully elegant neck. The face too, he thought, was beautiful, in what way he did not know nor could put words to. He felt a marvellous kind of vocal and mental strangulation as he looked at her. He was quite wordless before her. He did not know for sure if this girl was beautiful or just pretty, and it did not in the least matter, because there she was, standing in front of him, a bit apologetic-looking, her brown eyes full of light, almost by themselves asking him did he mind that she was such a busybody.

'Okay with you?' she asked, hopefully, fingering one of her cameras. 'Just one or two for the magazine—Jay said he thought you wouldn't mind—please be good to a working girl—'

He discovered his voice finally, though even to his ears it came out as a kind of wild yet subdued croak. 'Oh—yes—of course, Miss—of course—'

'Thank you, kind sir.'

He felt himself being drawn into her wide infectious boyish smile. It was more of a grin, really, a confessional grin, as if they were both in on some great secret, engaged in some great conspiracy, some absurd plot which they alone shared in all that roomful of people of so many other lives, destinies, personalities, dreams, dreads, pasts, presents and futures. Yet as she, this creature named Abbie, started snapping her cameras at him, not a head moved or turned in their direction, nobody seemed to take the least bit of notice of them at all, of what he instinctively knew was taking place between them

35

there and then, between his own improbable self and this rather crazy creature called Abbie. He looked on with a kind of slow astonishment as she started taking pictures of him, presumably to aid Jay's publicity plans; she wore black denim jeans, rather clinging, and she crouched, knelt, lay on her back and sides and in general adopted all kinds of outlandish madly athletic postures as she photographed him from almost every conceivable angle, her slim nimble fingers clip-clip-clacking and one thick black wing of hair falling from time to time down over her eyes, which she brushed impatiently back with a wide fine white sweep of her hand, cocking her head this way and that, screwing up her eyes at him in a most comical fashion, measuring him up, measuring the distance between them and the amount of light the day lent to her, going to the right of him, moving obliquely to the left of him, looking all the while straight at him, yet never quite straight at him, her feet always slightly apart, as were her lips, her one visible eye partly shut, her other eye invisible and rather invincible behind the lenses, which she shifted, changed, manoeuvred and readjusted with what seemed to him incredible dexterity, and always above the noise and the happy cork-popping din of the room he caught the tiny faint metallic whirr of her cameras as she worked, he and she somehow suddenly and rather ridiculously oblivious of the rest. He sat still, almost, just looking at her, watching her, her movements and facial expressions, with both awe and amusement, and the irony of it all, to his reckoning, was the fact that she seemed totally unaware of him as he sat there before her and those merciless demon cameras, because he imagined he saw more of her then as he sat so passively there than she could ever see of him behind her forest of lenses.

'Thank you,' she said finally, straightening up and stretching, giving him a tired smile. 'Mind if I dump these and come back?'

'Please do,' he said, careful not to sound too eager.

He looked for Laurie. He could not see her now, could not seek her out in that swarming friendly wilderness of a room. He felt a turmoil starting up inside him. Abbie returned and sat on a cushion at his feet, a glass of something in her hand. The room was bursting wide with people, spilling out on to the lawns, passing around drinks, faces flushed with sun and amity. Abbie had got rid of her cameras. She had been so active just a moment back, it seemed; now she sat so quietly, no longer a professional person, as she had called herself, hidden behind a forest of cameras, but merely a girl in black jeans and sweater, a rather tired young woman, holding her glass quietly in her hands, gazing down at the floor.

'I loved your book, Riley' she said, drinking slowly.

'I'm glad,' was all he could think of saying.

'Why is it so melancholy?' she wanted to know, rather dreamily twisting the stem of her glass between her fingers. He noticed how strong the outlines of her knees were under the jeans. Her lips became a bit moist, which excited him strangely. 'Can you tell me why?' she asked, looking up at him.

'Not very well,' he said, squeezing his lids tightly against his eyes. 'Maybe I'm basically a very sad and melancholy person—'

'Because of these?' she said, stretching out a hand and slightly touching the crutches.

'Yes, and no,' said Riley, rather savagely twisting his head away.

'I always wondered what it must be like to be a writer,' mused Abbie, spreading her feet, hands hanging over knees. She smiled a little bitterly. 'Wish I could write. Don't even write decent letters to my folks. You don't know what it's like to be always behind a camera, photographing writers.'

He said nothing, not knowing what to say, having no answers for her. Briefly he saw Laurie on the other side of the room, in the light of the French windows, the late afternoon sun bringing out copper glints in her hair, her face animated, yet intently reposed, as she listened and absorbed the talk.

'Am I boring you?' asked Abbie, with a false, forced naivety that was somehow excruciatingly pathetic.

'Oh, no,' he said, suddenly free and reckless. 'Keep talking.'

Abbie looked puzzled and angry. 'What the hell do you mean—talking?' she said. There was the beginning of a storm between her brows. 'For a writer you're not very explicit, are you?'

'I suppose not.'

He had so few words for her. Least of all, he had so few words for himself. He was clammy with perspiration and the voices were droning like hordes of insatiable gnats inside his temples.

Abbie looked at him with an intelligence and understanding he would always remember. 'Would you like some air?' she said.

'God, yes, I'd like some air.'

Abbie got up. She found a sneaker that she had somehow lost, slipped it on, then handed him the crutches and guided him surely through the throng of people to a narrow balcony beyond. From the thin edge of his eye he thought he saw Laurie turn her head in their direction, but he pressed on and eventually reached the coolness of the evening and the wide rolling green spaces of the garden below.

'I forgot my cameras,' said Abbie, petulant as a child.

'And I forgot my typewriter,' said Riley, loosening the crutches and hunching one buttock upon the stone lacing of the balcony. 'Hooray.'

'I'm a damn good photographer,' she said, moving away from him, crossing her arms, leaning her hip against the balustrade. 'Why did you come out here from the famous gathering in there, to talk to a stupid creature like me?'

All the noisy gaiety was there behind them, behind the glass curtains, all the bright talk, the facile tongues, the slinging repartee, the stinging wit; outside, the first early stars, the imperceptibly moving greenness, and Abbie in her faded jeans, holding her glass in her hand, leaning against the pillar, wistful, lost.

'Why are you here?' he asked her, wanting suddenly, passionately, to know. 'What brought you here?'

'Who ever knows?'

He stared out over the glimmering acres of lawn, finding no answers, no bearable solutions, no feasible reasons why he should be inside his own skin. He heard music from behind, from somewhere beyond the trees, felt the shadows of people, behind the music and the trees. In his mind he saw again behind lighted windows, again his wonder in life increased and his understanding of it lessened all the more.

'It's beautiful, isn't it?' said Abbie, remote, a bit forlorn. 'I was born here, right here in this neighbourhood. Yes, don't say it,' she said, jumping ahead of him. 'One has to be born somewhere if one has to be born at all.' She stopped and looked at him. 'Don't you feel that way about Ireland, Riley?'

'About Dublin, yes.'

She made a mock semi-curtsey. 'Of course,' she said, becoming again comically grave and solemn, with a kind of absurd elfish solemnity he would ever afterwards associate with her, a sudden kind of wonderful, absolutely unpredictable solemnity that was registered at once in her long, thin angular face, in the inflections of her voice, in the very movements of her facial muscles, so that she became almost another and quite different person. 'Dublin, of course. I have read Mr Joyce too. You know your city. I know mine. A city has so many faces.' She paused, passing a hand lightly over her hair. 'Just like people.'

What a cliché! he thought. Yet coming from her at that exact point in time it held such a tone of absolute sincerity, he felt this was no longer just chatter, slotted in between the whirr and clip of a camera, but real words coming from a real person who was finally really being herself; he felt a kind of humility in her presence, knowing that she was, perhaps now quite unknown to herself, showing him a part of herself, of her life, she might not otherwise reveal or know herself. There was an unwanted sense of melodrama in her words which some inborn fastidious quirk in him resented, and of which he felt she was all too keenly and deliberately aware; yet he had somehow this rather terrifying conviction that every word she uttered she meant.

He leaned over the balcony, looking down. Remote sounds came from the blazing glass universe of a room behind, the unceasing babel of talk, laughter, the harsh, haunting merriment of people released momentarily from the cages of their particular lives, particular hells, and altogether removed from the warm panic now of a sudden gathering inside him, yet he knew a kind of ironic calm, even in the midst of this gentle upheaval.

As Abbie was about to say something, Laurie appeared in the doorway. 'Riley?' came her voice.

'Yes,' he said, dragging his eyes away from the green haunting evening sky. 'Yes, Laurie.'

'Mr Jay Simon would like to speak to you privately,' she said, stepping nearer, slightly widening the doors. 'I think he said his library, just to the right inside the room. Shall I fetch Don to help you?'

39

'I can manage, thanks.' He hoisted himself once more on to the crutches, swivelling around, again alert and aware as when he woke up that very morning. He stood rooted in a pool of light. He waved a crutch a little erratically in Abbie's direction. 'Laurie, this is Abbie,' he said in a voice of deliberate pomp and circumstance, almost intoning the words. 'I have already forgotten your surname, Abbie—'

'Auld Lang Syne,' she said simply, 'with emphasis on the middle bit.' She moved forward hesitantly. 'May I lend a hand?'

'I said I can manage,' he repeated, standing as erect as possible. Then he grinned. 'But why shouldn't I let myself be supported by two such good-looking ladies, damn it?'

Easing himself slightly off the crutches, he allowed them to hold each of his elbows and support him the length of the floor to the green baize door of the library, which Laurie held open for him. Her hair almost brushed his cheek as he passed through; he cocked his head quickly back, seeing them moving a little uncertainly together back into the room, then the door closed and he turned to the light behind the long mahogany desk and the figure seated directly under the light, wreathed in a cloud of grey-blue cigar smoke and the fine oaken after-smell of brandy.

'Riley, bless you, old son,' said Jay Simon, getting up and moving with that same quiet-catlike agility, pulling out a deep black-leather armchair. 'Welcome to my inner sanctum. There is yours,' said Jay, plonking a tall glass before him, placing the bottle within tantalisingly easy reach, relighting his corpulent cigar and brushing fingers back over thin shingles of sandy hair, small pudgy brown eyes glittering with quick calculated amity. 'We just wanted to know, Sue and I, if you are enjoying yourself in America, and if we can help you enjoy yourself better? There's no mad rush to get back to Ireland, is there? Though I expect you miss your pints of stout—eh?' Jay smiled sunnily.

'Yes,' said Riley, noting the amber glints of light in his bourbon. 'Among other things.'

'Such as a little blue-eyed colleen or two stashed away here and there—eh?' Jay said with a large exaggerated wink, spreading himself comfortably in the chair, leaning back. 'It's a perfectly healthy pastime. I see you've managed to acquire quite a delectable specimen already—a nice girl, Abbie, truly a wonderful girl, absolutely dedicated to her work—a little bit lost, don't you think, a little bit stranded—eh?'

'I wouldn't really know,' said Riley, not so much evasive as somewhat perplexed that he should be expected to know so much about someone who was still quite considerably unknown to him. 'I liked meeting her.'

'I always get on to her whenever I want anything really special done in the photography line,' went on Jay. 'She always delivers the goods. She's what they call unattached, by the way, which should increase your interest considerably —eh?' And again the wide accompanying wink that was supposedly meant to convey a wealth of masculine camaraderie and understanding, but which to Riley seemed a gesture of inane burlesque vacuity. Then Jay straightened up and became abruptly business-like, the steel that lay behind that Buddha-like placidity now showing. 'Sales are rocketing,' he said briskly. 'Now there's talk—no, more than talk—a distinct possibility of a television documentary on you that will be shown coast to coast across the country, running to an hour and a half, which would of course boost the sales even more. We're sorting out the legalities of the contract just now, but we expect things to start rolling very soon—isn't it exciting, Riley?'

The question took him by surprise. 'What?' he said, confused. 'Oh, yes—yes, of course.'

'You're already quite a comfortably off young man financially,' Jay was saying, 'from your British earnings, but we're going to hit the jackpot as well over here with this masterpiece. That is why, Riley,' said Jay slowly but smilingly, 'we want you to finish the new book so much. In many ways it is the reason for you coming here in the first place. Martin and I— well, we felt you needed to break away from your environment, we felt your material was getting on top of you and that you needed to look at it from a distance—you needed to "cast a cold eye", to borrow from your compatriot Yeats. See what I mean, Riley—eh?'

'Yes,' he said, 'I think so.' He reached forward and slowly raised the bourbon to his lips.

'And it was sheer genius on Martin's part getting the Emersons to offer to help and have you as their guest,' Jay continued, face half-clouded behind the cigar smoke. 'I never met them before today, but Martin swears on the holy bible by them, and that's good enough for me. And you seem quite happy being with them—are you, Riley?'

'Oh, yes,' he answered, again slightly taken aback by the abruptness of the question. 'I couldn't be happier.'

'Good, good,' said Jay almost with a satisfied purr. 'We all want you to be happy as long as you're here, for in order to finish this new book it is imperative that you should be in the right frame of mind as often as possible.'

Riley had the absurd feeling that he was the passive subject of an intense medical examination and that the eyes of the man before him were the cold points of a stethoscope going methodically over him, but he remained silent and sipped his drink.

'For, let's face it,' went on Jay, 'with this book we are publishing you've written real literature—a novel of intense truth and passion, not a neat sentimental naive woman's magazine story of a crippled boy in desperately poor circumstances— no, by God!' Jay exclaimed, for the first time getting aroused, slapping the palm of his hand down hard upon the desk. 'This is for real—about real people trapped in themselves and spitting furiously back at life—people who may make you want to vomit at times, but people you can't ignore or pretend don't exist, and because they existed for you, Riley McCombe, you've made them exist for everyone who has picked up your book and read it.'

Except for the single lamp on a shelf behind the desk, the room was in rich dark brown semi-darkness, and the face of Jay Simon rose and glimmered like a salmon-pink full moon against the dim-shadowed bookcases behind. Riley's gaze was now riveted on that face with its look of almost fanatical belief, and the face suddenly could have been his own, not the vastly dissimilar contours, not the grossly different shape and texture, but certainly the same intense almost ferocious expression of conviction and absolute certainty about the direction in which the bulk of his life was moving. He felt in a new kind of presence, one that induced in him a kind of reverence, almost of awe, and he was glad for his own silence and took refuge in it.

'Which is why, Riley,' Jay was now saying in his ordinary bland voice, 'you have got to finish this new novel. You owe it to all the people all over world who have read or are going to read your last, and more important than that, you owe it to yourself, for I don't believe you will ever or can ever be truly fulfilled and at peace with yourself until you've typed down the very last sentence of the last chapter. Now look me in the face and say I'm wrong!' finished Jay, blowing away the smoke-rings and smiling.

'I'm looking you in the face, Jay,' spoke Riley at last, 'and you know what my answer is.'

'Good, good,' beamed Jay, rising and sweeping round the desk. 'Drink up and let's join your waiting public!'

They returned to the large aquarium-like room to be struck by the almost physical force of the party going on around them, amid the swirling swarming eddies of smoke rising like marsh mist from the thronging room. Jay's hand held his elbow and steered him steadily to a small empty space that opened up unexpectedly like an oasis between two brown-veined marble columns. He sat down upon a low plinth that joined the pillars.

'Don't go sprinting over the lawn now,' cautioned Jay, laying a hand on his shoulder. 'I'll be back with something similar.'

Jay moved smoothly back into the crowd, and for a while Riley leaned back against the nearest pillar, resting the crutches across his lap, looking on with an insatiable curiosity as the crowd thickened and thinned near where he sat, jostling against each other casually, good-humouredly, men patting sweat-moist necks and elderly bald domes with handkerchiefs; women holding their heads carefully like heavily-coiffured swans delicately moving and gliding through a sea of robust masculine appreciation; young girls with bare smooth shoulders and faces like pale lost lilies moving with beautiful languor through the throng, breasts curving, white balconies rising out of deep-delved gowns and summer dresses, some with thin gold chains dangling from wrists and ankles; young wives grown desolate and bored not inviting but coolly accepting the predatory male glance which the young college adolescent nymphets eagerly sought and devoured with fresh-eyed hunger

43

as they giggled their way through the long wine-rich music-loud evening, the whole garrulous wistful sanguine motley feeding whether they knew it or not upon each other for sustenance and succour. Riley for a while felt happily marooned, safe and distant, bound to his own small rock of self-identity, discerning, observing, drawing certain facile conclusions, summing up with sly witty innuendoes, cubby-holing all those variegated lives with slick brilliant expertise drawn from some inner reservoir of unsubdued malice. But he grew tired and restless; there was a slow pounding ache behind his eyes, and loneliness lay like a stone on his heart. He looked around him, feeling alien, foreign, a stranger, an outsider, an uninvited guest at some strange banquet where by a cruel quirk of fate he now found himself, more alone than if he were upon the glacial wastes of the moon.

'Hi,' said a woman's voice, startlingly close by. 'I hope my husband didn't give you verbal indigestion.'

He looked up and saw Sue Simon standing a little behind him, an arm twined around one of the pillars, a sandalled foot resting upon the plinth. He thought again how remarkably cool and melon-fresh she looked in all that heat, sweat and smoke; she had changed into a plain white-grey linen trouser suit, with a brown silk scarf caught round her throat, and her neat dark hair was trimly tied back, giving her the look of a healthy well-scrubbed boy-sailor. Save for a faint trace of lipstick she wore no make-up at all. She held a long slim glass in her hand. She was indeed, he realised again, a handsome woman.

'I saw your entry into his *sanctum sanctorum*,' said Sue, before taking a slow sip of her drink. 'Where no doubt he proceeded to sound forth upon the moral dangers of being a world-read best-selling author, especially being young and trusting in this depraved and depraving New World.'

'Oh, that,' said Riley, returning her slightly bantering smile. 'He was just being kind. And also very flattering.'

'Poor Jay,' she said. 'He broods over his authors like a mother hen—a grossly over-weight mother hen. You must try and tolerate his many peculiar traits, if only because he has so many fine ones.'

'I think I like him quite a lot already,' he said.

44

Sue gave him a rather penetrating unhurried look. 'You didn't have to say that, you know,' she said, still looking down at him, rubbing the rim of the glass along her lower lip.

'Yes,' he said, 'I know. I said it because I feel it is true.'

She smiled and nodded her head slightly. 'That's an excellent reason for saying anything. He is so good at giving people quite the opposite impression of what I know to be the truth about himself.'

'You mean he isn't as hard-boiled as he makes out?'

Sue's face was wistful. 'He tries to be hard-boiled, and sometimes he succeeds in convincing himself as well as other people.' She smiled wryly. 'Sometimes he *is* hard-boiled, and that's slightly better than pretending to be, but it isn't worth the effort it takes, and on goes the mask again, the well-worn mask of the hard-bitten whizz-kid from the Bronx, the self-made man who was a publishing tycoon before he was forty, cracking the big whip over the heads of lesser men, like writers for instance, whom he loves to treat with a sort of fulsome patronage, but of whom he is really though secretly scared to death.' She stopped. 'Do I surprise you?'

'A little, yes.'

'Are you surprised, I wonder, by what I say, or just because I am saying it in the first place?'

'A conundrum, no less,' said Riley, warming to the challenge she seemed to be throwing down. 'A little of both, I think— perhaps more by the what rather than the why.'

'Then you must be interested in Jay as a person, right?'

'I think I'm interested in everyone as a person,' he rejoined. 'For me, that must be the prime and initial interest.'

'That's either extremely naive or extremely perceptive of you,' she replied in her calm low-toned drawl. 'Perhaps a bit of both—'

'Perhaps.'

'Jay is certainly complex, all right,' she said, 'otherwise I'd never have gone out with him, never mind marry him. So he plays his own highly intricate and personalised game of the self-made man, the smooth dealer with the silver tongue and the heart of solid negotiable one-hundred carat US gold bullion. A little of Shylock and Svengali and Ebenezer Scrooge rolled into one, perhaps with heavy undertones of a rather

45

moronic Mussolini. And he's really quite good in the part, to the general audience, but I hardly come into that category after eighteen years of marriage,' she said, taking another slow sip, 'and from my seat in the stalls the cracks in his otherwise impeccable stage costume are all too painfully obvious. Of course he's an egotist—perhaps a bigger one than either me or you,' Sue smiled, 'but deep down—if I can employ such a cliché—'

'I've used worse ones,' he said.

'Deep down he's ridiculously simple, almost to the point of absurdity, as if he were still battling his bland Jewish way through high school, hellbent on beating all the other well-fed starters in the race, not even content with being a well-placed second.' Again she stopped. 'God, even to my ears all this sounds densely boring. I think you are a very patient man, Riley McCombe. And a rather nice one, if the truth be told. As told,' she finished in the same calm intently intimate voice, 'it must be.'

'Thank you, Sue,' he said, rather awkwardly, the clean linen whiteness of her sweeping over him now like a welcoming breeze.

'I hope this is the first of your many visits to Jericho Pines,' she said, already beginning to move away. 'Here approacheth your angel of mercy, and,' in a slightly more audible voice, 'I leave you two to it. Ciao.' And the linen coolness of her was gone.

His mind was clear and receptive to every single step of foot and every single inflection of voice in the whole of that enormous basilica of a room, as if he were merely indeed an oversensitive tape-recorder inscribing everything, every casually fallen word, half-perceived look or half-finished gesture, upon the thin super-sensitive stuff of his memory forever lying in abeyance behind the forever-moving lenses of his sight. He heard almost the mental click of the lenses as his ordinary eyes roved and moved here and there scanning the swarming human landscape before him, biting deep and indelibly into his brain. He was now all a camera, as hopeless and as dedicated as Abbie with her chain of cameras around her neck, and more alone than ever she would know, for he could depend on one camera only.

At last the promised drink had arrived and was now being

offered to him, though not by the well-manicured hand of Jay Simon.

'Jay asked me to take this to you.'

'Thank you, Abbie,' he said, putting the crutches carefully on the safe side of the pillar, taking the glass from her.

'You still don't remember my surname, do you?' she said, a little piqued, standing above him, somewhat defiant, challenging in the fix of her shoulders, a thumb hitched down into the waistband of her jeans, that long thick raven's wing of hair tumbling more than ever down across her eye.

He started to hum the air of Auld Lang Syne.

She stopped and her hand fell rather heavily on his shoulder, the pressure of her fingers pleasurable through his shirt. 'You're funny,' she said, her fingers tightening as she teetered slightly on her feet. 'So damn funny.'

'Oh, I'm the original Cyrano de Bergerac,' he replied, gulping down almost half of his fresh drink, finding some altogether unexpected tears burning at the edge of his eyes, again inwardly aware of his own direction. 'Except that my complaint isn't nearly as obvious as an overgrown nose. That at least was good for laughs.'

'Are we going all·maudlin?' said Abbie, stammering slightly, still holding his shoulder, her somewhat bemused deserted child's face not far from his own, so that he caught the scent of her hair swaying downwards.

'Yes, you're right,' he conceded, trying hard to focus his mind on something other than the delicious closeness of her, the shape of her small rounded breasts under the sweater. 'That's another of my unpleasant traits.'

'I'd like to get to know your better ones,' she said. She sat down abruptly beside him, putting a hand over her mouth as she gave a slight hiccup. 'I think I must be slightly drunk. Do you mind? It doesn't happen often.'

'Let me act as your mirror,' said Riley, 'If you will promise to act as mine.'

'Then let us both be mirrors to each other,' she said, 'albeit slightly cracked mirrors.' Abbie was silent for a few moments, legs stretched out, feet crossed, meditatively contemplating the somewhat scuffed tips of her well-worn sneakers, arrow-browed.

47

'I'd like to take you into the Village sometime,' she said quietly. 'I have a small place there, nothing much. Humble but my own. Have you been to the Village since you came?'

'No, I haven't.' He had a feeling it would not exactly be Don or Laurie's favourite haunt, but he did not say so.

'Oh, then you must come,' said Abbie eagerly. 'I think you'll like it. It's become a bit commercialised and almost respectable now, but it's still exciting and other-worldly and maybe you could use it as a backcloth somewhere in this new book you're writing.' She stopped and smiled, and again it was more of a grin which he found charmingly open and irresistible. 'You see, I've only got your aesthetic interests at heart.'

'Well, that's better than having no interest at all.'

'Would you like to come, Riley—truly?'

'Truly, I would love to come.'

'I'm an impulsive creature with an acute sense of time slipping by,' she said, 'so would tomorrow be all right?'

'Tomorrow? Well—er—'

'Am I rushing you?'

'Oh, no, not a bit,' he said hastily. 'As far as I know tomorrow is a free day, and it would be nice to relax after all this.'

'Right,' she said brightly, already considerably more alert and less soporific. 'Would tomorrow morning suit—about eleven? I have a small car and I know Randalswood very well—that's where your hosts the Emersons live, isn't it?'

'That's it. The house is called Ambleside, the last on the avenue leading down to the beach.'

'Do you think she'd mind—Mrs Emerson—a little upstart of a career girl like me whisking you away from under her nose at only our first meeting?'

'Tomorrow will be our second meeting,' said Riley, 'which will make it a little less incredible. No—Laurie won't mind. She says the more people I get to know over here the better I'll be able to understand and write about Americans, for the stage Yankee is just as obnoxious as the stage Irishman.'

'I guess that's true of every nationality,' Abbie mused. 'In my job I fall over them by the dozen every day.'

'I'd like to hear more about your work, Abbie. It must be very exciting.'

48

She shrugged her shoulders and gave a long sigh. 'It can be, at times, but for the most part it's a dull deadly grind. People tend to treat me at best as a nuisance, a necessary evil, and at worst as someone mentally retarded in a rather severe way. I guess they're right on both counts.' She paused and looked at him, a wistful half-smile hovering about her mouth. 'But sometimes it can be exciting, like today, meeting you.'

'You're making me blush,' he said lightly, feeling the warm sweat moist on his neck.

'Am I? I'm glad. I thought it was just the whiskey. Riley,' she said, turning eagerly to him, 'about tomorrow—if it's fine, would you like to see New York with me? I know Mrs Emerson—'

'For God's sake call her Laurie.'

'Laurie. I suppose she has taken you into the city often—'

'Once or twice—it isn't easy with the kids.'

'I'd like to show it to you through the eyes of a photographer,' Abbie said, her face becoming animated, throwing back that truant rope of hair impatiently. 'That sounds terribly conceited, but I think I could show you things and buildings and places from angles that you might not see otherwise by just going into New York to see a show or visit a museum or art gallery. There are so many hidden aspects of this city I long to show and reveal to you, if you're sure you wouldn't be too bored—'

'I wouldn't be bored, Abbie,' he said, no longer timorous of meeting her gaze fully.

Like a glad impulsive child having received a favour, she squeezed his hand happily.

'I'll show you around the Village first,' she said, 'there's someone I want you to meet there—a great friend of mine—he's a sculptor—he's been like a father to me, he and his wife have more or less adopted me—she paints too—they have a marvellous studio there—you'll love them. After that we'll drive around the city and spend the whole day there and eat whenever we feel like it—how does that sound to you, Riley?'

He was about to answer, the quick glad words about to tumble from his tongue, when something made him look up, and he saw Laurie standing a few feet away, the orange shawl across her shoulders, her handbag dangling from her wrist.

49

She came forward, her face rather tired and strained, her mouth a little tight.

'Sorry to break up the party,' said Laurie politely, 'but Don and I think it's time we were making tracks for home. It's been quite a day, one way or another, and we're both feeling rather pooped. Are you ready to take your leave, Riley?'

Almost guiltily Abbie withdrew her hand from his and stood up, and he thought the gesture both charming and absurd; yet he felt a certain constraint himself for some obscure reason, which he resented furiously, but he found his crutches and hoisted himself to his feet.

'Whenever you are, Laurie,' he said.

'I'm afraid I kept him longer than I should,' said Abbie. 'When I start talking I forget when to stop.'

'Oh, I'm sure Riley wasn't exactly mute himself,' Laurie said with a rather distant smile. She held out her hand. 'Well, it was nice meeting you, Miss—er—I'm sorry, but I don't think I caught your name—'

'Abbie will do fine—just Abbie.' They shook hands.

'Perhaps we may see you again sometime—' Laurie said formally.

Abbie smiled. 'I'm afraid so,' she said. 'Being the bold brash creature that I am, I've already inveigled poor Riley into a date with me—'

'Oh, yes?' said Laurie, her voice calm though her brows were raised a little.

'Yes, he finally succumbed to my blandishments and agreed to let me come out to your place tomorrow morning to pick him up—'

'To—pick—him—up?' Laurie repeated slowly, just managing to keep the hard edge of malice out of her voice.

'In my car,' said Abbie nonchalantly. 'I'm sure you've shown him all that's best in New York, but I thought he'd be interested in seeing it through someone else's eyes, and me being nothing really but a sort of animated human camera maybe I can show him things he might otherwise miss—'

'Oh, I'm sure you can,' said Laurie. 'Riley's always insatiable for new experiences—'

'The sign of a good writer,' rejoined Abbie, finishing off the remnants of her drink and crossing her arms, looking as though she were enjoying herself hugely. 'So I'll rouse you about eleven in the morning, Riley—' she turned quickly to Laurie, 'if that's all right with you, Mrs Emerson—the time, I mean?'

'Perfectly all right. I hope you have a good day for it. Ah, here's my husband now—Don, have you met Riley's friend, Miss—er—?'

'I'm Abbie,' she said, shaking hands. 'Glad to meet you, Don.'

'The pleasure is mine, Abbie,' said Don, large and genial, shaking hands warmly. He stepped back, looked at Abbie and then at Riley, and grinned broadly. 'You sure have an eye for pretty girls, Riley!'

Abbie smiled and turned to Riley. 'No goodbyes. See you tomorrow morning bright and chirpy. Nice meeting you folks.' And she glided away back into the crowd.

'You're a fast worker, friend,' said Don, moving to take his arm. 'A real pretty girl, that. How do you think she'd fit in on the Irish scene?'

'I've a feeling she's quite adaptable,' he said, propelling himself forward towards where he remembered the door was, Laurie going a little ahead of them, holding the shawl about her shoulders.

Just then Jay Simon broad-shoulderedly barged his way through the crowd and stood before them with the same infectious boyish grin sunshining his broad countenance, giving Riley a sly reproving look. 'Emulating Longfellow's Arab—eh?' said Jay with tremendous bonhomie, once again clasping him around the shoulders and almost but mercifully not quite kissing him on both cheeks in the French and, vaguely he remembered, the Russian way. 'Folding up your tent and quietly stealing away. Bold, McCombe, bold! Why the rush—there are still so many people I want you to meet—or should I say who want to meet you—can't you stay?'

'I'd love to—' began Riley, slithering to a standstill.

'Me too,' said Don with enthusiasm, equable as ever, turning to Laurie, whose face was hidden in semi-gloom as they neared the glazed porch doors.

'I think not, Don, really,' she said. She stopped and turned, smiling, extending her hand to Jay Simon. 'Thank you for a lovely day, a lovely welcome, thank you for having us, Don and myself, mere nonentities to you and your wife—'

'Nobody connected with our friend McCombe here could possibly qualify for that description,' said Jay, clasping Laurie's hand in both his own. 'We're all in on this epoch-making project together—eh? Just take good care of him and pack him up with all the right vitamins—he's a valuable piece of property!' And the way in which Jay Simon said it, with such infectious candour and camaraderie, it did not sound banal at all but strangely innocent.

'We'll take care of him,' said Laurie quietly, her hand still held by Jay, 'if he'll let us.'

'Don't you know you're irresistible, honey?' Don said cheerfully, patting his wife's shoulder. 'Say good night to your wife for us, please,' continued Don, shaking hands and making his way towards the exit.

'I will, I will,' promised Jay, passing with them through that long somehow absurdly Romanesque hallway, his face beaming like an autumn moon in an unreal twilight. 'I will indeed. I don't know where she's got to, but Sue's a remarkable woman—'

'Yes, she is,' agreed Riley, hobbling tenaciously along, feeling the sweat under his armpits already beginning to cool as they approached the still glimmering evening outside.

They paused on the patio, Jay taking a firmer hold of Riley's arm. 'It was Sue, you know,' he said with unmistakable pride, 'who was really responsible for you being here at all. I seldom read manuscripts if I can get out of it at all, but Sue was absolutely determined that we should buy yours, Riley. She stayed up one entire night reading it, and when I tiptoed into her room the next morning I expected to find long exhaustive notes of criticism, but no—on top of your mountain of manuscript she had scribbled just one word—"BUY"!' Jay laughed. 'So I, like a dutiful husband—being a shrewd publisher was merely secondary—I did just that.'

They all laughed. Riley looked up. The moon looked wan and indecisive, somewhat lost and stranded, like a virgin fresh from the cloisters about to enter the rude world of talkative, argumentative, hungering people, standing hesitant on the threshold, a pale slip of ephemeral innocence. And in its gleam Jay Simon, the jovial court jester with more than a touch of the master puppeteer in him, looked oddly, incongruously innocent himself.

The swish of the car tyres on gravel, the long winding drive back, the intermittent welcome intrusion of the moon slanting over blanched silver plains. Riley inclined his head back upon the car cushion, dreadfully tired, every ounce of his body exhausted, yet his mind wholly, painfully alert, watchful of every star. Don did the driving, his strong-boned sturdy knuckled hands upon the steering wheel pleasantly comforting and reassuring. In that funny resonant Midwestern drawl of his Don was quoting under the midnight highway glow the salty poems of Robert Service with the metallic tinkling of the panhandle in them, and the magnificent Rabelaisian meanderings of mad sad doomed befuddled Robbie Burns drowning in whiskey and poetry and love along sweet Afton's voluptuous braes. And Riley in his equally doomed heart sculpting jagged uneven shrapnel pieces of poetry in his own muteness as the innumerable beacons flashed incessantly past, the silent all-eloquent presence of Laurie in the seat behind forever in the forefront of his voyaging mind.

Don paused in bawdy midsong. 'You're very quiet, honey, back there,' he said, 'Why so? Didn't you enjoy the day? A bit ballyhoo, but didn't you enjoy it?'

'Oh, yes, I enjoyed it,' said Laurie, and to Riley her voice sounded thin, tired, remote.

'Then why the gloom?' Don wanted to know, negotiating rather a tricky bend and flicking a glance in the overhead mirror. 'It was Riley's day—why spoil it now?'

'Am I spoiling it?' she asked, pulling on her frail lace gloves. 'Am I spoiling it, Riley?'

'Oh—er—no,' he began, pulling himself up straight.

'I think I can answer for him, dear, for both of us,' said Don calmly. 'We both know, myself and Riley, that you're just about the most wonderful creature in the world, and we're both damn thankful that we know and love you—' Don managed to give Riley a playful nudge in the ribs, which was rather unnerving as they were just then overtaking some cars. 'What say you, friend?'

'Oh—yes, yes, of course,' Riley managed to say in between

holding on to his crutches and fear of imminent departure to eternal spheres via an American motorway.

At last Laurie spoke from the depths of the car, quiet, calm. 'She's very pretty, Riley.'

'Who's very pretty, honey?' asked Don when Riley did not immediately answer.

'I was speaking primarily to Riley,' said Laurie, not tartly, but a little tiredly, leaning back.

'Sorry,' said Don.

'Yes,' said Riley, with more defiance than he intended. 'Yes, she is.'

'Oh,' said Don, nodding his head sagely, smiling, his alert intelligent face lit in the flickering spaces of the overhead yellow orbs of highway lights. 'Now I've got you—that cute little lady photographer who took a shine to you—eh, Riley?'

'She was very friendly,' said he, a rebel star racing crazily ahead of them, burning into his eyes.

Turning his head slightly, he could just make out Laurie's face in the gloom of the back seat, studious, composed, contemplative, staring pensively down at her gloved hands folded sedately in her lap. The lights blazed down the seemingly endless labyrinth of highway. He was tired, drained, hopeful, and happy in a way that was indescribably sad. The racing, galloping star ahead kept dipping towards the faint glimmering horizon, but never quite making it.

III

He woke with a sudden, precise click of consciousness, his mind clear as a windowpane swept clean after a summer shower. It might have been night or day, early morning or late evening; it was impossible to say in the heavy tangible gloom that pervaded everywhere around him. The thick drapes were still drawn across the window, casting a penumbra that altogether dissociated the mind from all known margin of time or the inbuilt awareness of time's passage. He shut his swollen lids and tried to escape back into oblivion, into the mellow mists of alcohol now slowly, fearfully ebbing from his mind, releasing the sharp ferrets of thought and memory.

The low-beamed narrow ceiling of the room in Greenwich, her bachelor pad as she had called it, where she had brought him with touching trepidation, a place of splendid disarray, strewn with a chaotic conglomeration of random pieces of furniture caught in a paroxysm of startled contradiction, that seemed somehow comically to complement each other. He remembered what the house had looked like from the cobbled street—like most of the other houses, leaning precariously towards each other as if afflicted with rickets, narrow, hump-backed, little attic windows squinting like eyes in the foreheads of gnomes and gargoyles, allowing only pale infrequent patches of sky to infiltrate the humming gloom of the serpentine lane-ways that led off the wide cross-town streets and main avenues. She had stood there in the middle of that dishevelled beehive of a room, hands thrust into the pockets of her jeans, looking about her with a comical careless slightly befuddled air, as if wondering how they had come to be there, asking him did he mind the awful mess of it all and would he like tea or coffee . . . and rummaging in the cupboard for some of the sterner stuff.

He moved his totempole-heavy head, and, opening one eye reluctantly, saw the wisps of a still smouldering feminine cigarette rising from an ashtray on the small bedside table, the lighted tip giving off a vague flaky redness from the bowels of the marble ashtray. He turned over on to his back, closing his eyes, wanting to be sick, wondering with panic where he could be sick without ruining or despoiling anything, wondering where the hell the bathroom was, and wishing he were out in the open air. Jesus, a voice asked him which he did not readily recognise as his own, was he going to destroy the lovely cool linen of her bed by getting brutally sick on it? The sheets felt and smelled sweetly of good human sweat, and he was determined not to pollute their sweetness by his own gut-foulness.

He opened his eyes fully. They grew accustomed to the dark or rather the dense gloom of the room accommodated his sight, and he could discern draped over the back of an ordinary wooden chair the pale shimmer of a shift, terribly alone and innocent; on the bottom of the chair itself there lay a dark octopus cluster of cameras, straps dangling like fungi over the sides. The water and the music and the clean beauty of Botticelli and the aged faces of the ducks in the ponds in the Park and the laughing reflections of her in the plate-glass acres of Macy's in her tight black jeans holding fast and giddily on to his elbow in the mad human cattle-rush of a weekday noon and afternoon . . .

It was strange the way the tiredness had fallen from him on returning to the house in Randalswood; it had suddenly dropped from him like a heavy overcoat, and he no longer felt like sleep. They had some coffee and a late brandy, which Laurie refused, and as soon as he could he went upstairs to his room, changing into his pyjamas, relishing the cool of them against his skin. He switched off the main light, leaving the yellow standard lamp on, and stretched out on the bed. Presently he heard Don and Laurie come upstairs and go past his door to their room down the corridor; the room where Richard slept lay between, and little Midge, young as she was, had a room also, all to herself, dainty as a doll's house. She had invited him in there once, regal as any princess condescending to acknowledge the existence of a mere commoner, and he had found himself standing as clumsy as an elephant in her own fairytale corner of the house, afraid to move lest some careless movement of his crutches might upset any of the delicate Dresden china figurines which seemed to inhabit every inch of her room, her luminous blue eyes grave as she explained who had given her that doll and when she had acquired that one, telling him their names, madly exotic, which she conjured up herself, and itemising each detail of their costumes. Riley had felt as Lemuel Gulliver must have felt in Lilliput, large, cumbersome, horrific, perilous of crushing underfoot a single charming miniature form. Since that day Midge had invited him in again, but though he often thought of that fantasy room with longing, the fear of irreparably breaking something remained, and he would make up some plausible excuse for backing out of the gracious invitation, for although he might perhaps be able to substitute whatever he might have damaged, he knew, as in real life, that some things are irreplaceable.

It was long past midnight, it might indeed have been one or two in the morning, but the need for sleep had passed, and he lay wakeful and wistful on the bed, thinking back over that long crowded day, sifting the events, telescoping them, remembering faces and voices of strangers, the green and marble expanses of Jericho Pines, wondering in ways ambiguous and ambivalent about Jay and Sue Simon, about their lives, and in a less vague, more poignant way wondering about Abbie, that strange funny rainbow girl now arching over his thoughts, hearing perfectly once more her sudden tomboyish laughter, every inflection of her voice; she seemed somehow rootless, a stormy petrel of a thing, a prey to every chance whimsical breeze that might come along blowing her where it willed and she going indifferently or defiantly along with it to wherever the foolish captive music of her heart led her. All this he knew or surmised only with the remotest intuition, for her shadow had not as yet taken on substance in his mind, yet already a part of him knew her beyond the need for possession, beyond the hard factual knowledge of her, and this filled him with nervous elation, rendering sleep impossible. It was all so absolutely real to him now, that long scorching day seethed and foamed within him like surf, like brine hot and fuming from the sea, drowning out all other things, not letting him be, tossing him about in wanton turbulence.

And as he knew it would, the typewriter beckoned, lying on the floor in a silver pool of moonlight, squat, stolid, a thing of nuts and bolts and springs and screws and altogether unremarkable and mundane; but not to him, not now, for now it was Pegasus waiting to be mounted, waiting to fly him to whatever star he wished, whatever galaxy he wanted to explore, it was now the open sesame that would unlock any door, span any barrier of mind, delve deep into lost earth or soar miraculously and majestically above it to heights unimagined and bejewelled, the one thing now that would make him victorious and free. He arose from the bed and fumbled his way along the edge of it until he reached the large fly-winged armchair and lowered himself down into its soft receiving depths above the waiting body of the typewriter. In a kind of oblivious fever he lifted it on to the low stool, inserted a slim page of foolscap and at the turn and click of a switch the machine crackled into life as if quivering sensuously under his touch. There was nothing in his world now except the typewriter; he and it were utterly alone and isolated, committed to the night and to each other, alone with the need, the urgency, the hunger to empty his mind of images, shapes, sounds, shadows, lights that filled and thronged like mad marauding herds thundering truculent and triumphant until his head and heart ached with their brazen bellowing. Words poured from him, random and raging, roaring and ranting, swallowing up page upon page, his fingers flying over the keyboard of the typewriter like those of a demented pianist lost in some frenzied rhapsody of his own, a music only he could hear loud and deafening in his heart. Vaguely he felt the beads of sweat dripping down his forehead, stinging his eyes, drops of burning salty water anointing, scourging, blurring his vision. He brushed them impatiently away, flung them from him like spray, and went on pounding the keys, pounding out his own momentary salvation, unaware of the slowly brightening windowpane facing him, the first febrile chorus of birds in the trees outside, lost to everything but the rattling noise of the old typewriter under his fingertips and the louder more furious humming of his heart.

Some vague faraway something told him that tomorrow in cold reason he would look upon this mountain with dismay and destroy most of it in anger and contempt, fiercely reviling and ridiculing his own puny attempts at expressing the stirrings of heart and mind. But for now tomorrow was a thing of vast improbability, and if what he had typed yielded even a thin sprinkling of gold out of so many layers of dull dross, no star would have burnt in vain and been lost.

At last he looked up, the penultimate page almost completed, and was surprised to see that the glow of the standard lamp had grown pale and dead against the brighter light of day. He lay back in the chair, utterly spent now, his body lathered with sweat, his hair dank and wet, staring with surprise and relief out of the window at the new day in full-throated chorus. He looked down at the proliferation of pages spread like confetti upon the carpet, wondering where he had been, where the night had gone without him. There was a soft movement outside his door, then came a gentle knock.

'Yes?' he called out, rousing himself from his blank weary staring into nothing.

'May I come in?' she said, and he heard the slight tinkle of delf.

'Oh—yes, please do,' he answered.

Laurie entered, carrying a tray with a cup and saucer on it; she closed the door with her shoulder, coming forward and putting the tray down on the table.

'I brought you a cup of strong black coffee,' she said, smiling. 'I thought you'd need it. I heard the typewriter going from an early hour—'

'Oh God,' he said, guilty and contrite, taking the cup in both hands and taking a long grateful gulp. 'I hope I didn't wake the household with the racket.'

'Not a bit of it,' she reassured him, her hand briefly resting on his shoulder before she sat down on the edge of the bed. 'I couldn't sleep either, and lay there hearing you typing—like hearing knitting-needles clicking.' She looked curiously down at the pile of pages on the floor beside the typewriter. 'I was wondering what kept you up all night.'

The coffee felt good. 'God knows,' he said, sighing. 'I haven't looked at it yet, but I think it's a chapter in the new book—'

'A whole chapter?' she said, in a way that pleased him.

'Yes, I think so,' he said, sipping his coffee.

'May I?' Laurie asked, reaching for the manuscript, raising an eyebrow enquiringly.

He grinned. 'If you feel up to it so early.'

She stooped, gathered up the pages with both hands and settled back on the bed, rustling the paper into place on her lap, brushing back her hair absently as she began to read. She was still wearing her night-robe, pink, deep and luxurious, falling to her slippered feet, open at the neck, showing her suntanned throat. Her brown hair, sleek and smooth, was caught up in a bun on the nape of her neck, and the early sun caught it as she bent over the pages, elbow on knee, hand cupping her chin. He watched her intently, seeing her long dark lashes shadowing her eyes, patches of faded varnish on her nails. A small pulse throbbed minutely at the hollow base of her throat. His eyes travelled slowly to her feet, her toes almost visible in the thin pink slippers, something oddly naked, vulnerable, off-guard; it was the first time he had seen her dressed in such a free, ordinary, unthinking way, and he felt excited. He drank the last of the coffee quickly and looked out of the window at the cloudless morning sky beyond the swaying top branches of the trees.

Her silence lengthened, unbroken save for the rustle of paper, and again he grew alarmed and apprehensive, wanting to get inside her skull and discover what she was thinking, to invade her thoughts and send them scattering in wild disarray, to break that maddening calm of hers, that studious serenity which enveloped her, and excluded him from any real communication with her, shutting him off, holding him at bay, making him feel stranded. He did not want to look at her, he did not need to, for her presence filled the room and overflowed into his mind. There was an ache at the back of his eyes, and despite the recent coffee his tongue and throat felt dry, leathery, parched; the tips of his fingers tingled, sore and raw from the pounding at the typewriter, and it seemed that every muscle in his body was stretched taut and tight as violin strings pulled brutally to their limits. He could no longer take refuge in weariness; not now, with his every sense attuned to her slightest movement, hearing her quiet breathing, seeing behind his closed lids her calm intent face bent over his foolish vain multitude of words, imagining in spite of himself the outline of her body in the loose concealing robe. He pressed his eyelids tighter, his fingers gripped the arms of the chair in an involuntary movement of revolt; once more he felt the familiar irrational anger rising in him as her silence continued, as though she were microscopically examining every thought and feeling he had ever known, tracing the highways and lowways of all the lost laneways of his life back to their beginning, ferreting out with gentle insistence every small insignificant secret he might have kept and hoarded to himself from the gaze of the world. The long frantic labours of the night were less than the merest dust now, were blown leaves floating forlornly in empty space falling dismally to earth before his eyes; they were inane insane utterances stuck in the stuttering slobbering throat of an imbecile crouched on a bleak street corner yelling out, in futile rage and defiance under an indifferent sky, the broken words of all maimed and tongueless things that ever had sufferance under heaven.

Then she spoke, the last page fluttering from her hand.

'Words,' she said wearily, passing a hand over her eyes. 'Words. Oh, Riley, dear Riley, when are you going to get away from words?' And it was a question, a real agonised question.

His heart lurched down, down. He opened, closed, opened, closed, and finally opened his eyes, praying for release, knowing there was none, and confronted her with the brave desperation of a man facing a firing-squad, absurdly conscious of birds singing.

'Is that all you see?' he asked, and he was surprised at the quietness of his voice.

'No, no,' she said, her face showing annoyance. 'Of course that's not all I see! Give me credit, for God's sake. I see many things. You are beginning, Riley, you are beginning to write, to be truly a writer. But please, please watch out. Stop this crazy love affair with words.' She hoisted one knee, hands clasped around it, leaning back, staring desperately up at the ceiling. 'It will destroy you otherwise—'

'But it's the only way—' he started.

'—That you can write,' she finished for him, tiredly. 'Yes, yes, so you keep saying. I can't buy that, Riley, I really can't. You can go on writing that way—it's so easy. Bang, bang, bang. Words for the pure and simple sake of words. Wolfe did it quite well, and so did Dylan Thomas, but you have not the equipment or the capacity of either—really, you haven't—'

Oh God, he screamed inside himself. The birds were still singing. There was still mercy abroad in the world.

'I know I'm hurting you,' she said, looking him straight in the face. 'I know I am, and I'm sorry. But hurt is inevitable in criticism, real criticism. My God, Riley,' she said impatiently, tapping the pages on the bed beside her, 'at times I thought I was reading a very adolescent version of James Joyce! Don't make a face, it's true. Don't try to be an undernourished Joyce. You have so much other stuff in you, stuff that is truly fine and uniquely your own.' She stopped abruptly and looked at him with what he thought was supreme sadness. 'Don't you see?'

He rested his head wearily in his hand. 'Yes,' he said, 'yes, I see.' For no reason at all he remembered that the standard lamp was still burning, cold against the day.

'I don't think you do,' she spoke quietly, putting both feet on the floor and rubbing her eyes with her knuckles. 'I think you think I'm just being bitchy, don't you? Good God,' she said suddenly, comically exasperated. 'If only it was that simple!'

'A little praise goes a long way,' he said softly, shaking his head, staring forlornly down at the typewriter.

'Praise!' she said sharply, and he saw her hands tightening, spread out on each side of her. 'You need praise less than anyone I know. Do you expect me to fawn over you like all those people last night—like Jay Simon and the others, and that creature called Abbie?' She stopped, and her face was a sad afternoon landscape.

'You don't understand, do you?' he said, again speaking softly, a little wearily. 'You can't see what a word of praise from you would mean for me, can you?'

She continued to look stonily down at the floor. 'You've had too many people here and at home telling you how great you are. I'm not here for that, Riley.'

'What are you here for?' he asked in sudden overwhelming

irrepressible despair, twisting his head savagely towards her.

He saw the stark stricken look in her face, a look of fear almost, and immediately he was sorry, immediately he felt he could have cheerfully killed himself for the hurt he had given her; but it was too late. At once they looked dumbly at each other, lost, bewildered, trapped in a certain excruciating knowledge and certitude, and at once they heard the telephone ring in shrill persistence from her bedroom. Silently she left the room. He reached over and, with the tip of one crutch, expertly pressed the knob of the standard lamp and switched it off. He had started to unbutton his pyjama top when Laurie reappeared briefly in the doorway.

'That was your friend Abbie,' she said in an ordinary domestic matter-of-fact voice. 'From New York. Better get dressed. She's picking you up at eleven.' And she went with a soft swish of her gown.

Down the corridor he heard Midge in a bright linnet-throated voice starting to sing out a nursery tune.

Abbie looked almost the same as on the previous night at Jericho Pines, dressed it seemed as before in a tight sweater and clinging black jeans, her bare feet thrust into well-worn sneakers of an indeterminate grey-blue shade; the only new note of change he could see was a white and red dotted scarf, wrapped around her head turban-wise. She wore not the slightest trace of make-up, and had a clean healthy well-scrubbed look that fitted the day perfectly. She looked incredibly young and chirpy, all the tiredness of the night before gone from her, a clear gloss on her skin, tanned and vibrant.

It was a small car, a convertible with the hood down, and her long very slim legs looked almost ungainly in the cramped space between the floor and the steering column around which her knees stuck awkwardly like slender black shoots. His crutches stuck out of the back seat but at a safe angle so as not to present a road hazard; they both laughed as they tried to put them in the right position in the back of the car, Abbie saying they were his twin pillars of respectability and how very upright they made him. Laurie saw them to the car in the driveway, her manner cool, decorous and polite, saying she hoped they would have a good day, and Midge crept to the door to peep out, still in her blue pyjamas, bright hair tousled, and piped up to ask who was the pretty lady that was taking Riley away and would she bring him back. He looked back and saw them standing in the porch, gazing after them, Laurie's arm around Midge, rubbing her fair head thoughtfully. Then they were lost to sight.

'She doesn't approve of me,' said Abbie simply, as though merely expressing a fact impartially. 'Pity. I kind of like her, even if she does seem intelligent, which should put me off.'

'Is that why I don't put you off—because of my lack of intelligence?' Riley asked lightly, enjoying the cool rush of air on his face as the car picked up speed through the quiet tree-lined avenues of the pleasant town, broad smooth trim lawns rolling down from the shingled fronts of houses.

Abbie smiled, fumbling in the glove compartment and taking a pair of dark-brown sunglasses and slipping them on. 'Oh, I don't mind intelligent men,' she said, 'as long as they don't bombard me with it. It's intelligent women who scare me because I'm not the competitive type and I just rush for refuge behind my faithful cameras. I left them behind today, by the way,' she added, 'all play and no work being the order of the day—'

'That's good,' he said happily. 'You see, you are intelligent after all.'

She smiled, hands firm and steady on the wheel. 'I thought you'd appreciate that,' she said, then after a while went on pensively. 'I wonder why she doesn't like me?'

He felt uneasy, unwilling to be drawn into a hypothetical guessing-game like that, thinking how absurd it would be if he had to defend Laurie when all he wanted and craved was to enjoy whatever hours he might spend and share with Abbie.

'She probably looks upon me as a little smart-alec upstart,' Abbie went on when he said nothing. 'Horning in on her territory or something like that—what do you think?' she asked, briefly looking at him sideways.

'I think you're imagining things,' he told her, but it came out very lamely indeed.

Abbie looked surprised. 'Oh no,' she said, 'I don't imagine things like that, not about people. I haven't got the imagination for that kind of thing. I merely record what I see, like with my cameras, you know, and it's clear as day your good friend

Laurie thoroughly dislikes and disapproves of me.' She paused a moment, meditatively chewing her lower lip. 'I suppose it's because of you,' she said in an even, dispassionate tone, as it stating the obvious.

'What do you mean—because of me?' he echoed, and instantly regretted the question, knowing he would have to listen to her answer.

She gave him a quick amused glance, smiling as she returned her attention to the road. 'Oh come on now, sir!' she admonished mildly. 'Don't play the innocent with me. You're too smart a guy not to see—and don't say "see what" either!' she added, anticipating him. 'She's so jealous about you it's painful—'

'Don't be absurd!' he said angrily, feeling the elation and high promise of the day turn sour.

'You're the absurd one if you pretend not to see,' said Abbie. 'I should mind my own damn business, of course, but I'm an incurable busybody, and besides you're the only reason why she should choose to dislike me—now that's unkillable womanly logic, isn't it?' she said with triumph.

He gave an exaggerated groan. 'I wouldn't know the first thing about womanly logic,' he said, 'if such a thing ever existed.'

She gave a quick little laugh. 'You're funny. Okay,' she said briskly, pressing down steadily on the accelerator as they finally left Randalswood and reached the freeway. 'We'll skip the vexed subject as you obviously want, and head forward into today with a roar and a bang and a yo-ho-ho and a bottle of rum!' And lifting one hand off the wheel, she loosened the scarf and shook out her hair, letting it blow free, sweeping out behind her, a dark skein flying before his captive vision . . .

The day passed in a swirling kaleidoscope, a dazzle of green glare and gold before his mesmerised eyes, punctuating each moment with new bewildering wonders, vast vistas of stone and steel, cloud-touching concrete giants of innumerably-windowed buildings towering awesomely above the crawling crowded canyons of streets, casting enormous elongated shadows over the huge palpitating patchwork landscape of the metropolis; at high burning noon the heat beat in visible waves off the scorching pavements to hang palpably in the thronged air. The huge glass acres of the shop-fronts reflected and magnified that heat, mirrored too the rush and rustle of ant-like human hordes and vehicles caterpillaring their querulous honking horn-blasting way through the jungle maze of nerve-rattling thoroughfares choked with an engulfing avalanche of people passing each other mindlessly with bland oblivious alert indifferent anxious smiling frowning open-and-shut faces, milling together, never touching, hurrying, ceaselessly hurrying to individual points of destination and departure, white, black, yellow, nutbrown faces, skins, bodies of indeterminate hue, young, old, middle-aged, of indecisive years, straight, upright, bent, deformed, ugly, wrinkled, grinning grotesquely in the pitiless sun, stretching forth gnarled hands for pittance; proud, contemptuous, haughty, sweeping past with implacable purpose, impervious to everything save themselves and the things that lit and shadowed their lives, an intolerable multitude of people passing in a blur before his eyes, hard-skinned determined male faces, sombre-suited and hatted, or in garish flower-patterned shirts open to the navel, bare hairy chests heaving and sickly-moist with sweat, mountainous and bow-legged bludgeoning their way through with grunting truculence, teeth clamped brutally on fat unlit cigars; the softer subtler skin of women and thigh-showing young girls preening boldly at traffic junctions and pedestrian crossings, sun-browned limbs eloquent under wisps of insubstantial summer dresses or elegant svelte costumes and meticulous matronly suits, giggling, smiling with sunny pleasure or showing white even teeth in slight distant absent smiles at hard deliberate quizzical male stares of interest and appreciation, strangers many galaxies of time and circumstance removed from each other caught up for a fleeting breathing moment of time in a seething broiling whirlpool of ceaseless motion that beat and drummed intolerably upon his sight and hearing and the nerve-ends of his senses.

He beheld with a sudden stab of pain and pride and quintessential motherland-longing the banner of home, the flag of his wandering warring race, flying flamboyantly alongside the other national emblems of free and allegedly free nations blowing in the faint heat-laden breeze outside the tall glass menagerie of the United Nations building overlooking the sail-dotted East river, a modern pyramid built on the hopes and dreams and aspirations of the world, enclosing, entombing those hopes and ideals spawned from human suffering and despair, crystallised in the quick fertile minds of brave dauntless devious men and leaders of men holding the fate of the world in hands honourable or treacherous, strong, weak, blessed with the trust and fortitude of millions, bought with the roubles and ducats, the yens and rands and dollars of a miserable besotted few sworn to destroy all bridges and snuff out even the faintest candle that might lend light to lost human eyes.

Surveyed from a distance the building looked as fragile and vulnerable as the foolish brave hopes it symbolised and harboured, but once inside it revealed its dimensions, its cool glass infinities, its huge walls hung with the murals of many countries depicting national and international themes of peace, freedom, goodwill, grotesque parodies though these might have turned out to be, yet embodying the unconquerable quest of the spirit after the same imperishable gifts. Everything he saw in the colossal colosseum of modern times, every mural, frieze, fresco, triptych, every banner, flag, emblem, sculpture, painting, all held both truth and contradiction, hope and the cruel casual negation of hope, love and the apocalyptic annihilation of love; it held the future up as a thing of improbable brotherhood and probable self-destruction; mankind was both patient and physician, the doomed and the rescuer, the saviour and destroyer of itself, exactly as each individual man was unto himself, the plight and destiny of mankind being but a larger and ultimate statement of the plight and destiny of each and every man under whatever flag or code he may live. His crutches rang hollow and hard down the long echoing halls and corridors deep in the intestines of the building, and though the effort of walking, of lifting his weight off the floor at each step and swinging himself forward kept him in a perpetual lather of sweat, and though Abbie was constantly at his side, her hand on his elbow exerting a slight heart-stopping pressure, he could not suppress a shiver; no matter how elaborate or exquisitely executed the objects of art adorning the walls and floor spaces, he saw only the tinselled toys and tawdry things of hope around him, and was glad to step out into the glare of the sun again, its heat, pitiless though it was and greeting him almost with a physical blow, reassuring him that at least out here in the

67

broad hectic day people lived and walked with their hopes and fears, suffered and savoured the doubts and expectations of their days and nights and found the final fortitude or faced the ultimate despair with the last burnt-out vestiges of themselves unentombed in any glass mausoleum and undeterred, undeluded by any ideology that might once have been an ideal.

Outside on the glimmering pavement Abbie stopped and looked at him, adjusting the sunglasses higher on the bridge of her nose. 'So that didn't grab you, huh?' she said with the same direct simplicity and candour.

'It was interesting,' he said carefully, balancing himself and leaning back against the wall of the building they had just left.

'What didn't you like about it?' she asked. 'I'm curious.'

They sat down on the parapet of a low wall that ran along the perimeter of the main courtyard, he resting his crutches between his legs as the crowds passed unheedingly by and the street vendors plied their wares. Abbie regarded them for a moment, smiling impishly. 'I don't think I'd ever have the nerve for that sort of thing. I guess I'm a spoiled brat. But go on,' she said, turning her face back to him, crossing her feet under her, hands dangling over knees. 'Tell me what you didn't like about that glass mountain in there.'

'It made me sad,' he said after trying to think of something more positive to say. 'I don't know or rather I can't say why. What it holds out is so brave and splendid, so fine and good, and yet—and yet so obvious, so necessary, so endemic to the condition of man. It's like building a nursery for a kid who's always known the rough freedom of the streets, or a kennel for a dog that's never known any home but an alley.'

'What's wrong with that?' Abbie wanted to know, puzzled. 'I don't get you, kiddo. What's wrong with nurseries and kennels, for God's sake?'

He grinned and grimaced at the same time at her unstressed simplicity. 'Oh, nothing,' he said, 'nothing at all, both are admirable in their own way, except that you can't force the occupants into either after a certain period—'

'Well, seems to me,' she said stubbornly, staring intently down at the square paving-stones, brows still furrowed intently, 'both are preferable to either the streets or the alley—but then I admit to being drastically retarded.'

'But don't you see—' he began, and stopped, seeing how the afternoon sun struck her hair free upon her shoulders, turning it into a sort of dark molten flow. He gulped. 'Don't you see . . .?'

She took him then to the mecca of the money-maker, that counting-house of the world, a street of thick ponderous colour-less buildings where no sun shone, redolent with the almost tangible smell of old-musty, new-crisp bank-notes, where the people he saw were hardly distinguishable in tone and com-plexion from the buildings themselves, and hurried as grey shadows back and forth, tight-lipped and beetle-browed, clutching black briefcases underarm, hurrying by each other obliviously, carrying the monetary cross of the world on their black-clothed shoulders. The whole street resembled one huge bank vault, a solid gloomy strong-room barren of everything save the crinkling of hard currency. It was dull, drab, depres-sing, formidable, and it struck him as odd that this single soulless street should be the heart-pulse of the world's financial existence, drawing into its cold calculating tentacles every kind of glorified hawker and huckster that ever drew blood from a turnip. He was glad to be rid of its brooding deadly-serious gloom and escape out into the live streets once more, where the spire of the cathedral which bore the name of the legendary patron saint of his water-lapped green little island rose like a chalice of grace and beauty into the sky, an ornamental delight amid the towering faceless concrete stalagmites that tried and failed to crush it into insignificance by sheer dull density of weight.

Even at that blistering early afternoon hour a steady stream of supplicants swept up and down the wide stone steps seeking solace both from the sun and their own secret store of sins in the cool sombre depths of the church under the high vaulted roof swirling with dim soft green-filtered light falling like balm down upon them. It was an oasis in the middle of an asphalt wilderness, and no lingering longing after an all-loving all-powerful deity drew his mind there, but rather the more tempting and more elusive probability of peace and mortal comfort which he might discover and enjoy with simple animal pleasure and gratitude without pondering on whatever might lie beyond the welcoming cross and the waiting grave.

And then downtown again—Abbie was pursuing a zigzag course—at the turning of a street corner they were abruptly in some Dantesque hell. At first glance this thoroughfare was synonymous with all the others he had seen, busy, bustling, traffic-choked, raucous with all the maddening murderous myriad sounds of the city, and the crowds were the same, hustling, harried, harassed, heedless, hurrying on their separate ways with the same electric sense of urgency swelling and rushing onwards like innumerable frantic squirrels. But suddenly something else caught his eye, something which he thought was very odd and frightening; under a red-striped shop awning a man lay sprawled out upon the pavement, clad in rags that fell from his matchstick frame like strips of paper, arms outstretched and bare feet twisted crookedly together as though he were crucified upon an invisible cross. The afternoon traffic was building up, and Abbie drove slowly, so he could look quite closely at the strange inert figure on the sidewalk, almost in slow motion; the face, thin, wrinkled, monkey-like, spiked with a miserable mangy beard stiff with human spit, the hair matted and sticking up like congealed sticks of glue, a thin winy trickle of saliva zig-zagging down the side of the half-opened mouth; he saw then, in that frightening close-up scrutiny, that in his far hand this pathetic corpse of a living human being still gripped tenaciously between his claw fingers an empty dark-red bottle as if it were some kind of garish tabernacle which only death could release from him. And more awful than the grotesque gutted-out body, foul and defeated under the sun, was the fact that nobody seemed to cast it a second or even a first glance; people hurried on, either walking round it or casually stepping over it as they might a dead dog; a young man and girl romantically holding hands simply walked on either side of the beaten stupefied thing without loosening their love-locked fingers, not looking down at it even momentarily but continuing to gaze dreamily at each other.

And before his numbed senses could quite comprehend the terrible significance of it all, before he could recover from this encounter with absolute degradation and defeat, he beheld other figures littered at intervals along the sidewalks in varying stages of oblivion, propped up against walls, crouching in doorways, staggering blindly along with faces either dead and tenantless of all spirit or split in a terrible gargoyle grin of half-witted bestiality, bumping into people and pushed impatiently aside like so many troublesome nuisance-making animals. The fact that it was all happening in the broad swarming light of day, under the clear ordinary sky of summer, added a dimension of cold crawling horror; it belonged to the night, to the sinister shadows of dark alleyways where its terror might perhaps have been more acceptable and familiar; the night could have rendered it almost unremarkable, but these dazed defeated denizens of former men moved like zombies in the wide summer sunshine, in a street crowded with ordinary perplexed anxious uncertain life-loving happy people; and the blind and maimed in their ordinary midst, slipping down deeper into hell, into the living grave, the quicklime pit, disowned, discarded, damned and dehumanised, drawing brief doomed sustenance from the quick red poison of a bottle bought with a pittance of either coinage or human shame. And the sun shone bland and pitiless and there were the odours of good food and drink in the air.

'The Bowery,' said Abbie calmly, looking about her with cool professional eyes as she stopped at some red traffic lights. 'Not exactly Disneyland, is it?' Her fingers beat a little rhythm on the steering wheel as she waited for the lights to change to green, 'Now let's find a contrast.'

From the outside it looked, although bigger, like any other private home in that quiet sedate street of formidable respectability; imposing enough in a serious way, almost bare of ornamentation, a thing of grey-stoned dignity, looking as if it belonged to a retired scholar of fastidious attributes. They found a parking spot after some careful manoeuvring and Riley hobbled up the few stone steps to the entrance, Abbie staying a little behind in case of an injudicious movement that would cause him to overbalance backwards. Inside, the vestibule still looked as staid and unremarkable as any hallway of an ordinary house, except for the quaint appearance of a uniformed porter on duty standing behind a chain barrier collecting entrance fees and lifting the chain when these had been duly paid. After that everything was suddenly transformed; what had seemed seconds before a normal almost deliberately dull residence became a place of enchantment and exquisite sensitivity. The corridors and rooms were still those of a house, yes, where real people had once lived and loved and laughed and had elegant conversation and come to the sad inevitable mortal close; but now beauty adorned its walls, grace and loveliness and perfection were everywhere in evidence, the reality and dream merged beautifully as one to form a tapestry of enchanting charm and delight, the masterful creations of human mind and hand hung everywhere to bewitch the eye and send the soul into ecstasies of pleasure and tremulous joy. Luminous felicity shone out of canvas and sculpture alike, merging in a cadenza of delight with the furniture and carpeting and decor of each room so that not a single jarring note obtruded to unbalance the fine harmony that everywhere reigned. Lost and enraptured and altogether enthralled, only afterwards did he remember that Abbie walked at his side, that small groups of other people moved relentlessly through the elegant rooms discussing the paintings in hushed tones like worshippers in church; he was oblivious to everything save the treasure-trove of beauty immortalised by brush-strokes of genius into statements of heroic grandeur. And through the huge wide ceiling-high windows the afternoon sunshine poured, throwing honey-coloured shafts across the carpeted floors and falling diagonally upon the depicted scenes framed above him.

'I have always preferred this to the Metropolitan,' said Abbie afterwards as they sat by the water-fountain in the main hall, soft organ music in the background. 'It's so intimate and quiet —so relaxing, like visiting the home of a friend. Of course,' she went on, leaning back, her hands upon the parapet of the fountain, 'that's exactly what it was once upon a time, the home of the Frick family, who were very rich and accumulated this collection over many years. I like to come here to unwind and pick up a little culture on the sly.'

He had not spoken for some time, and she looked at him. 'You're very quiet,' she said. 'Anything the matter?'

He looked up, a little startled at her perception. 'Oh, not really,' he said hastily. 'I'm just a bit overwhelmed by all this,' and he waved a crutch in a wide arc to indicate their magnificent surroundings.

Abbie gave a slight ironic shake of her head. 'It's more than that,' she said, lowering her eyes and contemplating her fingernails. 'It's Laurie Emerson, isn't it?' and when he did not answer she went on. 'You had a quarrel this morning, didn't you?'

He stared at her, baffled. 'How did you know?'

She smiled, still examining her hands. 'Oh—womanly intuition and all that,' she said, her mouth curving in a smile. 'I just felt it. I have very sensitive antennae, just like my cameras. It was about this book you're writing, wasn't it?'

He gave a hopeless shrug. 'I give up,' he said. 'I confess all. Yes, it was about the book. Some of her criticisms made me very angry. I can't write the way she thinks I should write— I just can't. I can only write one way, and that's my way, for better or for worse. She treats me like a damn high-school kid, expecting me to write like a bloody textbook.' He stopped, realising he was getting quite worked up. 'I'm sorry.'

She smiled. 'That's all right, kiddo.' She laid her hand briefly on his arm in comical camaraderie. 'Relax. I know how it is. But why should she want to change your style? Why change a successful formula? Sounds crazy to me. But then I'm just a working girl who knows damn-all about things literary.'

'She means well, I know that, but no matter what I do I just can't get her approval—'

'And you want her approval that much?' she asked.

'I would like her approval, yes, from time to time,' he answered. 'She's an intelligent woman and I'd value her approval of my stuff, but all I get are lectures on English grammar and the necessity for conciseness in composition. It's maddening.' And unknown to himself he was tapping his crutch impatiently on the floor, a gesture Abbie beheld with amused eyes.

'Are you two in love, Riley?' she asked calmly.

This time he was genuinely astounded. The abruptness of her question rendered him speechless for some moments as the brilliant and gay Mozartian strains rose and fell about them.

'My God, what makes you ask that?' he said finally.

'I ask it because I think it,' she said with an unanswerable simplicity. 'After all, is it so unlikely? You have a fine mind and are not at all bad-looking,' she gave him a quick little smile, 'and she's a handsome mature woman. I'd say the necessary ingredients are definitely there.'

'But she loves her husband,' he said, as if stressing a funda-
mental incontrovertible fact to a backward learner.

'So?' she said, lifting an eyebrow. 'Come on, Riley, don't be
naive. One is capable of loving many different people in
different ways, and even of loving two people quite deeply and
passionately at the same time. You're not much of a writer
if you don't know that, my dear sir,' she finished, tapping him
on the shoulder in mock reproval.

He felt a kind of churning inside him, both at the thought
of what Abbie had just said and at her very presence there
beside him in the music-filled hall with Bach and Mozart
making the air radiant. His mind drew back in sudden panic
from both thought and presence; he was lost once more, lost
in the bewildering maze of emotions that were now flowing
through him in a torrent, tossing him this way and that way,
throwing him up and plunging him down, spinning him round
in chaotic circles till there was a great humming commotion
inside him. He felt like a man being pulled in two opposite
directions by two powerful forces of gravity, who would be torn
apart if he did not choose to relinquish one or the other of these
forces. And he felt tremendously incapable of making that
decision or even of putting his mind to the task of it; there on
the other side of the horizon lay the dream, a dream that until
now he had failed even to recognise and acknowledge, and
here sitting calmly beside him in black denim jeans was the
astonishing reality, with no aura of mystery or magic about
her, no mythical hidden depths, speaking ordinary words about
ordinary things, and that very ordinariness intrigued him
powerfully; her very simplicity drew him inexorably like a
magnet into the warm laugh and the challenge, the quiet
promise of her. He desperately needed directions now, a clear
path out of the maze, a trail leading to a finely defined conclusion; but there were no directions, none that he could read,
only opposing confusing contradictory voices speaking to him
in the wilderness that held him prisoner. It seemed his life
would always return to confusion and perplexed precarious
uncertain joys, that it would always revolve around the choice
of two directions trapping him whichever way he turned—
baiting him with impossible treasures, rare treasures of mind and
flesh, of promise that would never end, luring him on, voyaging

74

his hopeful wilful heart to things beyond the dreaming of it.

And then her voice. Calm, ordinary, quiet, so very quiet. 'You don't have to go back there tonight.'

The lurch of his heart caused him to grip the crutch very fiercely between his fingers until his knuckles whitened and throbbed painfully. His throat constricted, and he pressed his lids tightly shut for some moments.

'No,' he said, throwing back his head and looking up at the leaping spiral of silver water above them. 'No, I don't have to go back.'

She was looking unseeingly before her, hands clasped around one knee. He brought his gaze back to her; she looked terribly young, terribly vulnerable in a strangely impish manner, worldly-wise and knowing, unsure and trusting and utterly unknowing. He felt a tremendous tenderness for her, perceiving in her all the hurt and wounding which life held for both of them and for all who dared to trust and dared to give, foolish impetuous souls throwing themselves at life in beautiful abandon, picking their bruised selves up after each grievous fall to go in search again of that peculiar destiny that beckoned and cajoled and would never let them be. All this he saw in Abbie, the slim dark rose of a girl sitting next to him on the edge of the fountain with hands clasped round her denim knee staring wistfully into something she beheld and did not for a moment comprehend.

'I don't understand much about books,' she was saying, and he realised she had been speaking for some time before he became aware of it. 'I never was much good at it. I was weaned on Jane Austen and Mrs Henry Wood, so you see how retarded I am. Well-meaning and with a heart of gold, but severely retarded.'

'Abbie—' he began, and stopped, wordless.

'It's all right, kiddo,' she said playfully, rocking back and forth on the parapet of the fountain. 'I can't cook very well either. I can take some very good pictures though. That seems to be about my only virtue, though others think it's my greatest vice. You'll have to find out my virtues and my vices for yourself. Would you like me to take you to the Village?' Abbie asked him with that quicksilver switch of thought and topic that constantly caught him off-guard.

'I'd love you to take me to the Village,' he said with a grin.

They left the music and the water and the charm and rare elegance of it all, and went out again to the still broiling city and the something that neither of them quite comprehended . . .

They went through the Village early that evening, past the queerly designed and garishly filled shops and fashion salons and ritzy little out-of-the-way bars full of gloom inside, past basement clubs with outlandish names under grimy gritty no-colour buildings, from the subterranean depths of which issued the soulful strains of blues intermingled with the strident cacophony of modern melancholy jazz at once murdered out of existence by banshee blasts of babel rhythms flung out from basements next door. As they passed he saw young bearded men, some dressed soberly enough, looking a little embarrassed about it, but the majority of them in weird ragged clownish garb, their hair knotted, beribboned, matted, entangled, shiny with grease, dishevelled in a rather deliberate way, others flowing free and long and luxuriant as a woman's. Some sat hunched and huddled in doorways and on the pavements gripping stubs of pencils between their fingers, writing into torn notebooks, from time to time lifting their heads and mouthing incoherent snatches of slaughtered poetry like mad dogs baying at an invisible moon, turning hollow oblivious faces skywards as if towards a Mecca of their own which they alone perceived, delivering incantations; still others stood against walls or in doorways mindlessly strumming the rusty strings of decaying guitars, plucking out of the time-stained wood and quavering wire some shadowy sad melody out of their own lost pasts. Young girls, as oddly attired as their male counterparts, in blue jeans bestrewn with crazy cloth patches, wearing decrepit sneakers, some with enormous nineteenth-century straw hats which completely obscured their faces, sprawled like so many empty sacks upon stone benches, horizontal slabs of humanity, some mute and immobile like mummified residents of an open-air morgue, others gathered in groups talking in great animation to each other or to themselves or to no one in particular, hair wild, untended, looking up at the sky and hugging themselves tightly, joyfully, desperately, as though afraid they might at the very next breath be snatched from the face of the earth, and

76

though that very earth be dull and hard and cruel and indiscriminate in its choice of victim, yet they stood on it in all their wild lovely terrible innocence and hugged it to them, and the earth in turn held them captive and enthralled as animals in a cage.

He looked on the scene with insatiable wonder, lost and suspended in some ludicrous half-world between fact and fantasy. Yet these people moved, they spoke, gesticulated, and he knew they must love and suffer and endure the loving and the suffering like every human being on earth; he felt the last warm caress of the setting sun on his cheeks, saw the sombre shadows between the queer humpbacked houses, heard the lost-child-like wail of garbage-hunting cats behind tenement railings, and he knew it was not a dream but life played out in the painful light of day.

She led him into the Square, gnarled old trees trembling in their own particular Indian summer, gnarled old men on benches playing eternal games of chess amid a flurry and frolic of avaricious pigeons swarming the air and strutting arrogantly about on the cobblestoned paths almost demanding to be fed; the pigeons were lords here, this was their domain, their happy hunting ground, and they held absolute sway, resentful of intruders unless handsomely rewarded, flapping angrily about if the reward was not immediately forthcoming, following the visitors in great agitation and indignation, squawking shrilly, making a queer gurgling noise that was half reproach, half appeal, impervious to the seasons. Even in this warm summery weather the old men wore abbreviated woollen mittens that reached to their blue bony knuckles, crouched over the stone chessboards with the stone pieces, never speaking a word to each other, rubbing their stubbly grey chins, lost in extricating their undimmed senses, generals at war on cold stone benches in a bare battlefield, like their habitual neighbours the pigeons oblivious of everything, the people and weather, blind to whatever world that might lie outside their private concrete cosmos of gaunt trees and argumentative pigeons that was the Square.

They descended into the pungent gloom of a basement club; the hour was early evening, few people were about, and these were mere shadows crouched trance-like over little round tables, cigarettes drooping in their mouths, curling lines of smoke curving invisibly into the heavy sweaty air. There was an impromptu stage at the far end of the room, a narrow flat boarding raised a few feet from the floor; on it sat a young man twined around a tall spindly bar-room stool, bent over the guitar he was laboriously trying to play, a single green lamp spotlighting him, giving him a weird unreal appearance, as though he were sitting plucking twangy strings on a rock in some underwater cavern; the sweat stood out on the man's face, shining, and his green-hued fingers moved sensuously over the guitar strings as though over the body of a lover, though the sounds that they provoked were hardly those of love. Sometimes the shadow people at the tables would stir, to pick up a glass or to light another cigarette, then they would settle back into semi-somnolence again, faceless, detached, almost disembodied, hardly in life.

The coffee tasted raw, bitter; it stung his mouth and made its fiery way down his throat, as though compounded of boiling rubber and vinegar. The waiter was a hunchback, smiling an unaltering fixed imbecilic smile and rubbing a huge disjointed wrist across his forever moist lips, muttering a guttural something that might have meant thanks or a malediction. The green young man on the stage had stopped pretending to play and sat hunched on his stool staring down at the floor, his whole body quite limp now, so limp it seemed his bones and muscles had turned to jelly and that at any moment he would simply melt and seep through the floor and flow in a green stream to some unnameable limbo. Abbie whispered something to him across the table, but he could not see her face beyond the flickering half-spent candle stuck in a wine bottle, only the sheen of her hair, and he did not catch her words.

Reaching the street again, the sun struck at him; it blinded him, huge dark-red orbs swam before his eyes, slowly they faded, and he saw the same garish shops and tucked-away bars with their winking red signs, the ricketty old houses nodding to each other in the dying sun, the young people in their strange lost somehow beautiful middle-world, islands, some trying to make bridges to other islands, others no longer trying, already gone over the horizon from which there was no return, and he thought that maybe they did not want to return any more, finding in their wilful wistful self-exile some fragile precarious freedom only they could name and abide with. He felt somehow strangely envious of them; he did not quite have words to ascribe to that envy; they were perhaps quite irretrievably lost, but what were they lost to, he wondered. Was he himself not as surely lost as they, but without their desperate self-deliverance, their frenzied frightening isolation that seemed to act as a shield against the meaner barbarities and crueller expectancies of life? He almost came close to knowing that there were two ways in which a man could be lost; with possessions and without possessions, and if some day he himself had to make that awesome choice he was blithely confident he would choose the latter, to go naked into the open places of life where nobody owned anything or had claim to anything save the air they drew into their lungs, to follow that lost lonely course rather than stay on in that hide-bound menagerie of concrete tangible possessions, swathed in them, hemmed in by them, each one demanding a separate piece of oneself, finally turning oneself into divided loyalties, rendering one more ultimately lost than any one of these young oblivious people squatting serenely on the footpaths singing to their own existence in inarticulate tongueless celebration of that fact. Wildly he wished to walk among them and discover what their world might hold for him, knowing himself as lost as they, but their minds and faces were closed to him, he was after all uniquely alone, and he could only pass on.

'Will you put all this down on paper some day?' Abbie enquired with a certain mocking flippancy when at last they were alone together in her chaotic beehive of an apartment, she pouring drinks for them both into two plain corpulent earthenware tankards. 'Perhaps in this new novel you're writing?'

She set the two tankards down on a long wooden table and flopped down beside him on the dusty old-rose sofa, throwing one arm over the back, kicking off her sneakers and stretching out her legs at somehow ungainly angles.

'Only if it comes into the story,' he said, lifting the heavy jug to his mouth and taking a deep draught of the whiskey, with a pleasurable shock of assurance. 'But I'll put it down somewhere—it's too good to miss.'

'But if this book is about you being in the States and all that,' went on Abbie, reaching for her drink, 'or based on it, what you've seen today would surely come into it, wouldn't it? I mean, it must have made some kind of impression on you.'

'God, of course it did,' he answered, in his excitement almost finishing off his drink. 'My mind's whirling round like a windmill in a storm. I just want to dash back to my room and my typewriter and get it all down, forgetting about commas and full stops and all the rest of it—you don't depict the raindrops when you're painting a thunderstorm.'

'A fine literary turn of phrase, that,' said Abbie, curling her feet underneath her and regarding him with amused quizzical eyes over the rim of the tankard. 'I sometimes feel like that when I'm taking pictures—the technical details sometimes get in the way and make the picture as a whole look too carefully planned and contrived. But you're not thinking of dashing back to your typewriter this very minute, I hope?'

He smiled a foolish happy reckless smile. 'Not this very minute, no,' he said. His head was feeling deliciously light; his thoughts swam clear and sparkling like goldfish in a bowl, he could almost feel the texture of his thoughts, now smooth, now grainy, thrusting turbulently through his mind.

The smells, sights, sounds, reverberations of the day crowded in on him, dizzying him, giddying him till he felt gloriously insubstantial, free and felicitous as the breeze, full of a fine uncluttered airiness that made each moment a shooting star flaring across the orbit of his vision; he saw, felt, sensed all this with perfect perception, with eyes wide open and staring at the girl on the sofa beside him, yet not really seeing her as a separate entity at all, but as part of the unfolding tapestry billowing out before him in such turbulent brilliance.

Abbie's voice seemed to come to him from quite a distance, hushed, a little awed.

'You look so strange,' she said, whispering almost. 'You look beautiful just now. Like a visionary in the desert.'

Her words brought him back to the room and its cramped untidiness, the swaying curtains, the dusklight coming in through the window, her face like a pale flower in that dusk, her black hair, mauve glints in it, sweeping back from her forehead, her eyes dark, mysterious, unseen, watching him with soft unstirring intensity, hands cupped round her tankard as she leaned back on the sofa. Somewhere he imagined he caught the mournful wistful strains of a barrel-organ, but it may only have been part of the music filling his mind, softening the certain panic he was feeling in the dusk and shade and the eloquent stillness of her. A street light went on, throwing oddly-shaped shadows on the far wall, falling upon her hair.

He knew what was happening, felt the sweet enormity of it all, this certain something that was happening or was about to happen, yet still the strangeness of it, the unknown thing about it, frightened and alarmed his senses so that he shied away from her almost. Desperately, with a comic frenzy, his fingers bit into the fabric of the sofa, seeking its texture and missing it; no facile escape in the tankard now, for it was empty and he knew it would not be refilled, not now. His eyes sought frantically for something in the room, some object to fasten on to, to escape her face, her slow intent gaze, and found nothing. He tried to hear the real or imagined music down in the street, but if it existed at all it was drowned utterly by the deafening din and commotion now swarming in his mind and the welling confusion of his heart drumming wildly, beating at his temples, pulsating behind his now tightly closed lids.

'Riley,' she said, and her voice was unbearably gentle. 'Riley . . . please don't be afraid. Let me help you.'

He felt her fingers on his arm, soft, feathery, creeping upwards, touching his cheek, moving over his mouth, over his closed eyes, exploring him gently, in his hair, the nape of his neck, her quiet strong fingers drawing his head towards her, upturning his face to her own, the soft swift insistence of her lips moving over his face, finally, unhurriedly finding his own taut mouth, barely touching at first, tentative, tremulous as a bird, then hardening into need, demand, her hair falling over him, the girlness of her sweeping over him now in a sweet sudden rush of response igniting all of him. He felt the luxuriant softness of her breasts as she pressed his face in the vale of them with a soft lost little cry, felt her fingers touch his groin, moving with deliberate certainty, and he cried out too in ragged broken joy as they found the risen manhead of his life down there between his thin scrawny unbeautiful loins . . .

The faint pungent smoke from the cigarette in the oyster-shell ashtray on the bedside table found its way into his nostrils, into his sluggish brain; he heard or imagined the ticking of a clock somewhere, the after-smell of her still lingered, and still he did not know if it was night or day, and knew it did not matter at all, but perversely he wanted to determine that one single fact at least out of the tumult of everything else. He felt sick; his stomach churned, and he could not recall where the bathroom could be found. He gulped down the rising nausea fiercely and settled his head back upon the pillow, drawing his knees up into a tent-like hump under the sheets. Vaguely he thought he heard the splash of water coming from somewhere and seemed to discern certain discreet movements, things which he somehow always associated with a woman and morning.

He might have slipped back into sleep, or it might just have been the momentary closing of his eyes, but when he looked up her face was there above him, pale in the prevailing semi-gloom, concerned, her arms resting upon the bed, her hair tumbling thickly over one shoulder. She was wearing a blue woollen robe, and he caught the fresh soapy smell of her.

'How do you feel?' she asked, and when he did not reply she said softly, 'Oh Riley . . . I'm sorry, sorry. I so much wanted it to be good for you. What went wrong?' And she sank slowly to her knees and buried her face in the sheets and he saw her shoulders shake with quiet unobtrusive sobbing, her hands joined behind her neck.

And he did not know or did not understand what had gone wrong, back there in the night, in the night of failed promise, in the wide bed he was now lying in, and the intimate live darkness that had enveloped them. Her strong arms holding him, his own frail strangleholds desperately clutching this sudden unknown delight, the hot soaring need driving them on past words, past reason, past anything he had ever known or comprehended before, her low breathless urging against his ear, against his mouth, the feel of her breasts, the cushiony feel of her thighs, maddening him, rousing him to a rage of knife-like desire that desperately sought culmination in her, lifting him, lifting him. And the abrupt failure of that desire, its sudden fizzling cessation, the quick descent into ordinariness and deadness, her lonely cry of rage and then regret, her head upon his chest, tears subsiding, all of her limp then as he was, one arm thrown limply across him, and all stillness between them, despair and stillness, blotting out all else. And he with blind face and numbed lost heart staring into the now mocking dark, hearing the dull thud of his heart against his ribs, feeling nothing at all save the bitter bite of failure gnawing in his guts, wishing to be alone, alone with himself above anything in the world, alone with this failure, feeling the spoiled useless wetness between his thighs, alone to confront and suffer the scourge of this ruthless night of nothingness. And her words of kind solace rubbing acid into the wound. 'Don't feel so bad . . .'

She raised her head, brushing her hand across her eyes. 'Do you want me to take you back?' she asked.

He looked at her dully, wondering what she meant, for he did not know where he could now go back to, except the place of demented dreams from whence he had come in search of something he had failed to find and perhaps never would. And the thought came to him then that he might have left that something behind back there in the factory smoke and grime and asphalt and concrete wilderness of that other place. He smiled sourly at the thought.

IV

During the ride back to Randalswood in the early morning, the roads fairly uncluttered by the later commuter traffic, neither said much, Abbie's face set as she concentrated solely on her driving, the same scarf she had worn the day before caught over her hair. Riley stared stonily ahead, seeing nothing, everything sweeping past him in a fragmented blur, feeling almost cold despite the already warm sunlight, a deadness inside him alloyed with a self-loathing which logically he knew to be absurd but which refused to lift, and lay inside him like a weight. Gone was the promise and newness of yesterday, the electric sense of expectancy that had warned him more sweetly than any brandy from the famous Cognac vineyards; gone now any fragile hope the future might once have held in the shape of something yet unperceived by him and untarnished by the clear harsh stab of reality. Again he wished to be alone, completely inside himself, impregnable against the gentlest of intrusions, before a mirror, the mirror that only he himself could furnish, the merciless looking-glass of his soul which obliterated all cosiness and facile self-deceit and revealed in cruel perfect perspective the eager acceptance of praise and flattery from others. He knew he had to abide with this new knowledge of himself, though the thought terrified and flagellated him; it was as inescapable now as drawing breath, as eating, drinking, sleeping, opening one's eyes to the beginning of each new day however fiercely one might want to keep them closed forever. And he had so casually come upon this bitter new realisation of himself through her who was now taking him back to uncertainty and perhaps rejection, this strange lovely rather lost young woman, and far from anger, far from resentment, immeasurably far from hate, he felt, if he were capable of feeling anything at all then, immense tenderness for her, for her prodigal generosity of herself, her sunny willingness to give of herself, her genuine naivety in spite of the veneer of knowledgable world-weariness that she had so elaborately erected around herself. Neither of them could have foreseen even a fragment of all that had happened that evening of convivial bedlam at Jericho Pines; one moment they did not exist for each other, as distant as star is from star; the next moment she had entered his life and become as much a part of him as his very shadow. He understood now that she was as surely trapped in the web of herself as was he, that she too was seeking a way out of the maze and jungle of herself, and though she might be hounded and beset by different demons, her dilemma went as deep as his own.

Silently they entered Randalswood and drove though its neat leaf-shady slumbering avenues until they were just a block away from the Emerson house, where Abbie slowed and pulled in to the kerbside under some yellowing elms. She stopped the engine, then turned to him, leaning an elbow over the back of her seat. Her face and voice were soft, almost solemn.

'Riley,' she said, and when he continued to gaze straight on, she added, 'Riley, please look at me.'

Slowly he turned his head and his heart gave a sudden painful lurch when he saw the concern and pleading in her eyes.

'Last night was awkward for both of us, that's all,' she said with a quiet insistence. 'It can be the beginning of something real and fine, something positive and good for each of us—'

'Why?' he asked with unnecessary harshness, his voice flat, drained of emotion.

'Why?' she echoed, perplexed, taken aback by the unexpected directness of the question. 'I don't know why, Riley, I don't know why to anything. I don't know why we met as we did, why it all happened as it did—'

'Nothing happened,' he interjected in the same monotonous tone.

Abbie lowered her face. 'Neither of us was to blame for that,' she said quietly. 'These things happen between men and women

85

—listen to the voice of experience,' she said with a bitter brittle laugh. 'I guess we were in too much of a hurry—I know I was,' and she said it so wistfully it did not sound in the least wanton but lonely and lost as a child pining after some desirable and desired trinket.

He recoiled from the unbearable if unintended kindness in her voice, and looked up at the diamond points of sunlight dancing in the green canopy of leaves above them. He wished she would stop speaking and take him back to the lonely sanctuary of his room overlooking the broad lawn and the beach, where hopefully he might watch Midge at play and catch the brief illusion of peace.

'Please, Riley,' she was saying, as he stared up into the blazing leaves overhead dazzling and blinding him. 'Don't attach too much importance to last night. We were both unsure. We can learn if we want to badly enough—'

He blinked his eyes rapidly several times to dispel the in-flamed orbs imprinted on his retina by the sun.

'Why me, Abbie?' he said, looking steadily at her.

'Do you always have to have a why?' and her voice sounded exasperated as she gripped her fingers together in her lap. 'I tell you—I don't know why. Does it matter why anyway? You can ruin and kill so many lovely things by asking why. Isn't it enough that we met against such improbable odds? Isn't it enough that we shall have the knowledge of each other on earth no matter what does or does not happen?'

He caught the surging conviction, the fierce fervour in her words, saw it shining out of her face, and for a moment he felt naked and hollow and insignificant before her faith; but he was too soul-sick, mind-sick, gut-sick to gather sustenance from her words, all he wanted was to retreat into the lonely battle-field of himself and gather fresh resources for yet another assault upon the dark engulfing enemy of his own inertia and raise his thoughts above the swamplands of defeat lest he drown in the murky depths and be utterly irretrievably lost. For he knew he must be alone now and perhaps forever, that his loneliness was the first and last and only defence he had against life and its beautiful destructive lures and blandishments made to break and bend a man to its own demonic will and turn him from the true path and direction of his destiny, however obscure and unperceived that destiny might be. Henceforward there was only one way in which he could travel or wanted to go, and that way had to be uniquely his own, against adversity, against the dull sour certitudes of failure and defeat, even against the seduction of hope itself beckoning him out of his way with the gay uplifted finger of the comely courtesan trailing the heady perfume of promise and deliverance. If the world should hold a trap for him, it would be a snare of his own making, fashioned in his own image and apprehended by his own vision alone.

The green and gold glare of the leaves splashed down upon his face, and Abbie was saying, 'You don't have to go back. You could move into my place if only for a while and work there. I would be away working most of the day and half the night too sometimes and wouldn't disturb you at all. I know nothing about books or writing, I know damn-all, but maybe that would be a help rather than a hindrance, for you wouldn't be interrupted by all that scholarly discussion and criticism that Laurie Emerson seems to dish out to you whether you ask for it or not . . . you don't have to go back!' Abbie finished with desperate defiance, placing both hands on his shoulders and searching his face uncertainly.

'You know I do,' he said with tired patience.

Her hands fell away. 'You're in love with her, aren't you?' she said, not angry, not accusing, only sad.

He grimaced and passed a hand wearily over his eyes. 'Please take me back now, Abbie.'

She sat still for a moment, looking down at her hands, then she turned and switched on the engine.

The house seemed deserted as they drove up the driveway and stopped before the front door with its wire mosquito screen; in one of the second-storey windows a curtain swung lazily in the slight breeze, making a thin swishing sound in the clear sparkling air; the only person that seemed to be around was Cricket, now dozing as always under a tree, barely lifting his head and twitching his ears and languidly wagging his tail in drowsy greeting before promptly dropping his head and falling into limbo again.

'Probably gone to do the shopping,' said Abbie as she opened the door and stepped out of the car, coming round to his side and helping him out. 'Getting it over early. How sensible of

Laurie. Or perhaps the family is taking an early refreshing dip in the sea.'

He detected the acerbity in her voice as she helped him up the few wooden steps on to the veranda, but he made no comment, offered no countering witticism as yesterday he might have done, an unnameable weariness weighing him down like a physical thing so that his steps shuffled and dragged as if he were in chains. It was suddenly deliciously cool in the front living-room after the strong morning heat, and gratefully he sank into one of the cushioned wicker chairs. Abbie stood uncertainly in front of him.

'Do you think it would be all right if I got us something cool to drink?' she asked. 'Do you think Laurie—?'

'Oh no. The kitchen's just through that door.'

Left for a moment on his own, Riley leaned back into the curved comfort and embrace of the chair and closed his eyes, rocking slowly back and forth, letting his body fall into the subtle rhythmic motion until a gradual ease crept into him, giving him a momentary feeling of peace and familiar repose, as if he had never left this house that held so much haven and calm friendly shadows for him. A slight ironic smile passed over his face; something in the room, in the walls and bricks and timbers of the house itself, seemed to be welcoming him back, seemed to be extending to him a strange voiceless yet eloquent greeting creeping across the room to where he sat closed-eyed and body limp in the imperceptibly swaying chair; the tiredness was still there in his bones, in his mind, and the leaden ache of dulled memory still throbbed in all of him, but somehow here in this room, this house, these things were rendered less excruciating, less debilitating; today's pain making pain seem almost solace, softening the sharp edges of the new pain that had lately come unto him, making the wine of yesterday taste less bitter, offering no new vintage, no fabulous elixir scooped out of nowhere, but instead holding out to him the genial glass of quiet-tongued friendliness glowing richly in the depths. . . . He sensed something then, a certain presence, not far from him, and he opened his eyes.

'You finally came back,' said Laurie.

All he could immediately discern of her was her simple white linen dress; the rest of her was silhouetted in shadow against the glowing morning window behind her, so that for a fleeting succession of still-life-like moments he imagined her to be some kind of apparition belonging to another dimension, another place, another time, totally detached and dissociated from the neat orderly domestic room where he now sat.

'Have you eaten?' Laurie asked, and the very ordinariness of her question startled him and left him tongue-tied for a moment so that he could only stare stupidly at her. Finally he just shook his head. She came forward a little. 'There's some cold chicken and stuff in the icebox—'

'Thanks. I'm not hungry at all.'

Her voice was both tired and bitter. 'You didn't even bother to phone,' she said, still standing a few hostile feet away from him. 'I didn't know what to think, what might have happened to you. I stayed up till all hours, waiting for the phone to ring, Like a damn fool I waited and waited, not taking Don's advice and going to bed. Is this any way to treat people whose guest you are—is it, Riley, is it?'

He shut his eyes again, her words stinging him, slashing across his face like a whip; remorse and rebellion battled for possession inside him, both usurped by the weariness that overwhelmed him and rendered everything else only half-felt, half-comprehended save in some still conscience-stirring corner of his brain, and even then he caught only the thinnest tiniest resonance of reproach. He struggled to say something, anything in reply, when a movement behind him told him Abbie had returned.

'I found some cranberry juice—' she started to say, and stopped when she saw Laurie. For a moment nobody spoke, then Abbie came and handed Riley the cool glass. 'Hi, Laurie.'

Laurie looked at her a while before replying in a voice that was glacial in its formal politeness. 'Good morning, Miss Lang, If you will both pardon me, the family will be home from the beach soon and I must prepare breakfast—' She turned to leave the room.

'Oh, I was just going—' Abbie said hastily, putting down her glass on a small occasional table.

Laurie half turned and looked over her shoulder. 'Not at all. Stay and finish your drink and keep Riley company.' And she left.

Abbie picked up her glass and sipped it slowly. 'Well, at least the temperature has dropped considerably in here,' she said wryly. She turned to him with undiminished earnestness. 'Riley, what I said back in the car just then—it still holds. Won't you at least think about it? How can you write in such Arctic conditions?'

'It will be all right, Abbie,' he told her. 'It's understandable she should feel as she does. It was unforgivable of me not to phone.'

Abbie chewed her lower lip pensively. 'No, I'm the culprit, I'm the one who should have phoned. It was just that . . . well, I thought she might have persuaded you to go back, and I didn't want you to go back. I was being my usual selfish self.' She was silent for a moment, rubbing her lips along the rim of the glass, then she said: 'I'd better go—don't want to outstay my welcome.' She paused, regarding him. 'When will we see each other again—if ever?'

His fingers found and fastened around one of his crutches as he looked long and hard ahead. 'I don't know, Abbie,' he said, and he felt a muscle in his jaw twitch. 'I must work—'

'I don't want to push,' she said, hurt, 'but don't you want to see me? Can you forget everything so easily?'

A sort of blackness welled up inside him. 'No,' he said, 'no, I can't.' And he restrained himself from telling her how desperately he wished to forget, knowing she would not understand and not wanting to add to the hurt in her face.

She put down her glass. 'So long, Riley,' she said, then she stooped and kissed his forehead lightly, again a dark wing of her hair touching his cheek. 'So long, darling kiddo.' Next moment she was gone, her car roaring down the driveway.

He lay a little longer in the chair, then roused himself and, gathering the crutches under his arms, began to make his tortuous way upstairs. By some miracle, or perhaps because he was not consciously aware of what he was doing, he found himself on the second flight of stairs before he realised he was climbing them unaided. The realisation made him waver and wobble perilously, the walls seemed to swim and close in on him, he felt some kind of gravity pulling him backwards, and desperately he sought to propel himself forward; he did not dare look back over his shoulder for that would have spelled out certain disaster, he seemed suspended on one stair, swaying backward and forward, but more and more backward, trying grimly to regain a proper balance and knowing he was not going to make it—

There was a rustling movement from behind, and then he was being held and supported as her arms went safely and firmly around his waist, steadying him, putting him back on an even keel.

'God, that was close,' said Laurie, supporting him from behind as he mounted the final flight of stairs. 'Lucky I happened to be coming along. Never try that one again, Riley—always holler if nobody happens to be about, or just wait till someone comes. I don't want to be suspected of foul play.'

In his room he sank into the armchair by the open window, grateful for the cool touch of air on his face, and Laurie sat on the edge of the bed giving him a long concerned look.

'You all right? It must have scared the hell out of you thinking of that long fall back down the stairs with possibly a broken skull at the bottom. Can I get you anything?'

He shook his head, his heart returning gradually to its normal beat. 'I'm okay now, thanks.'

She sat there, in no apparent hurry to go, and he almost dreaded what she might say next, fearing it would be a return to the frost-bitten little cameo that had just been played out down below in the living-room, and wanting to shut his mind to it. But when she spoke her voice was calm and ordinary, as if nothing had occurred to wreck the old ease and felicity between them.

'I was on my way up to tell you that Martin Ruislip phoned yesterday from London,' Laurie informed him, plucking specks of fluff from the front of her dress. 'He wanted you, but of course you weren't here—' She gave a slight little cough in her throat, and went on, 'he's coming to the States next week, and will be staying with us over the weekend. He said sales of your book have jumped fantastically, and wanted to know how you were progressing with this new one.' She paused and gave a little perplexed sigh. 'I didn't know quite what to tell him, Riley.'

He felt an irrational anger rise in him, as if he were being scrutinised and spied on constantly, surreptitiously, and there was no way, no place where he could be alone with his own intimations of inadequacy, failure and loss.

'Why didn't you tell him the truth?' he said sourly, gazing out of the window down to the yellow beach, now slowly filling with people as midday approached. 'That I've reached a dead end and can't find my way out of it, that I have no more words to write and just sit and mope in my room waiting the arrival of a non-existent holy ghost . . . why didn't you tell him that?'

Her face and voice were impassive. 'It was not my business to tell him anything of the kind.'

Thrust and jab, jab and thrust, sally, retreat, advance, retreat, strike, withdraw, feint, deliver . . . he rose embittered to meet the rapier challenge of this absurd game of point and counter-point, this adroit fencing game of innuendo and barbed insinuation that now lay spread out like a battlefield between them. He felt the weariness fall from him.

'Not your business, Laurie? Why not? You seem to possess a positive talent for making everything your business if you want to—'

Her brows darted together and he saw her fingers tense. 'Are you saying I boss you, Riley? Are you saying I try to manipulate you just because I want to help you be the writer I know you can be?'

He forced the ironic smile off his face. 'I suppose I am saying those things, yes,' he said, propping himself up in the chair. 'I'm not ungrateful—'

'Oh, but you are, you are!'

'I am not ungrateful for the real and genuine help you've given me, Laurie,' he persisted, both hands now gripping the sides of his chair. 'But what do you want in return—blood? If it was only blood that would be easy, blood is after all such a cheap commodity, but no, dear Laurie, you want more, much more than my cheap blood.'

'I only want one thing from you, Riley,' she said, leaning forward, her shoulders, her face, her whole body set in an attitude of absolute and indomitable conviction. 'Just one thing. I only want from you the full realisation of yourself as a writer.'

He stared at her, marvelling at the faith or the arrogance of the woman, perhaps both, at once stung into rebellion whether it was one or the other. 'And you think you can bring me to that realisation—you honestly think it is your ordained destiny to help me—no, to make me acknowledge myself as a writer?'

'If I can help you realise your full potential as a writer,' said Laurie, her old fervour returning, making her eyes shine and her whole face become beautifully animated, 'is that such an ignoble thing? I realise it is arrogant, but the best motives and ideals in life are arrogant—they have to be if they are to survive and come to fruition. Don't you see that? Are you so blind that you can't see that?'

'I see one thing clearly,' he said, 'and that is that I must go along with myself, with what I believe to be the only way for me, even if that way can only be understood and made definable by me. I must be my own man, my own person, even if I end up being a beggar—'

She shook her head fiercely, drumming one tight white-knuckled fist upon her knee. 'You're talking great foolishness, Riley,' she said, her mouth contracted and grim. 'You're spouting clichés like any callow teenager defying the big bad world and looking upon everyone as his enemy, even the people who want to help him the most. You accuse me of being arrogant because I want to help,' she said, fingers spread out on both knees, gripping tautly. 'Don't you see it is you who is being immensely more arrogant by spurning that offer of help?'

He let out a sigh that resembled more a groan of exasperation, throwing his head back against the chair. 'My God—help, help! You use the word as if I were in dire need of an emergency surgical operation! Don't be so evangelical, Laurie, for God's sake. Let me pass through the fire I must pass through, let me pass through it alone, let me find out things about myself for myself, don't be always dashing ahead of me putting up road signals and direction signs—'

'You think I want to rule you, don't you?' said Laurie bitterly, though her voice was quiet, unshrill. 'You think I want to remake you in my own image. To you I'm probably no more than just another do-gooder, another frustrated suburban middle-class housewife so typical of the type people in Europe read about in their slick pseudo-intellectual newspapers and magazines—the all-dominant overbearing American matriarch ruling her husband and family with an iron fist in a velvet glove . . . In you, Riley, you probably think I see my salvation, my golden chance of doing something really positive for once in my life and escaping if only briefly from my neat orderly suburban claustrophobic jungle. The power behind the throne and all that.' She stopped and looked across at him, a slight lost ghostly smile fleeting across her face. 'Do I read your mind correctly, Riley—do I draw an accurate picture? Already in your face I see that I am not far off the mark. Well, if that is the truth as you see it, you might as well keep it—at least I won't take that away from you. . .'

Abruptly as it had come, he lost the will to argue, to contradict, to contend with her; it was detestable, seeing the hurt defeated look on her face, the vacancy, the emptiness and void in her eyes, the signs of utter dejection in the slope of her shoulders. Desperately now he wanted to take her in his arms, he wanted to clasp her to him fiercely, to comfort and reassure her or merely to love her beyond the need for words, beyond the arbitrary misuse of words spoken in panic or contrition, to give her his love beyond the barbed-wire fence of language. Yesterday in Greenwich might never have happened; it was a burnt-out dream, a smouldering cigarette in an ashtray giving off a bitter pungent smell, a measure of stale overnight brandy in a glass reflecting the listless morning, and a girl with bent head crying by his bedside. That long yesterday in Greenwich might never have been. It was insubstantial to what he was feeling now, seeing the tired sadness on the face of the woman whom he then knew he loved and needed more than any other human being on earth. She complemented his life, his being, everything he was or thought himself to be, she was the shadow and substance of his every thought, emotion, hope and dream; each morning arose and each day closed with her, the very star under which he sailed to remote fragile shores of promise and possibility, the stake at which his very life burned with free fierce intensity exploding into myriad brilliance in every corner and crevice of his mind. He wished and wondered if she could see it all revealed then in his face, mirrored in his staring captivated eyes; but her own eyes were elsewhere, were downcast and fixed listlessly upon the faded rose-pink rug at her feet, and silently, inwardly he gave a great cry of anguish and despair, knowing that through his own wilfulness and pride he was losing her, that she was sailing away from him, out of his little enclosed harbour of hope and redemption, leaving him anchorless and adrift, a prey to the merciless enmity of himself, a prisoner within and of himself. And he could only look at her now knowing he was killing the very thing he loved with every rash imprudent spurning word that had gone before.

She stirred. 'I think I hear the clan arrive,' she said, as the sound of a car came from the driveway. 'If you want anything—'

'Laurie—' he began, then sagged in his chair.

She stood by the door and looked at him. 'You look all in,' she said. 'Try to get some rest—I'll make sure the kids don't disturb you.' She left closing the door quietly.

She left, leaving him in a vacuum such as he had never known before, all dark and terror even in the warm broad day with the sun blazing and the white-capped waves breaking on the shore and people happily disporting themselves and children laughing and castle-making in the sand. He passed a moist trembling hand over his eyes and gazed down at his typewriter squatting almost at his feet, a black plastic hood over it, its long thin flex like an umbilical cord trailing across the floor, reaching to the electric socket in the wall by the window. He thought of it no longer as a friend, but an enemy, an alien thing, a snare waiting to trap and entangle him, a cunning adversary waiting to bait him into the daily betrayal of himself, spilling from its complex innards all the forms and fantasies that roved like wolves through his mind, trapping him into revealing the sinister ferret-sharp thoughts that plagued and tormented him remorselessly, the tears and phobias and dark wordless intimations that haunted and harassed and goaded him into quick raging useless rebellion in the loud silence of many an unending night. The hooded thing there at his feet seemed to be watching him balefully, malevolently, biding its time to catch him out in an unguarded moment, luring him towards it, offering false benisons, waiting until rage or despair drove him into its strangling maze of words, and the surge of his own misery and longing and impotent passion came flooding

95

out of him to splash upon the pages like blood, betraying him to the cool perceptive eyes of others.

This almost daily or nightly purging of mind and soul seemed to him obscene now, a deliberate and disgusting ritual of exhibitionism, a gesture of rare and astounding arrogance, flinging his petty cowering little thoughts out at the world like stones for others to pick up and examine out of mindless curiosity. He marvelled that he should have started doing it at all, that he had gone on doing it for so long; it was akin to emptying one's bowels in public, this constant regurgitation of one's innermost mind; it was not merely a waste but a senseless sabotage of one's life, this uprooting and updigging of memory and words, this diligent turning over of stones to reveal thoughts wriggling and squirming like worms underneath, moist and slimy and coated with loathsome deceit and sly ingratiating piety. It was a monstrous game of self-delusion, perpetuated endlessly, a spider's web spun out ceaselessly into space, winding and rewinding until ultimately one was trapped and imprisoned in its countless tentacles and smothered almost to extinction.

How better, how braver to keep oneself to oneself, apart, contained, silent, a mystery to all others, hugging the knowledge of oneself zealously within, shunning like the incarnation of evil itself the sham freedom, the mock liberation of words! How many pages he had violated and despoiled with the spurious vomit and puerile rantings of his thoughts! He felt remorse now for all the lost lovely little facets of his enslavement to the tyrannical thing lying at his feet; the pattern of frost on a windowpane in winter, yellow tufts of grass flattened by a sudden rush of wind, the shadow of low evening clouds sweeping over mountainsides fringing the humming city, the breaking images scattering over the surface of sluggish green canal water, red-bricked old council cottages gleaming in the arson at sunset . . . such things and others he had missed while he crouched insensitive and blind behind the typewriter pounding away the irretrievable days and nights of his life.

Even now, even here, at last alone in his room away from the tumult, the unexpected intrusions, the convoluted challenges of that trumpeting outer world of people and things where he had been so easily, so quickly lost so often, even now, even here he was not as intensely alone as he would have wished, that sweet and absolute solitude which he craved eluded him still, for the room was alive with the presence of the typewriter, swarming with the noisy battalions of his thoughts shooting like bullets out of the top of his skull. Sleep, restfulness, ease were far removed from him; he wished for these with an intensity that shook him, but the last shadow of peace faded with the dying of that wish, and the old folly, the old torment for words began to lay its familiar stranglehold on him again, infiltrating the sluggish channels of his brain, making him twitch and twist and knot himself up tightly in the chair. He felt caught in the maelstrom of wildly conflicting needs and impulses, wanting to remain still and knowing the absurdity of that longing, being pulled inexorably, almost physically to the typewriter, yet resisting the pull with savage perversity, riven down all his length, cursing and laughing within himself insanely, glaring at the squat inanimate yet terribly alive thing on the floor with mad ludicrous defiance, willing his mind elsewhere, anywhere, to fasten itself on to something else, trying to flash upon the sensitive screen behind his eyes scenes, words, faces, voices, tactile bodily contacts he might have witnessed, heard, touched in some tangible or imagined past; black and brown, white-spotted cows in a field lowing in bovine melancholy, huge swollen udders brushing the grass, a young man on a bicycle in white vest and shorts and a blue sports cap clamped upon his head, pedalling furiously down a narrow country lane, thin bony knees flailing up and down knocking against each other, eyes dark and fanatical in the scrawny face, receding into the sombre green and gold of the trees; a stout blue-ringed china mug strangely redolent of hot bread-and-milk breakfasts and childhood and the cool crisp smell of his mother's apron; the musty leathery smell of the sofa under the window in the front kitchen, the indented shape where his corpulent brother had just been sitting; the cold startling taste of snow on his tongue as he tumbled with his mongrel dog in the backyard. 'It will be a long cruel winter by the feel of the air' . . . he's forever sitting and staring out the window never saying a word . . . God never shuts one door' . . . and multi-coloured paper kites flying high over blunt chimney tops tethered to the earth by rough tenacious young fingers . . . His mind leaped at such images, pictures, sounds, smells, tastes enticed out of the past or out of nowhere, clutching at them now, trying to obliterate the present turmoil seething inside him and the hooded creature waiting, waiting in front of him, waiting as if to devour him. Tears in the wind stung his eyes once, long ago, but the tears and the wind were vanished now, and there was no solace anywhere in his world.

He raised his head and stared out of the window, seeing only the vast empty imbecilic blueness of the sky scoured clean and vacant of all motion that might arrest the vision; the sound of surf came like a mocking whisper barely audible, a quiet sybaritic lisp of derision lapping his mind. The room grew oppressively hot; the sweat stuck to him like gelatine coating his whole body, not even a leaf-frail wisp of breeze touched him now from the open window. His scalp felt as if he had plunged it into a basinful of steaming water, drops of perspiration trickled down his forehead into his eyes, scalding and searing, blurring his sight. Fretfully he tore off his shirt and flung it haphazardly away from him on to the bed where it billowed down into a white soggy heap. He kicked off his trousers and socks until he sat in his underpants only, cooler now but feeling still the trickle of sweat on his face and down the back of his neck tickling between his shoulderblades like some minute insect.

Lifting his eyes again to the window in blind quest of something to hold on to, a flutter of yellow swayed upon the edge of his vision, and looking down he saw waltzing up the driveway, bouncing a huge red-and-white striped beachball, Midge in a dashing swimsuit skipping along skittery as a pigeon, hopping from one agile foot to the other and singing a wordless little song to herself in a voice clear as mountain water, blissfully alone and engrossed in her world, a world of warm sand and cool summer grass, frogs croaking in hoarse concourse near slime-green ponds, a world of freckle-faced wonder and the spicy scent of cinnamon from the magical Pandora's-box-like kitchen on glad sun-ripened Sunday mornings dripping thick molten streaks of maple syrup upon the crisp checkered tablecloth, fresh-scrubbed lithe young limbs flashing across the brown-tiled parquet floor and the faithful dog Friday lumbering after in stertorous attendance, coaxed out of indolence by a child's gay irrepressible laughing call . . . The world of Midge was as known to him, to his imagination as the few though treasured books of wonder and fantasy he had come upon when he too was a child in a better time, and though hers was made of candy-floss and his own of hard breadcrust, there was yet an equal measure of mystery and unnameable uncatchable joy in their separate child worlds, and watching her frolic down below him now his heart could still follow her along that delicate eggshell path, sure-footed and full of light, on and on without pause, for that path had no ending for such as Midge whom he felt with utter certainty the years could not render less child.

She had gone, following her own pursuits of happy innocence and inconsequence, but leaving his mind clearer, refilled once more with hope and the ringing of tuneful things; the child all unknowing had undone one spell and worked another. With almost a convulsive cry of relief he turned to the typewriter, whipping off the sinister hood and switching it into quick throbbing life.

For a time, a long heartloud time it seemed, he sat still, not touching the purring living thing at his feet, listening in a sort of ecstatic silliness to its rhythmic breathing, its unobtrusive resonance, saying things only he could decipher and understand; then something began to emerge, something began to germinate and spread in his mind, a word here, another word there, a half-sentence, half-image, struggling feebly into shape, into light, into substance, painful as any birth, assuming substance and identity over an agony of time, pushing upwards through the hard brittle soil of his mind like strong unkillable plants bursting into triumphant bloom, gathering round a sunburst of yellow hair and small apple-blossom face and eyes of startling blue chasing the lazy cowardice out of him . . .

He sat, writing of that child and himself though he was only conscious of striking the keyboard before him in the hot room and the immense glittering day beyond the window. Tentative as a blind man he began, his mind hardly lighting upon anything tangible, his fingers containing everything . . .

> Child of light
> running down the eggshell path
> of your butterfly years

99

yellow tendrils
skying wild behind you
swept back by your delight

a flower about to open
about to gladden the world
petal by milky petal

gather me a daisy chain
made from your joy
to wear in my winter

when the glow of now
pales to the far scent
of fragile frost . . .

He stopped, wavering in midstream, the words slipping away from him, abandoning him, leaving him marooned, trapped on a high plateau from which he could not climb down to surer footing. He shook his head and glared venomously at the typewriter, as if trying to draw the passionately desired words out of its depths with forceps. He felt as if he could not breathe, as if invisible hands were about his throat throttling the life out of him, and he thrashed madly about like a beached harpooned whale. He threw his head back, as if imploring some mythical deity hovering unseen between himself and the ceiling. Suddenly from somewhere downstairs he heard or imagined he heard Laurie calling out her child's name in a quite ordinary, rather impatient, motherly way, and the requisite elusive sought-after words and images came sweeping back. Avidly he turned to the still pulsating typewriter, his hands poised above it like a comically encapsulated Chopin, frail and indomitable, fingertips ablaze with light . . .

'Margaret, where are you?' Laurie's housewifely voice.

Margaret of the marigold ways
running across deep October fields
drowning me in the pollen

of your madcap years
making pain seem solace
all child and sudden wisdom

amazing me . . .

A flick, and the machine fell silent. He looked in curious amazement at the printed pattern of words on the sheet of paper, intricately arranged as any painting or artifact, as if the words had themselves designed their own shape and order upon the page, free and absolute agents in themselves independent of his will and command. Where had it sprung from, this garland of words so subtly strung together? He could scarcely credit that what seemed to him this almost perfect flower, fragile and ephemeral as a breath upon glass, could have grown from the rank wilderness and arid stretches of his thoughts; one refined delicate jewel suddenly shining out of all the dross and maudlin mediocrity of the words that swarmed and throbbed and bellowed in his brain like so many maddened herds of cattle trampling him into insensitivity and dullness. As he stared at the string of gleaming words on the page before him he felt giddy and lightheaded, as if he had downed a draught of fine rare brandy.

Everything was one huge imponderable jigsaw composed of innumerable pieces floating around in space blown crazily about by wanton winds of thought; the greatest puzzle, the single most complex piece in the whole intricate tapestry of mystery and meaning was himself, the unknown and immensely unknowable thing that was himself stirring and breathing, dreaming and fulminating ceaselessly behind his eyes, behind his fingers, whispering, roaring, crying inside his skull, a prisoner raging and hammering upon the bars of his cell begging, cursing to be released. He felt himself to be no more than a receptacle, a mere vessel that was nine-tenths of the time empty until it came to be filled by forces sweeping in upon him from fields where he might wander for countless days dry and barren and brittle as desert cactus. Then like swift impatient men hurrying to their lovers at night to fill them with the pollen of their hunger and swollen passion, words came to him in an unstoppable surge and clamour of commotion flooding the wasteland of his mind, turning him into a highly charged battery of instant hysterical response, every part of him humming, speeding the swarming galaxies of images along the shrill nerve-lane of his body to the cumbersome creaking projection room in his brain where at last they were flashed out into inadequately shaped forms upon the vulnerable pulp of the waiting pages clamped tight in the teeth of the typewriter. And after the orgiastic frenzy of it all, the post-inertia, the slow draining of energy, of thought, of will, of any compulsion save that of dying, of sinking into a quiet soft-edged kindly death heedless of the closing of eyes and mouth or the obscene stiffening of limbs, the gradual delicious falling away into oblivion, comforting and deep with neither darkness nor light, sound or silence, panic or peace, but an intangible ineffable somewhere beyond the merest concept of these ready-made abstractions. It was more than calm after storm; it was nothing so graspable, so inevitable, so predictable, but was instead like the long nerveless sleep after tumultuous birth, calm fleecy-limbed dying after loud vivid life.

One moment he had been crouched like a wrinkled mandarin of a monkey before the typewriter; next thing he found himself lying on the bed staring up into the late afternoon shadows, not knowing if he had been sleeping or awake, unable and uncaring to account for the presence of lengthy unobtrusive shadows about the room. The window was still open, but no sounds came from the beach, not the remotest lisp of surf. He did not know how or when he had got on to the bed; he was unaware of having moved, of having switched off the typewriter and removed the printed poem from its grip. He lay wrapped in a kind of amnesia, knowing nothing beyond the moment that now held him, cushioning him in its soft shadowy cocoon. But something imperative was gnawing at him, something that would not be ignored or pushed away by the will or the absence of thought deliberately imposed; a terrible thirst preyed upon him, hurting his throat so that whenever he swallowed his own spit it felt like hard scraping metal bruising the delicate membranes like jagged wire rubbing against silk. He fought against acknowledging it, as always when he wished to shun anything willing his mind away from it, but gradually his thirst overcame him until it grew and grew and possessed him entirely, obliterating all else, clamping down on his mind like a vice, squeezing out all other conscious things; it lay wedged in his gullet, torturing, tormenting, setting up a fever inside him; he knew with a kind of wry rueful dread that it was a unique thirst, a thirst long dormant but now come into its own, a hard bitter biting thirst that no quantity of coldest water could satisfy or allay, a thirst that craved and demanded a fire to match and mingle with its own, a thirst embroiled in his guts, like a festering wound in his throat. It pervaded his consciousness remorselessly, spreading waves of longing through him, turning his tongue to hard leather and his guts to squirming coils of entreaty and desire; it screamed inside him, this implacable thirst, screamed like an enraged revengeful harridan clawing at him viciously with razor-like thrusts, slashing him brutally, goading him, setting free colonies of demented dervishes in his inflamed brain that danced and cavorted and obscenely gyrated before his captive vision, demonic marionettes in an impromptu nightmarish ballet released from some Dali-like hell-corner of his brain thrown upon the screen of his waking vision, grotesque gargoyles of detestation and mockery. He clutched at his throat as if to throttle himself, as if trying to squeeze the barbaric presence of thirst out of it, the fingers of his other hand gripping the sheets, tearing into them, sharp arrow-heads of fire beating behind his eyes, his whole body caught in a kind of rigid convulsion, muscles and sinews frozen like hardened lumps of concrete, his entrails sharp stiffened pinpoints of demand waiting to contract desperately into life again at the first warm sanctifying drop of the holy potion that others so inanely called alcohol. In a fiery moment of pain there passed before him a fragmented daguerreotype of a queer-shaped tree on a hill with a naked man slung at strangely contradictory angles upon it with a crooked bleeding beard-hidden mouth brokenly pleading for a drink . . .

He did not hear the door being opened, did not immediately hear any sound, but felt the presence there above him at the top of the bed, then heard the soft careful voice. 'Are you still asleep?'

Her shadow came between him and the still glimmering window, and the mattress rustled softly as she sat down on the edge of the bed. 'I looked in once or twice this afternoon,' she

said, 'but you were out like a light. You must be very tired.'
He barely felt the touch of her fingers on his forehead. 'God,
you're so hot. I hope you're not running a fever. Are you
hungry?'

His voice struggled up through the mucous slime that choked
his throat like vegetation. 'No, not hungry, but I—I could do
with a drink—'

He sensed rather than saw her smile. 'Not tea, I take it?'

He merely shook his head, his voice sunk again below the
coagulated layers of dried spit.

'I'll see what we have available in the medicine cupboard—
don't worry,' she added, and he still imagined he felt her smile.
'That's what we call the cocktail cabinet. Won't be long.'

It seemed to him that she was gone a very long time, that
indeed she had merely tricked him and would not be coming
back at all, merely placating him with promise in the hope that
he might slip back into sluggish slumber; and as he waited the
terrible iron tenseness increased inside him so that stretched
out there on the single bed he felt as if he were being pulled to
the utmost length of himself until he would simply snap and be
wrenched in two quivering halves. Then interminable ages later
he heard her in the room again and listened with infinite relief
to the tinkle of ice on glass. Again she sat softly down on the
bedside.

'Take this,' she said, handing him the glass that was half full
of the amber liquid. 'I think it's a good blend. We've had it
since about Christmas, I think. What do you think?'

He did not think; thought rushed from him like smoke out of
a suddenly opened window, as he took the glass from her hands,
spilling some of it in his haste, clutching it in both hands,
thrusting the rim of it between his teeth. The feel of the molten
liquid as it slid down his throat was almost excruciating; he felt
jack-knifed into life once more, the window exploding into
painful brilliancy, the shadows assuming marvellous meaningful
shapes dancing with eloquent abandon around the room,
flickering like exquisite fireflies in his brain; his throat burned
with a clear cleansing fire that swept away the clogging
excrement of drought and left it tingling and alive. The mist
that had scarved his eyes dissolved and he saw everything at
once with new and startling perception, aware of the folds and

pleats of the curtains and in Laurie's dress, the texture of which stood out as clearly as features in a rarefied landscape opening before his eyes. The line of her cheekbone was wonderfully sharpened and delineated; her smooth white throat rose above the dark blue of her dress and he had a quick impulse to kiss her suddenly impossibly desirable ears.

'I would venture to suggest that you were slightly dehydrated,' she said, watching him with veiled amusement. She bent and picked up the squat pot-bellied decanter from the floor, holding it up to the light and shaking it slightly. 'There's a drop more here if you'd like it.'

She refilled the glass that he immediately held out, and as he drank she rose and set about tidying the room, picking up his fretfully discarded clothes from the floor and hanging them carefully in the closet, straightening a chair cushion, pummelling another into shape, putting a framed photograph at just the required angle, placing miscellaneous objects in their apportioned positions, all of which she did without fuss or ostentatious gestures. While she was not formidably houseproud or even housewifely in any disquieting way, she had a habitual tidiness about her that sometimes unnerved him and made him acutely conscious of his own incurable chaos which his mind imposed upon the state of his surroundings as much as on his inner life; books left opened, manuscript pages littering the floor, half-finished notes lying around like confetti, drawers half emptied in impatient search for unremembered things, shoes, socks, underwear strewn indiscriminately here and there, disarray of the highest most inexcusable order proliferating into a state of confusion bordering upon unintended anarchy. He drank, intent on savouring the last warming drop, absorbed in the spreading circles and ripples of his pleasure, only slowly becoming aware that she was no longer moving about, but standing quite still by the window, looking intently down at the sheet of paper she held in her hand. She read it again, one hand resting on the side of the curtain, her lips moving slowly. When she was finished reading she stood at the window gazing out, one half of her face obscured to him in shadow. She looked at the single sheet of paper once more, then slowly turned to him, still not moving away from the window.

'When did you write this, Riley?' she asked softly.

He realised then that she had by chance come upon the small poem he had written earlier in the day, and he felt slightly defensive.

'Oh—that,' he said with a flippancy that failed. 'Some time today, I think.'

She again scanned it with her eyes before speaking. 'It's beautiful,' she said in a quiet intense whisper. 'So beautiful. I doubt if you have ever written a poem more beautiful than this.'

'Midge herself is the poem,' he said, swallowing down the last of the brandy and swinging his legs over the side of the bed, sitting up, 'not that piece of paper you hold in your hand.'

'Midge may well be the poem, as you say,' Laurie said, 'and I like to think she is, but you captured the poem, you caught the words out of nowhere and put them into shape on paper, put them into life. Are you going to show it to her?'

He flung up his head quickly. 'Of course not,' he almost snapped, as if being asked to display an abdominal scar.

'It would please her so much—'

'No,' he said in the same stern, almost harsh voice, then adding in a quieter tone, 'No, I don't want her to see it. You came upon it just by accident.'

Laurie looked at him, puzzled, frowning. 'Sometimes I don't understand you at all,' she said at length. 'You won't *let* me understand you, you won't let anyone get that close to you. You seem to suffer from some kind of inner claustrophobia—'

'That's so fanciful, it might have come from Woman's Own or True Confessions,' he said, not with scorn, but with a resigned air of tolerance.

She was plainly hurt, and became stung into vindicated reproach. 'You say it's fanciful because it suits you to think so,' she said, without deliberate effort assuming her old professorial mask once more, squaring her shoulders and leaning forward, hands on knees tightly fisted together. 'Whatever is unpleasant to you becomes either fanciful or irrelevant, and if that's your safety valve, fair enough. We all employ safety valves sooner or later. But in your case it isn't so simple, it isn't at all therapeutic, it's highly dangerous, because it comes out in your writing, it distorts your style and clogs up your thinking. That's what I mean by claustrophobia. You speak almost exclusively from an inner platform. You're morbidly preoccupied—I would say obsessed—with your own mental processes, you delve deeper and deeper into them and reveal them in minute detail, as if they were of the most profound importance to mankind. It's the most dangerous and destructive form of literary arrogance, of self-indulgence, self-gluttony . . .' She stopped, and he saw that she was breathing hard.

'Surely that's not the end of the list of my shortcomings,' he said with a desperately contrived mildness. Seems to me you compiled a much longer list the last time.'

She visibly composed herself before speaking again. 'Be facetious if you like, Riley, it doesn't alter things one bit. If you could be objective and honest with yourself to go through your manuscript again you'd see that there's something—more than something, a hell of a lot—seriously wrong with it. It's not incurable, but like every ailment it could end up malignant if you do nothing to prevent it spreading. I have faith in you, Riley—'

He could not stop the bitter words being torn from him like nails. 'And faithfully you chronicle my faults and stamp my few virtues underfoot.'

'That is simply not true,' she said with an obvious show of patience. 'It might seem that way to you, I admit, and I'm sorry if it does, but I know myself it isn't true. Why should I set out to be deliberately cruel and destructive in my criticisms? Don't you know that those who love you as a person and who care for you as a writer must occasionally hurt you if they are to help you to develop in either capacity?'

'Let me grow and develop in my own way and my own time,' he retorted, already feeling the brief euphoria of a moment ago evaporating and the brandy going sour in him. 'I can't be forced into growing either as a person or a writer. I must come to terms with myself first on both levels, but they have got to be *my* terms, not ones imposed on me by others whether out of concern or curiosity.'

'You're being petulant and conceited,' said Laurie, sadly rather than reproachfully. 'We all need help and advice, not only when we're young as you are now, but throughout our whole span of life, and in almost every sphere of our life. None of us can go it entirely alone for very long, certainly not indefinitely, and if we think we can we're not only fooling ourselves but laying ourselves wide open for grievous mortal hurt. And with you, Riley, it's all that more difficult, because you cannot grow as a writer unless you grow as a person, and vice versa. The one grows out of the other and comes from the same root.'

Her words came clamouring around him like busy inquisitive tenacious bees stinging him whichever way he turned; he felt baited, trapped, cornered, he longed to shut his mind to her, draw down a curtain between them, will her out of the context of his life at that precise moment; but her voice went on, level, controlled, yet animated and resonant with absolute conviction that mirrored itself in her eyes, full of a unique luminosity.

'Nobody is trying to force you into doing something you already know you must do,' Laurie was saying. 'Growth is a natural process, yes, but you can't just sit around waiting for it to happen, otherwise it might grow warped and twisted out of its natural shape, like a tree or plant left untended and uncared for, left to grow wild and unmanageable. The talent you have is like that, Riley—it needs constant care, constant pruning, it cannot be allowed to be choked in a proliferating wilderness of language, it must breathe and move with purpose and grace, unhampered by excess weight of words . . .' Laurie paused and was silent for quite some time. 'Don't you see any truth at all in what I say?' she asked quietly.

He took an equally long pause before speaking, and his words sounded hollow and dull even to himself. 'You cannot give people truth,' he said, 'you cannot hand it to them like alms or bread. They must come by it themselves, and more so if it is the truth about themselves. Time may cause me to change my mind, but this is what I believe now, and now is all that I know and all that matters.' He lifted his eyes, looked at her, then past her to the window.

Laurie sat immobile for another moment, then, laying down the sheet of printed verse on the typewriter, rose and quietly left him. He lay down once more on the bed in slow, almost imperceptible evening gloom, hands clasped behind head, wondering about the coming week that would bring Martin Ruislip to Randalswood in the hope and expectation of something which seemed dead beyond redemption now; wondering

108

about Laurie and what she had said, the anguish of his not being able to utter an ordinary undemanding word of love to her or a syllable of all that he felt, those words locked like prisoners inside him; wondering about little Midge and the poetry she spelled for him in the bright spray-flung innocence of her days; and the whole house below him catacombed with so many hopes and dreams, dreams that were tangible and unmysterious, that could be tasted and savoured and held solid and sure in the palm of the hand, free from the mists that obscured his own. Lying between waking and sleep, he imagined there came from some remote place in his mind the soft unobtrusive sound of a girl's voice, sobbing, in the dark unfeeling morning.

V

With grim tight-lipped determination that bordered on the fanatical, as if about to commit an act of total grandiloquent self-destruction, with a grim bravado theatrical in its very gesture, Riley inserted a long unblemished page of foolscap into the typewriter, flicked the ignition switch, and wrote neatly in the centre at the top of the page in bold aggressive black capitals: **UNTITLED NOVEL, CHAPTER FIVE.** It looked fine, that heading, assertive, definitive, sure of itself, and he stared at it raptly for some moments, thinking his own life should have a heading like that, a banner, proclaiming a definite point in time and direction, a definite stage of growth, shape, evolution. Why could not one's life be as a novel, he wondered quaintly, taking shape, outline, substance at each planned successive step along the way to a clear inexorable conclusion that would be rendered, if not joyous, then acceptable to reason precisely because it was so set, fixed—inexorable? So he mused, gazing at the simple legend starkly embellished at the top of the sheet of paper, letting such sweetly random thoughts run in a free aimless career through his mind, hardly knowing them to be thoughts at all, instead mere wisps of unthoughtout intimations ephemeral as smoke, sitting before the typewriter which throbbed expectantly at his feet . . .

Over a week had passed. There was only one more day left before the meeting with Martin Ruislip, one more day before they would all descend upon him in friendly but anticipatory concourse, Martin, Jay and Sue Simon, and God knew who else, no doubt all of them with nice rose-tinted thoughts of the vaunted Work in Progress that would make Riley McCombe that evergreen and perennial of clichés, 'a household name', and would bring themselves not a little reflected fame, prestige, and considerable lucrative returns at the end of the fiscal year, as was their just due for having promoted his literary pretensions so bravely. And there he sat, as if mummified, his mind a junkyard of useless eminently perishable wares getting rustier and more valueless even as he sat there staring at 'Untitled Novel, Chapter Five'. What did that signify, where was he in the book anyway—quarter-way, halfway, no way, nowhere? He prayed to be delivered from this evil of idleness and inertia, but knew that such deliverance must arise from within himself, and panic was the only dominant and prevailing thing he felt now. Panic and a sense of guilt that bit deeply into him making him clammy with sweat. He longed desperately for a drink, but the bottle which Laurie had reluctantly placed close at hand was already empty and he could not bring himself to ask for another.

He recalled what she had said about the manuscript, and her words now held for him a chilly ring of prophetic doom. Half of the summer had slipped past in a rich golden blur under an endless blue infinity of sky, and all he had now to show for it was an unwieldy indigestible gluey morass of untidy typescript, a Frankenstein's monster of a thing growing out of control and threatening to throttle and engulf him under its own sheer weight. He had squandered the past months engaged in a mad strangling self-defeating *amour profane* with words, a swimmer impossibly out of his depth and at last in imminent danger of drowning under the waves of his own bombast. Tomorrow threw its shadow over him and he shivered in the sudden cold darkness of today.

He bent his mind, his will, everything he had to the terrible task of writing, made himself forget all that had gone before, all the pointless prodigality and profusion of language, as if facing and starting upon a new day, the first morning of all, siphoning the best that was yet left in him, giving himself totally to the moment that was still his, marooning himself on the one narrow strip of untrodden land where he might break free from the murderous mazes which had confused and confounded him for so long and forge something new and clean and unambiguous, a tool he could handle and use with sureness and gradual skill. He began to write . . .

He did not know how long he had been writing, locked in his room, and it mattered not at all, for now it was not as it had been all the other times, now he was not lost or obliviously following a blind path; now he was seeing ahead, feeling, touching, hearing, tasting with needle-point sensibility every word, every nuance of a word as it came to him, as it flowed surely and strongly from him on to the page, supremely in control of everything that he thought, pieced together and transmitted on to the pages as they fell from the typewriter with a smooth regular rhythm to form an ever-increasing mound on the floor, words coming now in a calm unhurried stream instead of a frenzied chaotic engulfing avalanche. In the duration of a brief pause a certain sound slowly intruded into his mind, a soft tapping sound, and he became aware that someone was knocking on his bedroom door. When after he had uncertainly called out who was there, Laurie replied in a low anxious voice.

'Are you okay in there? It's almost midnight.'

With a slight incredulous shock he looked up and saw that it was quite dark outside and stars were glittering. Hardly conscious of getting to his feet, he somehow found his crutches and moved to the door, opening it. Laurie was standing on the landing.

'Are you all right?' she again asked, obviously concerned, and when he nodded in reassurance she sighed. 'What have you been doing locked up all day—writing another Book of Kells? Didn't you hear me knocking? I knocked a few times during the day, but got no answer. I could hear you typing away, though, and didn't dare try really hard to disturb you. Aren't you just starving after all these hours?'

He found it strangely difficult, even tiresome to speak, he had been silent for so many uncounted hours. 'No—not at all, not a bit,' he said, opening the door wider. 'Come in—that is, if you like,' he added hastily.

'Just for a moment, maybe.'

Inside, Laurie looked around, almost as if half expecting to see some sort of change in the room, then her eyes went towards the typewriter and the miniature pyramid of paper beside it. 'That wasn't there this morning, was it?'

'What?' he asked stupidly, then found her meaning. 'Oh, that. No, I just got through it today.'

Her eyes widened. 'All of that?' She went over and knelt down, lightly fingering the leaves. 'There must be close on a hundred pages here, Riley,' she said in unbelief. 'That's really something quite Trojan! May I glance through it, or am I disturbing you?'

Her voice was so eager, to refuse would have been brutal. 'Oh no, go ahead,' he said quickly, lifting one cramped leg up and down, balancing on the other. 'I was about to take a bit of a break anyway,' he lied.

He was sorely tempted to ask for a drink, for the same painful thirst was upon him again now that he had stopped writing, but she was already settling into a seated position on the floor, feet tucked under her, resting on one hand, turning pages, and he thought better of such a request. He went to the chair by the window and sat in it, stretching out, tired in a luxurious sensuous way. He looked out of the window; the night sky was brilliant, swarming with stars, and one in particular caught his eye, a huge one of a fiery red-brick hue glittering like the enflamed eye of a belligerent bellicose giant, not wrathful, but glowing in mock friendly ire, lighting up its own portion of sky, flickering on and off and on unendingly as if the imaginary sky-dwelling colossus was blinking delightedly because his radiance outshone that of all the other starry minions around in the vasty infinitudes of space. He felt a peculiar warm contentment spread through him, a swift lyrical familiarity with everything that moved and breathed and pursued its ordained purpose on earth or in space; he was apart as always, alone, following his own course, yet he was aware of the existence of things within and outside the separate but ever-widening range of his own knowing and sensitivity, aware of being part of the whole intricate consummation of life that was perpetually going on about him every waking and sleeping moment, every shadow of a second in which he drew breath. The knowledge of this, of his own unique participation in the unending perpetuity of things known and unknown, visible and invisible, comprehensible and vastly mysterious, filled him with a certain awe, a certain unmistakable indescribable intuition of curious peacefulness that went immeasurably beyond anything he had known before.

It was as if he had been given a sudden, stupendous revelation of himself simply by being alive at that precise singular moment in time, as if a mirror that was dim and clouded before had suddenly cleared and he could look into the infinite layers and depths of it and see all that it allowed him to see, perfectly and unerringly, with both surprise and precognition, startling him into this contentment that now pervaded him. He found himself gazing reverently at the great red star hanging luminously in the heavens and he felt its intensity burning into his eyes like blazing coal, the sharp cold fire of it penetrating him almost physically. Was it Mars, he wondered, that legendary god of warring majesty wandering agelessly across the skies striking fear and fascination into the minds and hearts of all who gazed at it from the questioning earth below? Or again was it the reflection of some demonic tormented spirit fallen from lordly heights to remain forever chained to the same zealous earth in eternal atonement for some great unmentionable outrage against the other gods? Lightheaded with such fancyings, he continued his rapt gazing into the luminous night, feeling weightless, formless, soaring, and from a great height looking down at himself in the armchair by the open window, his thin angular face oddly glowing, full of a mad transient transparent beauty at wild variance with the indwelling defiant face that was his at every ordinary turn and pass of time. Suspended between dream and reality, between fantasy and fact, from his great mythical height, he saw with perfect clarity the swaying curtains, the subdued glow of the lamp behind him bathing the room in soft subtle shadows, and Laurie reclining on the rug, her face half in shadow, reading the things dark and bright that he had written, his own created things sprung from his sad savage warring with himself. All this was revealed to him now, to his other self then voyaging somewhere in the intricate oceanic spaces of his mind briefly unbound and outside of the stumbling fumbling wretched caricature of flesh that habitually housed and enslaved him. He looked with exasperated sad compassion upon that other everyday self, the pale thin hawk's face mirroring his dreams and dilemmas; with sharp unconquerable tenderness, with the pain and mystery of love, he looked upon her now reading his words, the yellow lamp-glow upon her brown hair, lost to him as he lay dream-held by the midnight window gazing blindly at the bright bewitching star hanging gigantic in the sky.

The spellbound moment vanished and dissolved like wind breaking the glassy surface of a lake. With a rustle and crisp flutter of paper, Laurie let the last leaf fall from her hand to the mounting pile on the rug, the slight sound intruding into his mind, bringing him into the room once more, the certain feel of the chair under him, the cool night on his forehead. He turned to her; she was sitting quite still, head bent, staring at the floor, fingers moving slightly on her knee. She stayed so for a long while, as if unaware of him or of anything, then she looked up, meeting his eyes. She smiled slowly.

'Riley,' she said, at length, speaking in a hushed unsteady voice. 'Riley, my dear, it's wonderful . . . I can't believe the same man wrote it. I always knew you could write like this sooner or later, and now at last you have. I'm so thrilled for you, Riley—thrilled and proud of you!'

He could not make himself trust what she was saying. 'You like it, then?' he said with deliberate caution. 'You mean you think it's good?'

'Good? It's literature, Riley—real literature. If you never write another sentence, what you've written today would stamp you down as a writer of great talent, a talent almost approaching genius.' She was kneeling now as she spoke and her face was animated in a way he had not seen before, that of a young girl suffused with excitement, her eyes shining. 'This single chapter, this single section has transformed the whole book and made all the previous pain and struggle worthwhile. I'm delighted, Riley, and I know Martin will be delighted as well when he reads it tomorrow. You have made the break-through I always knew had to come—you're on your way now, Riley, and nothing is going to stop you!' And then she did what he had been both craving and almost dreading since nearly the first time he saw her face; she rose and in one quick flowing movement came to where he sat and, putting her arms around his shoulders, pressed her lips fully upon his own.

It was a totally spontaneous act, almost an unconscious one on her part, and the pressure of her lips was light, unquesting, and almost immediately she had moved away, but the touch, feel, scent, nearness of her engulfed him overwhelmingly, and they stared, startled, at one another for several moments, her face almost pale, lips somewhat apart, her eyes slowly filling with the unwilling knowledge and meaning of all that had just been expressed and released between them in one unthinking simple gesture of ordinary pleasure in another's personal progress. She passed a hand across her eyes, seeming to sway slightly, and looked back at him.

'I guess we could both do with a drink,' she said unsteadily, 'if only to toast that remarkable piece of writing.'

She went and shortly returned with a half-full decanter of whiskey. She poured and gave him a glass and they drank in silence. She went and stood by the window, looking at the sky.

'What an enormous star!' she said, glass in hand. 'Have you seen it?'

Her voice sounded relaxed, standing with her back to him, yet he thought it contained an undercurrent of nervousness, of disquiet, as if she were talking just so as not to let the silence speak too loudly between them.

'Yes,' he said, taking a slow sip of the brandy and almost not tasting it. 'I've seen it. I don't think it's real.'

She turned. 'What do you mean?'

He shrugged. 'I don't think it's really there,' he said. 'I was sure it was only there in my mind, like a dream or an image or a poem, as such things come to the minds of madmen. Now that you say you can see it, I think we are both mad.'

Laurie looked away, back to the sky and the great hanging star. 'You could be right,' she said quietly. 'Maybe that star isn't out there, maybe nothing is real any more.'

'I think you and I are real,' he said. 'I think you and I are very real, perhaps the only real things left.'

She was quiet, then said very softly, 'And Midge?'

He in turn was quiet, before saying, 'And Midge.'

She finished her drink and turned from the window. 'I think I'll say good night now, Riley. Is there anything I can get you before I go?'

'I think now I have all I am likely to want,' he said.

'Good night, Riley.'

'Good night.'

When she had gone he turned to the window and looked for the star. It was still there, but half veiled by a cloud now. He switched off the light, knowing he would still be awake when morning broke.

'I must say you're looking remarkably well,' Martin said with the surprised tone of one making a considerable discovery, almost as if he had come on a mercy mission across the Atlantic expecting to see his erstwhile protégé in the last stages of tuberculosis or cancer or some quaint and romantic malady popular among literary and creative souls. Martin continued to scrutinise him, even raising a quizzical eyebrow. 'Yes, remarkably well,' he repeated, almost insisting on it. 'I never saw you looking so perky. Laurie's good influence, eh?' added Martin with a fatherly smile.

'Naturally,' said Riley, grateful that she had just gone to fetch drinks.

'I'm delighted I persuaded you to come,' Martin went on cheerfully. 'It's been good for you in every way.'

'I needed little persuading.'

'Ah, but I seem to remember your expressing some slight doubt when first I put the suggestion to you—not about coming to the States but to Laurie and Don,' Martin remarked with sly humour.

'True,' Riley conceded. 'I didn't know what to expect.'

'I think you expected the worst. But it's turned out rather beautifully, eh?'

'Oh yes.'

They were sitting on the front lawn in the refreshing shade of the trees; Martin had arrived half an hour earlier, dressed with his usual propriety in a dark perfectly cut sober-looking suit and brown leather shoes above which whenever he crossed his legs could be seen dark blue woollen socks. A white handkerchief stuck out in a neat triangle from his breast-pocket, and Riley observed with some amusement that the tie was of the same colour as the socks. Martin Ruislip was indubitably the quintessence of English sartorial discretion, and while Riley had not been anticipating this meeting with any great enthusiasm, it was good to be in his friend's company again, and he was now looking forward to the arrival soon of the Simons and relishing the complete contrast, both in fashion and, he imagined, almost every other way possible, between the two men, almost as violent as the difference between muffins and pizza.

Martin looked tanned; he explained he had spent a month's holiday in Gibraltar that summer while engaged in writing his biography of a famous public figure who had become a renowned if not always respected cabinet minister towards the latter days of his life and whose personal secretary Ruislip had once been for some years. Martin hoped the book would arouse controversy and even possible litigation, though he concluded with a forlorn air that probably nobody would take a damned bit of notice of it; what was more unnerving was the fact that the publishers were the firm he worked for currently and in which he was a director, so if the book failed commercially insult would be added to injury since the money thus lost would indirectly come out of his own coffers. Not every writer, Martin mused entirely without malice, was as talented or as fortunate as Riley, and he was seriously thinking of stoically renouncing the lure of the quill and sticking to the editorial blue pencil, which at least paid the bills and the modest bachelor apartment he had near Hyde Park, even though he had always nursed a strong secret desire to starve to illustrious death in a garret, preferably with a bottle of French brandy under the dilapidated mattress. Such were the dreams of ordinary mortals like editors. Riley wondered what dreams, if any, Jay Simon might worship deep in his cash-register consciousness, if indeed he could afford dreams.

'I have had tidings of great joy from our mutual friend Laurie,' Martin was saying, straightening the creases in his trouser-legs. 'Though she did also say that you were going through a certain Sahara phase. Jay will undoubtedly want to know how *far* you have got with the book. I'm not very interested. I want to see how well you've written what you have done. I won't ask you how well you think you're writing,' smiled Martin, 'for writers are usually the last people to know. I daresay I shall presently see for myself.'

Riley felt apprehensive, and also a certain distinct irritation, as if he were being put on trial without having been properly cautioned or even indicted. His better sense assured him that

Martin was genuinely looking forward to reading the revised chapter which Laurie had praised and which was all that he would now show him, but he felt intimidated, cornered, pinned down, having perforce to justify himself, to stand up to intimate scrutiny through the eyes of this affable eminently likeable but intensely shrewd and perceptive man, as well as the smiling yet gimlet eyes of Jay Simon. He felt he was being placed under a microscope, and he writhed. He knew he was being unreasonable and hypersensitive about what was after all a very ordinary transaction between people who had something to offer and something to buy, yet he resented the very smell of the marketplace, the sound of the auctioneer's hammer tolling out the best price, the haggling in the wings, the decisions taken that would dramatically affect his life but about which he knew next to nothing, all committed to cold neat incomprehensible legalistic print signed with a facile smile and a flourish over afternoon cocktails. He looked now at Martin Ruislip and saw a smiling witty compatible fellow-creature, and for all his brittleness and sometimes his oiliness he knew, from his only meeting with him, that Jay Simon was just as non-threatening and as genial, indeed almost benign; still to his incurably islanded mind both men symbolised something he could not understand, a life-force beyond his own, engaged in things he did not remotely grasp, things far from sinister yet completely outside his comprehension even though those same things could dictate the course and texture of his life. All summer the beautiful yet demanding eyes of Laurie had been upon him reflecting hope, hurt, joy, sadness; a rich entrancing scrutiny, but a scrutiny still. And the probing was now to be continued, intensified, perhaps brought to the boiling-pitch; he felt he owned nothing any more, nothing of himself, not even the words inside his head were any longer his own, but were sifted and sorted and measured and finally spread out for all to see; he felt as if the very entrails of his body were on public display.

'Don't foreshadow doom,' said Martin, as if seeing the thoughts spinning round in his head. 'This is no inquisition. You look as if we were about to hang, draw and quarter you. Relax, man!'

Riley roused himself, contrite. 'Sorry,' he said. 'Just feeling a bit nervous, that's all.'

'I understand, but there's no need to be nervous, no need to be anything except encouraged and elated. We all have the utmost faith in you,' Martin went on. 'Especially Laurie. Her faith in you knows no bounds, and I suspect it's her opinion you look for and value most. Am I right?'

'Perhaps,' was all he could think of saying, the question being so slanted towards the only obvious answer.

Martin joined his fingers in his lap. 'You're an extremely lucky man to have a friend like Laurie, you know,' he said in quite a solemn tone, craning back his head and peering up at the branches. 'Extremely lucky. She must be a tremendous help.' Martin paused meaningfully, as though for an answer, but when Riley did not speak he continued, his voice positive, insistent almost. 'She's easily the most intelligent woman I know, kind, perceptive, gifted with an uncanny insight, able to make decisions firmly. You could not wish for a more ideal and admirable companion, and I take more than a little pride in the fact that it was I who introduced you two. A marriage of true minds indeed.'

Again, this time with greater certainty, Riley felt the anger, the bile rising in him; Martin was making such an issue of Laurie's virtues, reciting them like a litany, an inventory, lingering on each one as it came to mind, as if Riley were patently incapable of recognising and acknowledging these qualities in her for himself. In the eyes of practically everyone he had met since coming his indebtedness to Laurie Emerson was something he could never remotely hope to repay; it was as if to their way of thinking he had never written anything before he had met her, as if he had never existed except in a vague formless way on a primitive island full of mist and bog and smelling permanently of cabbage, a wild, rugged and barren hump of land sticking up out of the far main like a twisted fist, where the naive natives went without shoes and planted interminable potatoes, went from market town to market town on ragged browbeaten downtrodden donkeys and recited the rosary at least three times a day and aloud when drunk; a twilight place of holy candles perpetually burning on altars and in the windows of grey-faced thatched cottages strung along the arid slopes of mountains, always the air dark with the soft rain and the clouds so low one might almost walk through them.

He was sure this, despite his previous success, was how they saw him, and for most of them Laurie was moulding and re-making him into the creature he was to become, fashioning him with that alert keenly honed quicksilver intellect of hers into a sensitive industrious being, with a sizeable mantle of success about him, a primitive come down from the mountain to this suburban haven of exquisite manners and fastidious learning to be neatly trimmed and groomed and slotted into his pre-destined cubbyhole to which Laurie alone held the key. It seemed they could only interpret and come to accept him through her, could only visualise him through her eyes and look upon him as a creation wrought from her hands. So his love for her battled with this resentment of the role, real and imagined, that she played in his life; he found himself embroiled in two struggles centred round her, the one the necessity to be independent of her and therefore remain at least partly whole and intact, and the other to curtail this crippling resentment and suspicion and not be waylaid into useless and corrosive animosity towards her by his own distrust and narrow-mindedness. Even Martin would have him believe that this woman was now integral and totally indispensable to him, to his writing, and though in his heart the truth of this might echo, it was galling to have it practically pushed upon him by others, to have others, even inconsequential casual acquaintances, tell him what he already knew but feared to acknowledge. As in writing, as in everything, in accordance with his very nature, he had to set his own pace, make his own way, follow the directions he had marked out for himself, and trace by trial and error the full stop at the end of each chapter.

There could be no other way for him. If he had to, he would lose everything, abandon everything in order to seek things out for himself however blindly or with what folly. He would not be an open book for anyone to come along and read with easy assurance and perhaps a certain harmless ridicule; if he had to, he would stand away even from love, if love meant an un-conscious measure of invidious familiarity eventually breeding not contempt, but unthinking acceptance of him as a person, something more deadly, more deadening to the spirit than indifference itself. The acquiescence into which love might lead him filled him with all the loathsome terror of nightmare. If the dark wildness that was in him were to be tempered down and withdrawn, he would be as good as dead, an anaemic inanimate thing, a thing of blood and bone and nothing more, brainless, eyeless, without words for the saying of his dreams, without music for the celebration of each day, as good as dead. Though he had had no say in the beginning, the end and all things leading to and shaping that end would have to be uniquely his own and of his own contrivance.

'You're certainly in a thinking mood today,' said Martin. He looked at his watch. 'You haven't uttered a word for close on five minutes—and for an Irishman that is distinctly uncharacteristic!'

He looked up guiltily. 'Oh, I was just thinking about things,' he said, attempting nonchalance and predictably failing. 'Mostly about the book, you'll be glad to hear.'

Martin smiled infuriatingly, shaking his head. 'No, not about the book,' he contradicted amiably. 'If I may put it like this, you hadn't got the book-look on your face. I've come to know writers rather well and I've come to the conclusion that what they are thinking is usually written on their faces as clearly as the words they write down on paper. You've been thinking, but not about the book.'

'You talk like someone with a crystal ball,' said Riley, piqued. 'God, I'm thirsty.'

'Did I hear someone mention thirst?' said Laurie, coming from behind them carrying drinks on a tray. 'Sorry for being so long—someone on the phone who just wouldn't get off.' She set the tray down on the long wooden bench between the deck-chairs. 'I hope the wait will be worthwhile.'

She looked immaculately neat and young in a plain-cut yellow dress, her hair caught up behind and with hardly any make-up on. She sat down between them, taking a glass from the tray.

'What shall we drink to?' she asked gaily, poising with glass mid-way to her lips. 'I think there's only one possible toast—don't you, Martin?'

'Of course, my dear Laurie,' replied Martin, lifting his glass in turn. 'I normally abhor the pretence of drinking to anything, but once in a while it's nice to have something really exciting to raise your glass to. To our friend Riley and his obsession with words!'

They each tilted their glasses towards him ceremoniously and he picked up his own, feeling rather foolish, as if he were on stage facing an audience, though he knew this was just a bit of fun which they were staging for his benefit. All three of them took a formal sip, laughed, then took a proper portion, and the feeling became relaxed and easy as they settled back. The liquor tasted good, with little or no ice in it as Laurie knew he liked it, coursing through him sweetly, making the air brighter and the leaves shine with an even more scintillating greenness. The curious unsettling morbidity gradually ebbed away and, leaning back, he looked at them both with new and contented interest, once more delighting in their company and still hearing in that part of his mind especially attuned to it the soft sighing of surf down the shore. All misgivings vanished and the jade intermingling shades of the trees flickered delicately upon their faces.

'Where is Don?' asked Martin presently. 'I haven't seen him since I arrived. Surely he isn't working today—sabbatical sacrilege?'

Laurie looked down at her glass. 'Oh no. He and the two kids went sailing this morning—you know what a nut he is about that damned old tub of ours. He treats it like another man would treat a mistress,' she added, accompanied by an unsteady laugh. 'They should be home for supper. Maybe it's just as well they're away, as I imagine you and Jay would want to be alone for a while with Riley.'

Martin raised an eyebrow. 'Oh, we're not going to start reading what he's written with poor old Riley present,' he said. 'We're not fiends. We wouldn't dream of subjecting him to such medieval torture.'

'I'm glad to hear it,' Riley remarked. 'And it's only the revised first chapter, anyway.'

'Only one chapter? Well that's better than nothing. Did Laurie make you tear up the rest?' laughed Martin.

'Something like that.'

Martin settled back more fully, sipping his drink. 'Your letters anyway are miniature masterpieces, Riley,' he ruminated, 'really splendid. But they have lacked one thing ever since you arrived here.' He paused significantly.

'What would that be?' asked Riley, good-humouredly accepting the cue.

'The note of romance—what else? What's happened to that rare romantic soul of yours which was so much in evidence at home? Is it something in the Irish weather that brings it out more?'

'That's an interesting theory,' said Laurie.

'You really mean that since he's been here he hasn't fallen in love even once?' Martin said with tremendous mock surprise, addressing her directly.

'You'd better ask Riley that, I think,' she said, tapping her fingernail against her glass, making a small delicate tinkling sound.

'Am I permitted to pry?' asked Martin teasingly, with great good humour. 'I merely want to reassure myself that you are alive and well and as dedicated as ever to the perennial pursuit of human happiness in a tight sweater and skirt—unless of course your tastes in feminine fashions have become more sophisticated.'

An invisible cloud had come over the sun; he felt a sudden chill, a sudden rigid aloofness from them there in that bright afternoon garden warm with the scent of fresh beautiful growing things in the air. He caught again pungent cigarette smoke willowing snake-like from an ashtray, saw the dark glimmering of dawn through the curtains, felt soft hair touch his face, the strange lost crying of her in the dark . . .

'Did I perchance happen to strike a sore tooth?' said Martin. 'You have such a strange look on your face, Riley.'

'What?' he asked, hardly hearing. He looked at Laurie; her head was bent as she gazed at her glass; he looked away to the sound of the shore, wishing he were down there, alone. 'Oh, that's all right, Martin. A woman of no importance, to steal a line from Wilde.'

Laurie lifted her head and sipped. 'I always thought that was a particularly cruel title,' she said.

'Ah, yes,' Martin put in, 'but in the hands of dear Oscar even cruelty became a rare art—'

'That doesn't make it less cruel—' Laurie began.

'No, but decidedly more decorative,' insisted Martin, obviously enjoying himself. 'To the born satirist nothing is taboo, and Wilde was the satirist par excellence . . .'

Martin continued talking, with Laurie now and then answering, but for Riley the day no longer held warmth; he heard only the sound of words, not the words themselves. Against his will he was back in Greenwich, in that haphazard cluttered-up intensely lived-in room above the narrow streets, the garish neon lights over the shops and bars and all-night clubs, the electric tingle of excitement in the air alongside that of quaint ancient peacefulness that almost tangibly stamped itself on the cobblestones. Again he saw her face, sad, as if she were already on the road away from him, away from where they once held briefly together. Without knowing it his glass was empty and he automatically refilled it. He was aware of Laurie's eyes on him as Martin continued to talk. Her eyes were questioning, unriddling his thoughts, but he could not meet them, not then, with his mind fastening upon that other time, that other chaotic joy and panic, and he swirled the liquid slowly around in the glass, flecks of sunlight sparkling in its depths. He heard the grating screech of tyres on gravel and looked up; a large limousine was coming to a halt a few feet away from them. The Simons had arrived. Both Laurie and Martin got to their feet, Martin striding forward.

'All hail!' Martin said, then kissed Sue affectionately on the cheek and stepped back to look at her appraisingly. 'You're more captivating then ever, my dear Sue, however do you do it?'

'Hard work and a baby every year,' Sue replied in her calm placid voice. 'How are you, Martin?'

'As splendidly English as ever, can't you see,' Jay chimed in, clamping Martin round the shoulders and giving him a mock roguish dig in the ribs.

The two men chatted for a while as Sue came up and shook hands with Laurie, then Riley.

'You didn't visit us again as you promised, young man,' she said. She looked very chic, very cool in a dazzlingly white trouser suit, her tanned throat open above a satin blouse. 'May I hopefully take it you've been too fiercely engaged on the opus all this time?'

'On and off, yes,' he said, glancing beyond her as the back door of the car opened.

The men approached and Jay greeted him and Laurie with

his usual bonhomie and exuberance, talking all the while with that irrepressible panache which carried one along on the swift winning flow of his conversation that would streak off on diverse scintillating tangents without warning and hardly without pause, his round bland face gleaming meanwhile with the flush of his own oratory. Sue, however, had caught the glance which Riley had flashed towards the car, and presently turned to him smiling.

'We brought along a friend of yours, Riley,' she said quietly, as if speaking to him alone, while Abbie hovered uncertainly on the fringe of the little gathering. 'She's here on another working mission. All right with you?'

Sue put her hand on her husband's arm, stopping him in voluble mid-stream. 'Jay dear.'

Jay, surprised, turned round. 'What? Oh, gosh, of course—do forgive my terrible manners,' he said, going forward. 'Martin. I'd like you to meet Abbie Lang, a good friend of ours and one of the best snappers of snaps in the business!'

Martin bowed formally and shook her hand. Laurie, still standing a little way back, smiled and said hello. Abbie turned, fingering her cameras nervously.

'Hi, Riley,' she said, patently unsure.

'Hello, Abbie.'

As they all settled down Jay seemingly kept bringing him into the conversation, which was after all generally concerned with his writing, but Riley could not ignore the presence of Abbie, who seemed intent on getting her cameras and lenses into proper working order, and he managed to look in her direction from time to time while replying to the comments and remarks being put to him. There did not appear to be anything different or changed at all about her. She was dressed almost exactly as when he had last seen her, dark sweater and jeans and well-worn sneakers, hair falling loose about her shoulders. She appeared slightly more slender than before, her hips in the clinging cloth smoother, the shape of her breasts more delicate. She looked pale beneath her tan and her eyes held shadows that had not been there before. She was kneeling on the grass sorting out her equipment, absorbed in her task, taking no part in the talk that was going on under the trees. The words buzzed about him and he did not know if he was making intelligible responses or not, for the larger part of his mind was on her, the awareness of Laurie floating on the edge of his perception like a distant star. Once, pausing to reach for her glass on the ground beside her, Abbie looked over at him at a moment when he happened to be watching her; their eyes held; she did not pick up her glass, seemed immobile for that brief heartbeat of time, looking at him with dark unveiled intensity. Her look entered into his marrow. Then she took a quick sip, and went on with her work.

'And when may we expect the pleasure of your company once more at Jericho Pines?' Jay asked.

Riley dragged his mind back. 'Whenever you want me,' he replied.

Jay stood before him, broad and genial, glass in hand. 'Not that I want to interrupt the flow of genius,' he said, that peculiar Cheshire-cat-like smile on his face, 'but we're giving a little party tomorrow evening, one of our writers has reached the bestseller list for the first time and Sue and I thought it merited a little celebration. I'll send someone to pick you up about seven-thirty or so—is that okay?'

'Yes, that would be fine.'

Jay turned to Laurie. 'Of course you and your husband will come too, Mrs Emerson?' He smiled and held up his hand in apology. 'Sorry—I do have your permission to call you Laurie, don't I?'

Laurie moved out of the shade, perceptibly closer to Riley. 'Of course,' she rejoined. 'I'd be delighted to come along, though I can't answer for Don—he isn't exactly a party man, if you know what I mean. He'd much rather stay at home with the Scientific American or the National Geographic and a cold beer, or play some Berlioz after the kids have skedaddled to bed. He is really very homespun.'

'I am, too, at heart,' Jay admitted with a sigh, 'but in my business you don't get much chance for slippers and magazines and other such luxuries. Then may I take it we'll be seeing you too tomorrow night? Good, great. Don't bother to take the car —I'll see to the transport. Martin, of course, this is indirectly held in your honour, too,' said Jay, turning. 'It isn't often enough you bestow upon us the pleasure of your company this side of the Atlantic.'

So an hour or so went by, convivial, bantering, the day clear and warm with a slight cooling breeze barely stirring the leaves. Riley felt distinctly odd; there was something unreal in the situation, something out of context, sitting there on the lawn listening to the bland clever talk, his mind in confusion rotating like a fairground chairoplane gone mad between Laurie so quietly articulate at his side, and the slender blur of controlled animation that was Abbie, moving about the garden absently fondling her ubiquitous cameras, now playing with Cricket when that languid creature was not entirely comatose, now strolling off among the trees towards the muted sounds of the beach, hands clasped lightly behind her back. His thoughts hopelessly oscillated round those two separate and singular points of absolute polarity, swept back and forward constantly like leaves caught in a cross-current, no sooner fastened on one then the other claimed his attention. It was like being caught up in some bizarre and baffling game of which the players themselves were only vaguely aware, his mind being shuttled from one to the other through intricate patterns of movement seemingly observed by him alone. He sat there in the deck chair in a state of dazed near-bewilderment, though his face was calm and he mouthed appropriate words from time to time with that part of his brain that was clear and detached from both women.

Don arrived back, tall and bronzed, wearing his nautical cap with the red anchor on it, walking with that peculiar gait of his, shoulders sloping forward, arms hanging loosely at his sides, smiling and peering shortsightedly at his guests, in shorts, his bare legs hairy and muscular. As always he spoke slowly, drawling his words, stretching each syllable like elastic, measuring each comment he made carefully, methodically, his movements synchronising precisely with his deliberate speech. The man was big, ungainly, a little awkward in the perpendicular, and to the casual onlooker he might have seemed rather depthless and innocuous; this impression seemed almost to be of his own carefully contrived making, yet though his eyes were small and needle-pointed behind the thick lenses, they were intense, acute, boring into things, scrutinising shrewdly everything that came within their vision, the head, though balding somewhat, was massive, leonine, held high always in a Southern aristocratic manner. Every inch of him betokened pride, yet he was not supercilious; it was ancestral rather than personal pride, pride in the hard-working disciplined tradition of his heritage rather than complacent satisfaction in anything he himself might have achieved. The handshake offered was strong, uncompromising, courteous, and summarised the man behind it. Large, and taller than most men, he did not superimpose his presence on any gathering, and he could be surprisingly inconspicuous in a room big or small, managing to remain unnoticed and almost out of sight standing quietly in a corner with a drink in his hand, speaking only when somebody spoke to him; he was not an aloof person, he seemed to enjoy good conversation, but he very seldom instigated it and generally preferred to listen, with unfailing courtesy even though there might not be anything exactly stimulating worth the listening. It was possible to like Don Emerson without ever remotely coming to know him; he was not anything as obvious as an enigma, simply a man who would rather choose a deliberate if unlikely anonymity.

Midge was also there, and at once claimed or rather accepted the limelight that was immediately turned upon her. Bright-headed, demure and tomboyish all at once, she won with effortless ease, with a tilt of her deer-like neck and a crook of her beckoning finger, the willing attention, the instant allegiance of all, diminutive lady come into her own, holding court there on her front lawn, breaking into tiny sunbursts of merriment without prompted rhyme or reason, retelling in gilded detail the adventures of the day's sailing across the Sound, skipping from sunlight into shadow as she acted out each exaggerated example of the things that had and had not happened, fey, insouciant, golden. The child was like a firefly dancing in a circle of tall sombre trees cast deep in shade; she dazzled from one to another, daring and delightful, nimble, fleet-footed, sunnily engrossed in an ephemeral ballet all her own; it was as if a minute atom of the radiant sun had fallen from the sky and landed on the grass at their feet. Midge outshone the day itself and gathered them all up in her small hand. Beside her, Richard her brother and senior by two years remained merely part of the background, a shy undemonstrative rather brooding little boy, inevitably with a book of some sort under his arm, wearing a continual forlorn puppy-like pout on his face, looking rather like a dispossessed cherub searching for a lost niche.

Jay came over to Riley. 'Well, the moment of truth has arrived,' he said in his smooth pleasant voice, mopping his forehead. 'Martin and myself will get down to the business of reading your output up to date. While we're doing that would you object very strenuously if Abbie took a few promotional pictures of you, Riley—down on the beach, in the room where you work, banging away at the typewriter—that kind of thing?'

'I don't mind a bit,' replied Riley.

Jay's fixed smile broadened. 'I know it's all been done before, but we might catch some new and unusual angles, and anyway it will be better than for you to sit here biting your nails while we go over the script—don't you agree? Good, great.' Jay looked about him. 'Where is Abbie, by the way,' he said, shading his eyes from the sun.

'Right here, Mister Bossman,' Abbie called out cheerfully, coming up from behind. 'Just looning about.'

'Ready to start shooting?' Jay asked her.

'Ready when you are, sir,' she answered mockingly, saluting him, then turned to Riley, 'and of course you, Riley.'

He finished his drink. 'I'm ready.'

Abbie looked around, eyes narrowing. 'I think the beach first,' she said, then looked at Laurie who was nearby. 'Then, if it's okay with you and your husband, Mrs Emerson,' she said, slightly emphasising the formal appellation, 'I'd like to take some pictures inside the house and show Riley at work in his room.'

'That will be fine,' Laurie replied evenly and pleasantly. 'Shall I tidy the room up? As you may know, Riley isn't the tidiest person in the world.'

'Oh, that's all right,' Abbie told her quickly. 'Just leave everything looking like it always does, no fancy frills, just natural.' She hoisted the camera strap more securely round her neck. 'Shall we get cracking?'

It was nearing evening, people were drifting homewards for supper, and they had little audience. Abbie had a sudden brainwave and asked Midge to come with them, and the child needed no coaxing. As always, Riley felt acutely uncomfortable in front of the camera; he fidgeted and grimaced, feeling tremendously foolish, but unlike others before her, Abbie never uttered a word of advice or asked him to sit in such a way or look in any particular direction; she hardly spoke at all, hidden and invulnerable behind her cameras, her absorption and unobtrusive presence helping him relax, and he became once more quite natural with Midge, almost excluding Abbie and the whirring cameras.

'Is that the beautiful lady I saw the other day?' asked Midge solemnly. 'The lady who brought you back in her car?'

Riley nodded as she squatted in the sand beside him. 'The very same lady.'

Midge was silent for a while, watching Abbie some yards away. Then she turned her face up to Riley. 'Is she your girl-friend?' she asked, scooping up handfuls of sand and letting it fall through her fingers. 'Will you be married to her like Mom and Dad and live in your own house?' Midge stopped playing with the sand, as if waiting for an answer, regarding him with grave blue eyes.

He managed to sound amused, looking out to sea. 'I don't think so, Midge,' he answered. 'We really don't know each other very well.'

Midge was insistent. 'You like her a lot though, don't you?'

'Oh, sure,' he said, watching a fleet of seagulls gliding far out, their wings hardly stirring. 'I like most people—'

'But you like that lady a lot, don't you?' Midge went on, unyielding, sinking her tight little fists in the sand.

'She's a nice lady,' he said to the unrelenting inquisitor. 'I like nice ladies.'

Abbie was busily taking shots, too far away to overhear, her shadow moving obliquely across the sand.

'Do you like Mom?' was the next question put to him by Midge the beautiful and merciless.

'Of course I do!'

Midge looked at him, screwing up her eyes. 'Are you going to take her away from Dad?'

He looked down into the small oval face confronting him, feeling suddenly bare, unarmed; he could see the creamy freckles on the child's nose, yet in that instant immeasurable miles seemed to have opened up between them, putting them at a great and lonely distance from each other. He could only stare, transfixed by the cruel innocent directness of childhood.

'No, Midge, I'm not,' he said after he had controlled his breathing with an effort. 'But why should you ask me such a thing, what put it into your head?'

Midge shrugged, as if the subject were not worth considering any more. 'Oh, nothing,' she said, then pointed at the little armada of gulls he had watched a moment before. 'Look, those birds are swimming in the sky!' Her voice was vibrant with pleasure. He was still floundering in the wake of her previous remark when she settled back in the sand and said in a quite ordinary little gir''s voice, 'I heard Dad say it to Mom the other night.'

He was quiet for a moment. 'Say what, Midge?'

'That he was getting to be afraid of you,' answered Midge, digging her heels into the sand. She craned her face up at him, squinting in the sun. 'Why is Dad afraid of you?'

She was only a child, just five, but he knew he could not be glib or flippant with her, he could not evade her suddenly penetrating gaze; she was at that moment more intuitive, more uncannily perceptive than any adult person he had known. It was not mere childish curiosity, not unthinking inquisitiveness welling from the nowhere regions of childhood; she was possessed of an unnameable something that made her dart straight to the hidden heart of things, things that by the average dictates of nature should have been beyond her comprehension and indeed that of most people, the grey tidy unventuresome minds of her pretentious elders, like herself. But these things buried in secrecy below the facile devious thoughts of everyday she found out as if in an ordinary moment of childish chance she had dug deep in sand and discovered strange shells far under the surface. She did not, could not analyse such things, nor did she need to; they were simply there, where she had found them, and she simply picked them up and presented her discovery to others. She was still looking up at him, waiting.

'Midge,' he said, calm now and speaking without hindrance as to an equal, 'Midge, we are all a little afraid of each other. We don't always know why this should be so, but people are strange creatures, you can never get to know them the way you

132

get to know animals, the way you know Cricket. Our friend Cricket is so fine and beautiful and intelligent compared to some people, I would say most people.' He paused and gazed across at Abbie, crouching in the sand still taking her interminable pictures, her hair blowing in the stronger breeze from the sea. 'I can't answer your question, Midge,' he said, 'because I don't have the answer. At least not all of it, only a very small part of it, and I don't have the words to tell you that small part, perhaps because I don't understand it myself. I hope your father will stop being afraid of me, because there is nothing to be afraid about.'

'Are you going to tell him that, then?' the child asked, drawing masks in the sand with her forefinger, brushing strands of aureoled hair back from her eyes.

'If you want me to, yes.'

She giggled out loud then, as though the preceding conversation-piece had never been, pointing as the new sand-portrait she had just made. 'Look at that funny face!'

He looked down and saw that the face she had drawn bore a striking and rather unflattering resemblance to his own.

Abbie returned, trudging over the sand, winding and unwinding the spools of her cameras, leaving footprints behind her.

'What have you two been chattering about?' she said as she came up and halted in front of them, giving them a sly conspiratorial smile. 'I've never known you to talk so much, Riley—'

'Midge is rather infectious,' he said. 'She brings out the repressed speechifier in me.'

'Out of the mouths of babes,' said Abbie softly, her shadow falling across them.

He looked up at her sharply. 'Are we through down here?' he asked, his voice suddenly cold.

'Sure,' said Abbie easily. 'Midge, you're a natural, a real natural. You're going to be a famous model one of these days.'

'Oh no,' replied Midge seriously. 'I'm going to be a mermaid.'

'Just relax and look like you're in the middle of a chapter,' Abbie said as she peered over at him through her viewfinder, index finger poised on the button. 'Look real creative.'

'How the hell can I do that with you snooping around me?' he said sourly. 'It's a blank page in there, you know,' he growled down at the typewriter.

She grinned, tossing back her hair. 'Then write something on it—anything—it doesn't have to be Intimations of Immortality or Dante's Inferno, you know. Just a jumble of letters even—it won't show in the photographs anyway—I just want you looking like you're hard at work, oblivious of everything around you—okay?' Even as she spoke she kept clicking away from different angles.

'I feel such a bloody fraud,' he grumbled gloomily into space.

'Aren't we all?' she said cheerfully, moving about the room, twisting herself into comical semi-crouching postures.

'Do I have to join the circus?' he said, bending forward in the chair, kneading his fingers together, a fierce frown creasing his forehead. 'I feel like a performing monkey—all that's missing is the barrel-organ. Abbie,' he said, twisting around as she crouched behind him, 'Abbie, get me a bloody drink, will you?'

'What about Laurie? I mean—'

'Will you please get me a drink?' he said patiently.

'Anything you say, sir, anything to make my job easier,' said Abbie, coming around and taking another shot. 'I think I'll join you as a matter of fact,' she said, again looking at him through the viewfinder. 'Helps me act more natural too. Won't be a sec.'

When she was gone he sat and looked out of the window. Sunset: the sky swam with fiery arson-red warrior clouds, dashing pink daubs on the walls of his room and shedding a fire-like aura on his clasped hands. He was aware of Martin and Jay downstairs somewhere reading his manuscript over sandwiches and tumblers of drink, dissecting it word by word, sentence by sentence, surgeons going about their business, excising, cutting, threading together; he felt as if he were being dismembered, sliced up, patched and sewn, stitched, quilted into a pattern he had never intended, grafted into alien flesh, into a world he had never made. He imagined if he listened fiercely enough with all the rest of his mind closed he could even hear their voices through the floorboards underneath him, even catch the long meaningful pauses as they reached absently for their glasses, eyes glued to the pages in their fingers, the scratch of their pens as they made notes in the margins and between the double-spaced lines of sentences, annotating each error, underlining each questionable nuance of emphasis, littering each page with innumerable question-marks, comparing notes.

'The plasma has arrived,' the voice of Abbie breaking into his hounded thoughts, decanter in one hand, glasses in the other, pouring. 'Cheers.'

The imaginary ominous vocal rumblings from below slowly faded and the enflamed sky took on a more softened look. He put down his emptied glass and looked at her.

'Right,' he said. 'I'm ready.'

'Good for you, kiddo,' said Abbie, putting her half-filled glass on the window-ledge and bringing her cameras to the fore. 'That helped us both, I think. Just forget I'm here.'

'I will.'

She gave him a look at once pained and amused. 'As easily as that, eh?'

He did not reply as he bent over the typewriter and started fingering out the words of a poem that had just then flashed through his mind, the words fitting the image as snugly as a tailor-made suit. A poem about a girl half-asleep on a deserted dune dreaming about a beautiful non-existent lover sailing across impassable seas to her under cold spellbinding stars with romantic tatooes on his hairy forearms, her inner soliloquy interspersed with fragmented images of her mother's grave, scenes at the biscuit factory where she worked, improbable prairie dogs roaming through asphalt streets, and the lush grass in which she lies bedded high on a summit over a silver scimitar bay . . . a wistful sad wry end-of-summer enigmatic bit of a poem coming like the better poems out of nowhere, like the resurrection of things that died in the mind before they could be caught and shaped in the forge of sustained thought.

When next Abbie spoke he almost jumped, forgetting that she was in the room.

'Bravo, Riley, bravo!' she exclaimed. 'That was great. You looked just as if you were really at work—'

He raised his head, giving her what he hoped was a look of supreme withering reproach. 'I was.'

'Oh, really?' she said, picking up her glass and coming to stand beside him, peering down at the sheet of paper in the typewriter. 'What did you write?' She knelt down and read what he had written. Then again, more slowly, half forming the words with her lips; finally she sat back on her heels and looked up at him, puzzled. 'Would I sound stupid if I were to ask you what it means?'

'Does it have to mean anything?'

She paused, reflecting. 'No—no, I guess not, if you put it that way. Still, I'm one who likes to be able to say I understand —know what I mean? I like to be able to grasp things, turn them over in my mind and know what it's all about—'

'So which is the more important—the poem, the book, the painting itself, by itself, or your own interpretation of what it should mean?'

'I think that's one and the same thing,' answered Abbie. 'At least it is for me, bird-brained creature that I am.'

'What you're saying is that you don't derive pleasure from something you don't understand, something you can't rationalise, is that it?'

'I don't know. That sounds a little simplified. I get much pleasure from a Picasso and some pleasure from a Kandinski, but the pleasure would be greater if I could understand each of them a bit more. Is that very dim-witted of me?'

He reached forward and picked up the decanter from the floor. 'Dim-witted, no,' he said, filling his glass and putting the decanter down between them. 'Just a bit short-sighted, perhaps. What is there to understand about something that gives you pleasure—*why* should there be anything to understand? Do you have to justify the pleasure by rationalising the source of it, by coming to terms with the reason for it? We know that sunsets and dawns are caused merely by the earth's atmospheric makeup, due to an entirely logical scientific phenomenon, but does that knowledge help to increase our pleasure in watching the sun rise and set?' He drank. 'I doubt it very much.'

'There's some truth in that, I agree,' said Abbie, kneeling back, holding her glass in both hands. 'But isn't it also true that knowledge and understanding must add to whatever pleasure we get from certain things—I mean, the more meaningful they become to us the more we can learn to enjoy them?'

'I don't accept that at all,' he said, sitting more upright in his chair. 'Why should everything be subjected, even subjugated, to reason? Why not enjoy things simply because they are there, without wanting to lift a finger and say, "Ah, I understand that, I know what that means"? Pleasure and understanding are two separate things. By understanding the motives for murder or war does it make it less horrible or more horrible? I think the horror remains just the same, whether we know the reasons for it or not. Likewise bravery or pleasure,' he added.

'You're not talking much like a writer now, you know,' said Abbie, gently chiding. 'I always thought writers were people who never took things for granted, who went on asking questions and trying to find out things all the time, investigating life, so to speak. You seem to be saying the opposite, to be saying in fact, "Don't ask questions, just take things as they are." It's not very imaginative, is it?'

'Asking questions is one thing,' he insisted. 'Wanting and expecting to know the answers is quite another. If a writer has a duty or a function at all—and I'm not sure that he has—it is to ask questions, not to supply the answers. If the answers are there they will appear eventually, but the writer's task is to set the questions in motion and let the answers come when they will—'

'In other words, you supply the bricks but don't necessarily build the house, eh?' Abbie interjected.

'If by house you refer to truth, then that will build itself,' he said. 'Truth may be hidden, but it is always there. I just don't see the sanity in running after hidden meanings in everything all the time. Does a child ask why a sweet or a cake tastes so good, and if he knew would it taste even better?' He drank, a little mournfully. 'That's the great magic of childhood. We just reach out and grab at pleasure, accepting it as a right and not a privilege. We're not afraid to be happy, as later we come to be.'

Abbie gazed steadily into her glass. 'And you, Riley—are you afraid to be happy?'

He was quite a time silent. 'Of course I am,' he said. 'What intelligent person isn't?'

'I guess I'm not very intelligent, for being happy is

everything to me, I want to be happy every hour of the day and night.'

'And it doesn't scare you?'

'Oh sure, sometimes, but it scares me more when I'm not happy. Then I feel there's something wrong with me. I feel I'm walking through a long dark tunnel with no light at the end of it.'

'To live in hope of happiness is a futile waste of time,' he continued after they had been silent for some time. 'Sometimes the bravest thing anyone can do is to live without hope, without the illusion of hope or happiness.'

'You sound so dirgeful,' she said. 'I think we all must have our illusions. I know I couldn't go on without mine. Hope keeps me going. I think it's the one thing that does keep me going. Hope of being impossibly, madly, deliriously happy all the days of my life, which may be terribly naive of me, but it's the only way I know how to keep alive without going mad.'

'You equate happiness with love.' He spoke in a remote lethargic way, hunched forward now, elbows on knees.

'Of course,' she instantly replied. 'As naturally as I equate birth with life, death with dying, or more facetiously Barnum with Bailey. To me the equation is obvious and inevitable. I simply don't need to think about it. Oh, I'm not completely dotty. I know all that stuff about the pain and sorrow of love and so forth, and God knows it's true enough, but why should we make love out to be such a long groan of misery? The way people think and feel and write about love, it emerges as a kind of perversion, a kind of maudlin masochism.'

'You're talking now about the obvious—about the love between man and woman,' he said with ill-disguised, heavy and rather pointless cynicism.'

Abbie lifted an eyebrow. 'I don't have your penchant for the mystical and obscure. Sure, I love nature, and literature, and my fellow-man and all that stuff, but that's love of a different kind, a kind of universal love of one's own species. I don't think about it much, except in times of earthquakes or epidemics and political assassinations and things like that. Then I sort of start thinking about God. But all the rest of the time I'm thinking about myself and relating myself to some single unique individual, some special man, thinking about what that kind of love would mean to me. . .' She stopped and took a slow sip of her drink, her face in profile warmly lit by the sunset. 'I didn't mean to get into such a complicated argument,' she said, as if not wanting to let the silence linger and lengthen between them. 'I'm terrible when I get started.' She paused. 'You didn't even phone or write. Why?'

'Why? I asked myself that, more than you know. Maybe it was I had so little to say, or what I had to say was too late for the saying of it.'

'I never wanted you to say things to me just for the saying of them, Riley,' she said, leaning her shoulder against the window-ledge. 'I hated leaving my apartment, even for work, in case you might phone and I wouldn't be there. I haunted the mailbox every morning. Always the same. Nothing. Again I ask—why? Am I so repellent to your memory that you'd rather obliterate me completely from it? Don't you ever think and remember? Was it all so very hateful for you?' Her voice was far from ascending to any level of hysteria, but was quiet, controlled, somewhat defeated.

'Hateful?' Riley repeated. 'God, no. I have thought, Abbie, I have remembered, often, so very often, when I have finished writing and switched off the damn typewriter and lain in my bed in the dark hearing the leaves outside and seeing the moonlight creeping about the room. Oh, I have thought and remembered. But what am I to think, what am I to remember? I remember the good you brought to me, the joyful giving of yourself, but I think of the terrible impossibility of it all.'

'Impossible? Why impossible? That's not exactly a favourite word in your vocabulary, is it, Riley?'

He shook his head, finishing off his drink. 'Don't ask me why, Abbie. You must know and feel it as much as I.'

'I think I am in love with you.'

She said it without special emphasis, certainly without passion, without histrionics of any kind, merely as a statement of belief, leaning back against the window-ledge, legs curled under her, not looking at him but staring ahead. A kind of insensate anger seized him, coupled with wonder and a growing undeniable excitement; she was utterly undemanding, and for this he was relieved, for he was tremendously aware of the tightrope upon which he was balancing, yet he felt also an irrational resentment, a sulking juvenile pique at this very passivity of hers, so distant from what he remembered of their last time together, when he had glimpsed a world he had never before entered and the gates of it had crashed shut in his face. He reached for the brandy, seeking refuge in it, trying to bludgeon his senses into oblivion or at least ambivalence, but she stretched out her hand and placed her fingers on his wrist, staying him.

'Have you no words for me?'

'I have no words for myself, Abbie.'

'Do you despise me? Despise me for throwing myself at you so brazenly that night?'

'If I despised you, I would have to despise myself even more, and neither is remotely true.'

'Why, then—why do you shun me? You've hardly looked me in the eye since I arrived here today. Is it so difficult?'

He took a deep breath. 'It is—difficult,' he said after an effort. She took her hand away and he filled his glass. 'Abbie, please help me, please understand. Nothing like that . . . nothing like it had ever happened to me before. It was like— like almost climbing to the summit, only to slip and fall down into nothingness again. I felt cheated—cheated of for once being whole . . .'

'At the risk of sounding wanton,' she said into the pause, 'I could say we can both still make that climb.'

'It's not that,' Riley replied, resting his elbows on the arms of the chair. 'It's no longer just that. You were not to know, were you, that I was a virgin?'

She lifted her eyes to him. 'And you know now that I was not?' she said.

He laughed briefly. 'That's clearly not relevant,' he said. 'You were as virginal in your intentions as I was in truth that night. Something in me drew you, and for that self-awakening you will always have my love, such as I am capable of loving anyone, a capacity that is severely limited. No. It is something else, Abbie. Something other than the enjoyment of flesh with flesh. I don't think I could ever be whole merely through that—'

Again her voice was very quiet, but all the clearer for it. 'I did mention the word love, remember.'

'That's just it!' he said, almost wildly. 'Love! If we could have accepted each other as we were, needing each other in one respect only, without wanting to hear the fanfare, the drums beating, the trumpets blowing, the cymbals clashing, all the birds of the world wild and singing in our heart. . . . I was not made for such clamour. I feel threatened by it. I fear it would swallow me up, make me not less, but different from what I am, and what I am is all that I can cope with.'

'Why are you so afraid, Riley?' she asked, her voice puzzled and sad. 'In all your life haven't you let another person come close to you, really close, so that they could look at you and say "I know you"? Why should you be afraid of that? Most of us go through life wanting desperately for others to know us, but you seem deliberately to prefer remaining alone, a loner, an outsider by choice rather than fate. Why? Do you fear that people may take away something from you that you could never substitute, something that would in some way cripple you far more in mind and spirit than you are now in body?'

She was speaking with a quiet implacable insistence from which there was no escape, and again his cowardice came to the rescue, and he lifted the glass to his lips.

'As you said, I have no words for you, Abbie,' he said. 'No words for either of us. I may lack every shred of courage, but I must hold on to myself at all costs, I must not try to escape through other people, through their love, kindness, understanding—call it what you will. God knows I don't wish to be alone, to remain forever on the outside, but in the end I would rather be trapped within myself than to lose myself in others. I want to build upon the little I do know of myself, so that if others should want to know me there will be something to know.'

She shook her head vehemently. 'No, dear Riley, no, that won't work, that won't wash. Don't delude yourself—please don't delude yourself. You talk of not wanting to escape through others, but don't you see that life is full of escapes in every shape and form? Even love is an escape, an escape from the terror of not being loved, of being alone and unwanted, of being left to the sad colourless devices of ourselves. The glass you're holding in your hand now, Riley—that is one hell of an escape as we all find out sooner or later. And there's nothing wrong with it— we all need to escape from something or other, perhaps most of all from ourselves, it doesn't really matter what form it takes so long as we don't hurt other people. You say you have little love to offer others, but how do you know—have you ever tried? Have you ever let yourself love another person without thinking of yourself and how it might affect you?'

The sun had almost retired, the horizon was a gleaming blade of red and gold, shimmering, and the slowly gathering evening clouds moved about the sky like ships ablaze. The beach would be deserted now, save for a few lovers lingering among the dunes; later as it grew dark and the first stars came out neighbours would gather, light bonfires and have barbecues, laugh and sing and swim in the cool night waters, splashing each other amid squeals and guffaws, with here and there a footloose dog yapping madly streaking in and out between dripping sand-stained bodies. He closed his eyes, the burning blur of the clouds lingering behind them.

'Love, Abbie,' he said, holding the incandescent glass in his hand. 'I don't know about love. Your love is different from my conception of love. And I grant that conception is a narrow blindfolded feeble-minded thing. Far from being a dove it is a hawk in a cage waiting to pounce and sink its claws in as soon as the door is opened. No—I don't think I could love anyone without first thinking of myself. I told you it was a narrow conception. I can only plead ignorance, and even that ignorance I guard zealously against unknown intrusion.'

'Then you will be a prisoner all your life, Riley,' Abbie said, melancholy and impatient at once. 'You'll end up having nothing, not even that precious self you're so devoted to. If you've no room left for anyone but yourself you'll suffocate, you'll die of claustrophobia.'

'Must you indulge in high melodrama?' he asked tiredly. 'Don't you know most of us die tame unexciting lack-lustre deaths exactly the way most of us live? Death as a poetic concept no longer holds true. How many van Goghs do you know personally or even know of? Even Dylan Thomas went out like a common drunkard and probably choked in his own vomit. I'll most likely die in a nice warm bed in dull disgusting middle-age in newly-pressed pyjamas and a large half-eaten meal by my bedside, a demise of no character whatsoever. How will that affect your grandiose theory of my end?'

Abbie was laughing quietly. 'You may exasperate me with your stubbornness and stupid pride, but you can very often make me laugh just the same. Ah, Riley,' she sighed, putting her long since empty glass on the window-ledge, 'what am I to make of you? What am I to do about you? You're such a child really, a gauche ungainly juvenile playing at being a man, and your acting is atrocious. Has Laurie no redeeming influence over you at all—has she failed as badly as I have?'

This remark stung him, hurting deep in at the quick. 'Laurie? Why should she have any kind of influence over me in the first place? Why should people want to influence me anyway? Why can't they take me as I am without trying to remake me as they see fit?'

His anger was obvious, but Abbie took it very calmly. 'You're being very vain and very pompous,' she told him. 'You're very hard to take as you are, kiddo. And you're not being quite honest with either yourself or with me. I was speaking of Laurie Emerson, I was not referring to "people". I think you'll agree there is quite some difference. Do I have to spell it out?' He did not answer, and she remained silent for a few moments, sitting cross-legged on the floor. 'It's all right, Riley. I have a good eye for such things—'

'What things?' he challenged.

'So I do have to spell it out? She's in love with you, friend. I don't know about you, but that much is certain. You may think she's merely over-possessive, and of course she is, she's that type of person, but it goes much deeper, and if you can't see it you're blinder than I thought.' She held up her hand as he was about to say something. 'I'm not speaking out of malice. I am jealous, as jealous as hell, but I am also being objective, or at least as far as I can be, feeling as I do. To use less dainty language, the woman is nuts about you.'

His anger was real now. 'You say you've a good eye for such things,' he said, gripping his glass. 'What you really have is a silly snooping romantic feminine mind nourished on True Romance magazines and coloured by a succession of dismal love affairs—'

'Why are you so angry?' she asked, genuinely puzzled. 'Of course I have a feminine mind, but I don't see why its gender should make it less observant than yours. As for my love affairs

—would you believe they amount to very few? They may not have set the world on fire, but they were far from being dismal. The first was with a kid I met at college, a fine upstanding specimen of idealised American youth, crew-cut, clean-shaven, baseball type, adored Momma's cooking. His name was Theodore Filbertson, Junior, for God's sake. The last was a nutty pie-in-the-sky week-long affair with a much older guy, married of course, not quite old enough to be my father, but old enough. His one enduring passion was the science of graphology—he used to correspond with people all over the world just to study their handwriting and analyse their hidden psyche. I think what he really fell for was the way I wrote my r's. He said the letter r was the most aggressive one in the whole alphabet. His name was Cedric. So you see, when you talk about a succession of lovers you flatter me—a beautiful thought, but alas untrue. And believe it or not, I've never read a woman's magazine in my young and lovely life. I was too busy being a woman. All of which has nothing at all to do with Laurie.'

His head was beginning to ache slightly. He was acutely conscious of her, the dimensions of the room seemed to be shrinking, drawing them closer; he could quite easily have reached out and touched her, knowing full well what the touch would mean. He felt the same tingling instant arousal as before, as if drowning in the heavy pollen of her fresh vibrant young beauty. She was a challenge he could never hope or dare to meet; she was looking out at life with bold bright eyes, eager, expectant, claiming all, a receptacle for whatever joy and adventure there might be waiting for her in the world, totally committed to and absorbed in the moment in which she found herself. The pace of her life streaked ahead of him, highly charged and generating seemingly inexhaustible energy; he felt she would continue always to spin fantastically away from him beyond his orbit, however willing she might be to remain captive in his heart. She was as unfit and untrained for cages as he was himself, even though the door was left unlocked and the bars were velvet; she could only be free in the unhindered winging of her way, forever seeking without really wanting to find a haven. He imagined love for her meant the unfastening of locks, the opening of shuttered windows letting in an abundance of light, all the poetry of the world rolling in upon her in deep warm waves of music, a lotus flower in perennial bloom; he believed this was so for her, despite her air of worldly sagacity and nimble-witted toughness. It was as if love was a theme that had been specially orchestrated for her, to suit her every mood and intent, every nerve and nuance of her mind, and she expected him to be able to read the musical score as easily as she could listen to it and respond to it, but he could not.

'I'm sorry if I upset you by mentioning Laurie,' she said.

She was being a child once more, a contrite repentant child holding out her hand to be slapped; he felt a quick tenderness for her, an absurd protectiveness, he wanted to gather her up in his arms, to safeguard her against the wiles of the world about which she gave so great an impression of being blasé and consummately certain of herself, but to which she could, he knew, so easily succumb and fall victim. The sunset fell upon her, bathing her unashamedly, and his trapped gaze took in the shape of her breasts in the dark shirt, the clear thrust of her nipples showing through. She was leaning her head back against the window, eyes closed, the buttercup-smooth slope of her throat unbearably vulnerable and desirable, arousing in him things he did not wish to meet and acknowledge. There was about her an almost palpable aura of sensuality, carnal, unintentionally provocative, the deep luscious bloom on a rose in the hazy height of summer; it welled out of her from within, hung about her like vapour, like gossamer, luxuriant, heady, rich. He saw again the creaminess of her limbs, the white streaks across her hips and thighs and breasts where the sun could not caress her, felt again the soft fullness of her, her armpits holding a special odour, a special mystery, subtle, redolent of feminine hiddenness, his senses caught in the web of her loosened hair . . . He shut his eyes hard, as she would close the shutters of her cameras, trying to erase these images, to wipe from the sensitive retina the sudden flashes of memory the past projected, trying desperately to rid his brain of such scalding tantalising imprints; yet he saw even now how the cloth of her jeans moulded her thighs, delineating them to perfection, meeting finally in that peerless perilous apex . . .

'Riley,' she spoke in a hushed, lost voice, her eyes closed, perfectly still, 'Riley, why can't you love me?'

It was not a plaintive little wail of girlish distress, but rather the low remote crying of a lonely woman speaking from her own inner solitude.

'Oh, Abbie, please,' he said, his heart twisting over.

'Please tell me.'

'I can only love you as I do now,' he said, staring out into the glowing evening. 'Only as my stunted senses allow.'

He saw the movement in her throat as she swallowed and opened her eyes, gazing up at the ceiling. 'I'm sorry. That was stupid of me. I guess we can all only love as we are able.' She turned her face sideways towards him and smiled, winking in sudden comradeship. 'I'm okay, kiddo. No more sad songs for me. Just remember Greenwich wasn't the end of the world, for either of us. Try to think of it as a beginning, even if you never see me again. Promise?'

'That's an easy thing to promise, Abbie.'

'Ah, but don't promise it easily.'

'I won't.'

There was a discreet tap on the door, then Laurie's voice. 'Can I come in?'

Abbie got to her feet, pulling down the waist of her shirt that had ridden up a bit as she sat. 'Sure,' she called out. She set about busying herself with her cameras as Laurie entered.

'Are you through?' Laurie asked. 'Supper's ready. You both must be ravenous.'

'I could do with a bite of something, yes,' Abbie admitted. 'Sorry we took so long, Mrs Emerson—'

'Do you find it all that difficult to call me Laurie? I'm only called Mrs Emerson at PTA meetings and church functions or when Don takes me to one of his business dinners. It makes me feel quite staid and conservative—which I may well be, except that one doesn't relish being reminded of it.' Laurie came further into the room and sat on the side of the bed. She was obviously in a mood to be convivial and conversational, warmed perhaps by a combination of drink and good company, and perhaps by something he could not now guess at or surmise.

'Thanks, Laurie,' replied Abbie, once more adjusting her elaborate necklace of cameras round her neck. 'After we finished grafting we got to talking—were we really that length of time?'

146

'I really didn't notice myself, to be truthful,' answered Laurie, looking mysteriously happy. 'It was really a revelation, listening to these two literary gentlemen downstairs dissecting Riley's work so learnedly as they sipped their cocktails. It was like watching real-life open-heart surgery.' She turned to him. 'I'm not anticipating things, Riley, but from what I heard and from the sheer look on their faces, I'd say they're just dotty about that first chapter. Typical of Martin, he concealed his excitement somewhat better than Jay, who is going about purring now and just about licking his chops. Sue Simon contained herself very well also, but even she has a kind of glazed glint in her eyes. I don't think you have a thing to worry about. Forgive me if I've spoiled you hearing it from themselves, but I just had to come and tell you the good news.' Her face was so expectant of his approval that he could only look at her and smile, nodding.

'That's great,' said Abbie. 'Do you think there's any chance that I might steal a glance at the masterpiece, Mr McCombe?'

'If you want to waste your time, go ahead,' he answered, feeling the same oddness and sense of unreality being together with these two women, unable and unwilling to cope with the two polar-opposite forces of mental and physical gravity.

'Do you think we could sneak a small celebratory drink before we descend to the rarefied company below?' Abbie suggested, stooping and picking up the decanter from the floor. 'Laurie?' she enquired, holding it towards her.

Laurie smiled. 'I don't see why not.' A glass was found and Abbie half-filled it and then her own. 'I think we both should drink our own private toast to Riley,' said Laurie. 'The fanfares will come later on in the evening.'

'I'm all for that,' Abbie seconded, turning towards him with the decanter. 'How are you doing, friend?'

He held his hand over his glass. 'I'm doing fine, Abbie.'

They raised their glasses in salute to him, and more than before he was aware of the absurdity and comical irony of the little cameo taking place in front of him. He wanted to tell them both to go to hell, to roar out at the inane performance they were putting on apparently to boost his morale, which now was rather static anyway and innured if only temporarily against deflation or shock. Of the two, Laurie was the more animated, the more loquacious and eager to converse; he had never seen her in such a fey mood, witty, humorous, full of bonhomie, asking Abbie about her work, the intricacies of her trade, her family background, her university days. She was certainly the more elegant of the two, dressed to just the apt point of perfection, poised, correct, her mature beauty in striking contrast to Abbie's coltish charms, making the younger woman seem almost unkempt, untidy, even a little dissolute. Abbie indeed looked a bit bemused by this new and totally unexpected revelation of Laurie's nature; she sat listening as Laurie elaborated upon some point with all her usual finesse and delicate unobtrusive humour, her hands gesturing eloquently in mid-air. Her cheeks were rather flushed, thus heightening her finely boned features and adding to the gentle attractiveness she exuded. He sat looking on without speaking, intrigued by the contrast between the two, both puzzled and amused at the whole farcical scene as if it were all an elaborate piece of dumbshow being privately performed for an audience of one.

They went to join the others downstairs. Martin and Jay managed to look tremendously secretive, Sue only slightly less so; frequently they spoke in whispers, as if conferring together on matters of much moment, nodding their heads gravely, pursing their lips, studiously disregarding him, or giving him profoundly thoughtful and speculative looks as if he were a stranger and they were trying to assess him without showing too obvious an interest. He found the atmosphere odd, but amusing, almost surrealistic, as if he had wandered into some painting which he had merely been looking at a moment before.

Don stood by the fireplace, ready to join in the talk, but seeming a little cut off, not exactly excluded, but remote, on the fringe of whatever was taking place; he had changed into grey flannel trousers and a multi-coloured open-neck shirt, and most of the time stared pensively at the floor, drink in hand almost untouched. The three women sat close together in a little circle, Martin and Jay shared the same couch, and Riley was tempted to go and join Don, but he had not the remotest idea of what he should say to him; he suddenly realised he had never really spoken with Don at any length in the months he had been staying in the house; he knew him very little if at all, and he wondered about this in an idle fashion for some time, even to the point of guessing what Don thought of him, such a strange unpredictable unorthodox guest in a household eminently conservative. He sadly missed the magical presence of Midge; and he wondered if she were already in her bed, though she invariably tiptoed into his room in her fluffy pink robe and slippers to kiss him good night on the cheek, a ritual that had begun almost from the beginning. He felt restless and bored in the presence of these adults each locked within their own small conclave and he was even losing interest in what Martin and Jay might have to say to him, they were making such an enormous secret out of it.

Slowly he became aware of something else; once or twice he looked up to catch Don's eyes fixed upon him in a most peculiar way, thoughtful, perplexed, uncertain, like someone who is continually on the point of saying something, of asking a question perhaps, then thinking better of it and remaining silent and watchful. At first Riley thought he was mistaken, that he was imagining such things because he was tired and uneasy, but it happened too often for it to be mere coincidence, and as the evening wore on these looks of Don became more pronounced, lingering upon him more and more, almost unknowingly, with a kind of melancholy intense abstraction, as if he were not looking just at Riley himself but at some ponderous problem which Riley posed and represented. He did not for a moment believe these looks were meant to be offensive, or to render him uncomfortable, but nevertheless he grew distinctly uneasy as they continued and was glad to join in the conversation as often as he could. He knew then that something would have to be said, something would have to be broached between Don and himself, if not that night, then before very long, and this knowledge, this expectancy, became a hard muscular knot in his stomach.

He went through supper like a zombie; he was only vaguely aware of having some kind of chicken casserole with a wine that looked pale pink, anaemic, as if it had been diluted with the dye from rose petals. He hardly tasted what he ate or drank; he saw himself going through the motions of eating and drinking, that was all, performing these basic functions with automated precision, he did not even smell the food. With the exception of Don, still in a thoughtful inlocked mood, eating as desultorily as himself, the others went through the meal with relish, all the while talking, exchanging anecdotes, laughing in a free relaxed way, drinking a good deal of the wan-looking wine. It seemed Laurie was in her element and enjoying it, completely overshadowing her husband, every svelte inch the perfect hostess, smooth, unflurried, giving equal attention to everyone, accepting the compliments of her guests graciously yet with a certain subtle imperiousness, as if it were her due. She was particularly attractive that evening, her hair drawn sleekly back from her temples. She had changed into a dark blue dress that left her shoulders bare and discreetly revealed the opening of her breasts. She easily outshone the other two women, even the normally chic composure of Sue looked slightly un-prepared and uncertain, though she carried herself with her usual lethargic aplomb, and Abbie, beautiful though she was, was rather tense and nervous, even when she laughed; she was obviously trying not to look in his direction, but despite this her glances were frequent as if expecting, even imploring him, to give her some kind of lead, to guide her tacitly along on terrain with which she was unfamiliar and uncomfortable, but he merely observed her looks without the least response, advancing mechanically through the meal which seemed to him interminable.

It was over at last and they went into the sitting-room, Laurie politely declining any help with the washing-up, saying she and Don would see to it later. It was becoming oppressively close inside the house, and Jay suggested they go and sit outside on the veranda. As if this was a prior understanding, the three women on some pretext or other managed to remain inside, and as if taking the cue Don wandered off to another part of the house. So Riley found himself at last alone with Martin and Jay, fellow-conspirators in some absurd private game of which he felt he was now about to learn. After the heat of the house the air was delightfully cool and refreshing and almost instantly he began to feel much better, much more responsive to things around him. It must have been at least nine at night, yet the sky was like that of early evening with dusk coming down; the stars were startlingly brilliant and near, hardly twinkling but glowing steadily like fluorescent dots. The trees stood out sharply etched against the luminous horizon, hardly a branch stirring; even the blades of grass could be seen clearly below them on the lawn, almost visibly separate, as if they could be counted. Jay stretched himself and sighed, holding his arms aloft.

'Smell that salty sea air!' he exclaimed, going over and leaning on the rail of the veranda. He turned round to them, half sitting on the fence. 'You know, men, that's what I miss about Jericho Pines—the ocean. It's a swell house, a beautiful house, elegant and spacious, and we're happy down there. I guess I couldn't live anywhere else.'

'You've a marvellous home, Jay,' said Martin, sitting in one of the comfortable deck chairs, one leg casually resting upon the knee of the other. 'I make up the slightest excuse to leave London and come to the States just to stay at the Pines.'

Riley could see the broad flattered smile spread over Jay's face.

'Sure, sure,' said Jay, crossing his feet. 'It has everything we want, except ocean. That's what I miss, the salty tang of the brine. Guess I'm a frustrated mariner at heart. Bought a thirty-foot motor boat last fall, called her the Sprig of Green, a compliment to my wife's Celtic ancestry, you know, but it's moored down in Maine and any time we feel like going for a spin in it we've got to drive nearly two hundred goddamn miles—four hundred if you count the journey back. Sue likes the coast well enough, but she's not the nautical nut that I am.' He slid the cigarette holder from the inside pocket of his jacket and lit up, blowing smoke-rings thoughtfully. 'That's why I'm toying with the idea of leasing a cottage or bungalow of some sort somewhere on the coast. Being out there skimming over the waves at fifty, sixty miles an hour—Jesus, that's living!'

'The only sailing I ever did was a ferry across the Channel,' said Martin mildly, rubbing his nostril. 'And I recollect it made me violently ill. I'm a devotee of terra firma.'

Jay expanded his chest, letting out the smoke slowly. 'You don't know what you're missing, my friend,' he said. 'I feel free as a bird out there off Cape Cod, all business matters forgotten, no difficult authors to pacify over Pernod cocktails—with you the shining exception, Riley,' Jay added, giving him a quick flash of teeth. 'Have you ever gone sailing—if so, what do you think of it?'

Riley cleared his throat, feeling they were taking notice of him for the first time. 'I went out with Don and Laurie a few times,' he replied. 'A bit scared the first time, but now I like it very much. I agree it gives you a sense of freedom.'

Jay blew on the tip of his cigarette, making it glow. 'Ah, yes, but then he has a sailing boat, hasn't he? I couldn't be bothered with that. All that jumping up and down, tightening ropes, loosening them, trying to catch the wind, climbing masts like a goddamn monkey—what an exhausting way to enjoy yourself! I don't exactly relish cutting my hands to shreds just in order to brag that *I* can sail—'

'Some people find martyrdom extremely pleasurable,' Martin put in.

'Everyone to their taste and all that,' said Jay, 'but give me the power of the timbers vibrating under my feet every time, the roar of the engine at full throttle, everything spinning past in a blur, cutting through the waves . . . ecstasy!'

To Riley's dismay they continued to talk like this unconcernedly for some considerable time, Jay as usual making the most noise, talking mostly about the endless delights of being on board the Sprig of Green, just himself and Sue, for they usually left the children at home in the care of a nanny, he explained, and at such times it was like going away on their honeymoon all over again. Sometimes, he said, they would take leave of absence for almost a whole week, leaving all business in the capable Teutonic hands of Jay's secretary, a lady of rather Amazonian proportions called Margita Massberger.

He jerked his head up guiltily as he realised that Jay was speaking directly to him, having missed the beginning of what was being said.

'. . . Always had faith in you, never doubted for a moment that you had it in you, but we were quite unprepared for such—such a masterstroke of prose, prose that at times reaches heights of pure poetry without in any way departing from the purely prosaic theme of a family struggling for survival in a working-class ghetto—'

Martin's cooler voice interrupted. 'It isn't perfect, of course

—too long-winded in parts, needs tightening up, and this very long chapter will have to be rearranged—'

'Of course, of course,' said Jay almost with impatience; he seemed so anxious to reassure Riley of their unequivocal approval that now he was liberally indulging in his customary spate of prodigal platitudes, even if he did not know it himself. 'Nobody's perfect, for God's sake!' he exclaimed, waving his cigarette in the air and pacing up and down the porch, the epitome of an excited and very excitable impresario threading the boards of a stage. 'Nobody's asking for a miracle, but Riley's almost given us that, don't you see? There'll be some editing, sure, maybe a hell of a lot of editing, but, judging from this wonderful start, it will be like chipping away at a marble statue that's almost perfectly executed to begin with. This book,' said Jay, stopping between them and repeatedly ramming his clenched fist into the palm of his other hand, 'this book will be a hundred times better than his first! He's writing something that will sweep the world! I've never read anything as marvellous as this chapter! Okay—so I'm more emotional than you, Martin, but what the hell?'

At this point Martin looked distinctly embarrassed and made a low polite noise in his throat. 'And Sue—we all know what a cool number she is, never a hair out of place, never flustered even in a thunderstorm—you saw how moved she was today, Martin. It's my business to know writers, to assess them, to almost live with them, and I've been doing just that for almost a decade now, but never have I come across one like Riley and I feel privileged, honoured, elevated to know him.'

Riley watched the scene in amazement, too bewildered to feel embarrassed, hearing himself being spoken of in the third person, having the weird feeling that he was not there at all, that he was eavesdropping, overhearing a conversation not meant for his ears, hiding behind a door with his ear glued to the keyhole. Jay Simon stood there almost quivering with excitement, with conviction, like some visionary stricken with some tremendous supernatural trauma, almost incandescent. Riley looked across at Martin, who was studiously absorbed in examining his fingernails; he wished to God there was a drink handy if only to break the hypnotic trance which Jay was creating with the feverish surging flow of his words. He strained his hearing to catch the voices of the women coming from behind the lighted window screen behind him, but his mind could not clutch or fasten even to that. He did not know if what he was seeing was a carefully contrived act, a performance perfected over the years to beguile young and not-so-young impressionable authors into greater creativity, or if indeed Jay Simon really was as genuinely enthusiastic as he now seemed; it did not matter one way or another, because it was happening anyway, it was having this effect upon him and, he imagined, upon Martin, of both embarrassment and wonder, resentment coupled with a certain perplexed admiration for the sheer bravado and élan which the man so palpably exuded and communicated to those in his presence. Genuine or simulated, Jay's rhapsodical attitudes invariably made an impact and struck a response whether of pleasure or distaste or, as so often, a compound of both; he certainly could not be ignored or lack an audience, hostile or otherwise. If it were mere histrionics, then he excelled at it, but Riley grudgingly felt that Jay meant every word he uttered, a thought that was in itself both intimidating and absurd.

Then Martin cleared his throat. 'Don't mistake my silence, Riley,' he said, turning to him. 'I fully share Jay's excitement over your manuscript as it now stands. I simply lack his effusive fluency, that grand American flair for the grandiose so consummately encapsulated every four years in their presidential campaigns—'

Jay looked startled. 'Now hold on, buddy—'

Martin smiled magnanimously, settling back in his chair. 'No offence, dear man, no offence. In fact, quite the contrary. When we go to the polling booths to select a prime minister it is like walking to the strains of the Funeral March from Saul, whereas you dear Americans when electing a president cavort and high-kick your way to the tune of Dixie or Marching Through Georgia—admirable! More reminiscent of Mardi Gras than straightforward serious politics, but completely admirable, I assure you.' Again Martin directed his attention to Riley. 'As I say, don't for a moment misinterpret my silence. I think you are well on the way to writing an excellent book, a very excellent book indeed, and I shan't go into detailed critical opinion at this stage—that would only distract you.

The thing for you to do is to get on with it and leave everything else to us. Agreed, all?'

Jay nodded emphatically. 'Absolutely,' he said, lighting up another cigarette. 'Absolutely. Just be assured that we're with you all the way, Riley,' Jay added, giving him a hearty slap on the shoulder and squeezing his arm in genial yet implacable camaraderie. 'This is going to be the biggest promotional job our firm has ever undertaken, and we're going to pull out all the stops—nothing spared, no avenue unexplored, no medium neglected—this book deserves the very best at our disposal, and then some more. And taste—have no fear about taste,' said Jay, gesticulating with his hands. 'Everything will reek of good taste, from the jacket cover illustration down to the number of the Library of Congress Catalog card! Have no fear. We Americans might talk loud and dress loud, but when it comes to taste—' Jay pursed his lips and made a kissing gesture with his fingers.

To Riley's unworthy but undeniable relief the three women came out at that moment to join them on the porch and after a time the talk drifted away from the topic of the book and again drinks were passed around. Laurie was still in quite an effervescent mood, and conversation soon seemed naturally to revolve round her; if anything, Abbie appeared to be quieter even than Sue Simon, standing by the rail, apart, staring out towards the ocean, occasionally sipping her drink. She looked wistful, out of touch with the other two women, unusually withdrawn into herself.

It was finally time for goodbyes, shaking of hands, glad expectations of meeting the following evening. Abbie lingered just a moment or two behind the others to press her hand quickly into his; her fingers felt cold. He barely caught her whispered farewell, then she hurried down the porch steps to catch up with the others, and soon the big limousine had purred smoothly down the driveway and into the still luminous night.

He and Laurie went in. Don, who had just come back from wherever he had been, came hurrying in with a guilty look on his face; he had been reading in his room, he said, and had not realised how late the hour was until he heard the car driving off. Laurie patted him reassuringly on the arm and suggested all three of them had a nightcap. He poured for them both, but declined one himself, saying he had rather a bad headache. He bade them a tired though courteous good night and went upstairs.

'Poor Don,' sighed Laurie, seating herself in a chair facing him. 'He's not really what you might call a drinking man and as a social mixer he's hopeless.' She looked over at him, smiling. 'It's been quite a day, hasn't it, Riley? You must be feeling very happy and pleased with yourself, knowing what Jay and Martin think about that chapter.'

'Yes, of course.'

They finished off their drinks in silence. Laurie stood up and put the glasses back in place. She came and stood by his chair, her fingers very gently resting on his shoulder.

'I'm happy,' she said softly. 'Very happy.'

He did not speak, remembering that Don had had the same puzzled, almost pained look on his face as he left the room. Having Laurie stand there beside him seemed the most natural and most dangerous thing in the world.

VI

Early the next morning Laurie came in to say that Abbie was on the phone with the news that there had been a change in plans for that evening; the party at Jericho Pines was still on, but it had been put back until midnight, and having the day free until then Abbie wanted to know if Riley would care to go to an early evening performance of a new experimental production of Hamlet—it had received very good if controversial reviews and she thought it might be exciting . . .? He looked at Laurie.

'Why not go?' she said, reading his unuttered question and smiling. 'You've worked very hard these past few days. Shall I tell her to come and pick you up this afternoon?'

'What about tonight—?'

'Don't worry—I'll meet you out there, no need to drag you all the way back here. Abbie's waiting—shall I go and tell her?'

'All right. Please.'

He sat in the darkened theatre, observing with equal intentness the profile of Abbie beside him lit by the dim pallid penumbra of the stage lights, that strange subdued firefly glimmer that certain faces assume in live darkness, and the living re-enactment taking place below them on the stage, the replaying of so many interwoven themes, the music within the seashell, play within a play, life within a life, the merging and intermingling of so many variegated lives, each instantaneously making comment, passing judgment, and comically, solemnly, sadly wondering about the other, jesting, coherently jabbering, haranguing, jinxing about like animated puppets, like so many

157

garrulous gargoyles, mouthing erudite trenchant lecture-room language couched in the most current epigram-spewn idiom, while the mouthers lounged and strutted, reclined and languidly strolled about the universe that was the stage, in costumes as remote from the present as are light-years from the moving hands of an ordinary clock. He leaned avidly forward in his seat, shoulders hunched, a ball of tension, fascinated, transfixed, living the unfolding drama upon the insular unlimited stage, yet drawn again and again to Abbie's face beside him, calm, absorbed, her eyes luminous and remote.

He felt a quick sad thrill of emotion, feeling her remoteness, feeling himself anchored in a sea of people, not knowing a single one, not touched by a single spontaneous look or gesture; the only thing that now seemed overwhelmingly real and relevant to him was the galaxy of human fear and faith and fruitless fulminations taking place upon the stage. His mind leaped forward to catch the soaring maddened words:

> O God! I could be bounded in a nutshell,
> and count myself a king of infinite space,
> were it not that I have bad dreams . . .
> A dream itself is but a shadow . . .

The tormented taunted face rose before him, riven by murderous rage and indecision, enkindled with wild longings forever lost and buried under a recurring landslide of self-loathing and despair. And the face upon the stage was his own looming out of darkness, out of the further reaches of his life, fixed upon an undiscovered star, mocking him, reviling him, and the hounded doomed voice was his own telling him of fabled things swarming in the undergrowth of his wonder and panic.

> O! that this too too solid flesh would melt,
> Thaw, and resolve itself into a dew . . .

His mind throbbed with the swift bitter anguish of the words finding a solitary echo in his heart, wounding him, and riven with reluctant truth he turned with mute passionate entreaty to the girl next to him; her eyes remained fixed upon the stage, touching him not, and he was left only with the sad majesty of the words. His pain carried him for a shadow of a moment beyond the words to the pulse of the agony itself, the amalgam of longing and defeat and unkillable hope that was life, spilling over into the moments, hours, days, years that was the count of everyone on earth existing briefly in their own proud pathetic truth.

The people below on the stage were no longer merely acting out a part, were no longer postulating puppets laboriously dissecting the mental skeleton of a long-dead man, but were suddenly real people engaging their own destinies, trapped in their own identities, speaking from their own indecisive hearts, sundered in two as all real people are, manacled to themselves, trying to reach each other, alone yet desperately not wanting to be alone, making fragile bridges and sadly, bravely failing to bridge the imponderable distances dividing minds, hearts, ideals, dreams, desires, the implacable sword-thrust of thought bisecting life itself. And these people upon that artificial platform came to him, speaking to him out of their private pain and elation, speaking to him alone out of all the shadowy multitude that sat in mute ranks around him. Briefly he forgot Abbie, drawn away from her and the moment that held them by a merciless moontide-pull of words he could not and did not deny.

The curtain came down and the lights went on, hurting his eyes. They looked at one another, blinking, bemused, Abbie regarding him with a faint surprised smile. She reached out, her hand resting briefly on his.

'I won't be long,' she whispered, rising from her seat.

He watched her tall dark form move up the aisle through the crowd now surging towards the spacious foyer; he watched till he could no longer see her. Then he looked about him, hesitant, uncertain, yet full of curiosity. The darkness had been so intense, so intimate, that now under the cruel globes of light everyone seemed exposed, caught out, naked with that intangible pervasive nudity which no voluminous layers of clothing could conceal or hold at bay. The faces swimming around him looked startled, bemused, apprehensive, dreamlike; necks craning in languid exploration and half-expectancy, mouths yawning, opening and shutting mechanically, fingers passing pensively through hair, fat men, fat women with hands folded complacently upon rotund abdomens, staring ahead, staring into their own private nowhere, svelte young women in silk and fur stoles looking ostentatiously indifferent as their young men blandly looped an arm around their shoulders in playful amorous pretence; a man a few seats away snoring blissfully, the wind whistling down his hairy nostrils, a huge metal snake on the buckle of his over-burdened belt.

He sat in his seat waiting, waiting not only for the return of Abbie, but for something to happen, something he could not name or label, for something to emerge from inside himself that would give quick sharp relevance to it all, to the teeming life that was broiling about inside him as he sat so sedately in his cushioned seat in the great whale-belly innards of the theatre and the isolated pockets of living sensibility in dull humorous evidence all around him. He yearned for participation, for that fine mellifluous unrehearsed mingling of improbable affinities; yet, even as he so wished, he knew with the old immutable conviction that this was not to be, could never come to pass in the span of his time, captured as everyone else in his shroud of mortality, his crucible of blood and bone, forever endeavouring outwards, yet anchored, fixed in his own bondage far beyond his willing. Once more the people about him became shadows, and his ordinary seat held him down implacably.

Suddenly, there was somebody next to him; he looked. A youngish dark-skinned man smoking a gargantuan cigar—this experimental theatre was an exception to the general no-smoking rule—extending out of a many-coloured holder wedged between thick glistening pinkish lips. The man had a flat well-spread huge-nostrilled nose, close-cropped kinky black hair, and eyes in which bitter black berries swam in pools of ham-pink liquid. All the stranger wore was truncated faded blue jeans, a sweat-landscaped T-shirt covered with weird printed designs, and toeless blue and white sneakers on wide-splayed feet with huge knuckly ankles around one of which dangled a thin beaded chain of bronze glitter. The cigar smell wafted strong, and was oddly redolent of early-evening intimacy and the mysteriousness of woodsmoke in shrouded inaccessible hills.

'Wanna smoke, man?' the man asked, looking straight ahead at the unlived-on stage, smoke billowing lazily from his nostrils.

Riley managed to stammer no out of his startled surprise. 'You sure, man?' the dark man persisted, crossing his legs. 'Oh—yes, yes, thank you.'

The stranger turned with swift absurd anger. 'What the goddamn hell is you?' he spat out. 'I'm friendly, is all. Don't you goddamn well smoke? Have a drag, man!'

Again the almost voiceless reply shook into incoherence.

'Talk to me, man,' the stranger urged, squeezing the cigar-holder savagely between his teeth and speaking with comical yet frightening irritability, uncrossing his legs. 'Talk to me, damn you. Please, man, talk to me. Anything.'

He felt the sweat breaking out on him under his featherweight linen jacket, and with it a swelling urge to erupt into insane hyena-like laughter, an urge he could check only with an intent ferocious effort of will. He said nothing, focusing all his attention upon the velvet drapes of the stage sinuously moving in some imperceptible draught.

The man hunched closer, inhaling swiftly and as swiftly letting the smoke funnel out through his nostrils. He brought his face closer. 'The stars, man, the stars,' he said in a low confidential whisper, as if imparting a profound, secret, passionately held belief. 'The stars is my friends, my buddies. They talk to me down all that air, man, out of all that god-damn sky. They tell me things. Think of that, man! Listen,' the man said urgently, with a mad desperation, the smoke from the cigar half veiling the queerly lit eyes that so eagerly sought approval and trust. 'They holler down the air that I'm beautiful. Do you think I'm beautiful, man—do you?'

Panic assailed him and he groped blindly for words, finding none for this hounded unanswerable creature, who seemed mindless and invulnerable to any words that might be remotely offered. A large broad-fingered hand clamped down on his knee, squeezing painfully, yet with an oddly childish insistence that somehow cancelled out fear.

'You alone, man?'

Riley swallowed hard, but his throat was dry and no words would come. The unwanted pressure continued, the fingers kneading into his flesh, creeping higher, the man all the while staring at him with fanatical greed.

'You dumb or something?' hissed the stranger, blowing

smoke into Riley's face, plucking the cigar out of his mouth with frantic impatience, eyes no longer dreamily lidded, glittering lividly. 'You don't wanna smoke, don't wanna talk, don't wanna tell me I is beautiful. Jasper's my name, and Jasper's beautiful. Jasper's made out of beautiful black jade.' His fingers clenched together, as if impelled by some blind inchoate force that seemed palpably to sweep out from the man. 'Jasper's got bread, man, Jasper's got real bread. I'se no poor ole nigger. You alone, man?'

Riley wanted to spit in the black distorted face that swam inches away from his own, wanted to cry out at the pain of the iron fingers digging into his flesh, wanted to scream and laugh at the mad ghastly farce of it all with so many anonymous hundreds all around and nobody sparing the absurd spectacle a first or second glance. But no words would come and his muteness screamed inside him. The fingers clenched harder still and the man's breathing deepened, the black skin glistening under the lights.

'I gotta pad in town,' the man confided, eyes rolling, dilating and tightening alternately. 'We can drink, play some sounds.' He pushed his face so close their noses were almost tipping. 'I won't bother you none. Just wanna talk.' The clenched fingers had loosened and were now softly stroking Riley's knee in an amazingly silky feminine caress. 'Won't bother you none, man, I declare. No, man, not ole Jasper. I is gentle as a lamb.' The voice, that had just been speaking in a soft sing-song undulating way, suddenly rose a shrill frightening octave or two. 'You're shit, man, just ole white shit. You got no words for a black boy. I could squash you like a fly—whish!' the man whistled out through his teeth, his cigar making a taut vicious swathe in the air. 'Beautiful black is Jasper. Ole white shit is you. Why dontcha like me, man—why dontcha like smoke? You dumb or something?'

Heads were beginning to turn, faces looking around towards where they sat, but in his desperate farcical alarm he only discerned mouths opening and closing and eyes finding him out with the radar-thrust of curiosity, amusement, sly knowingness, remote hostility—two worlds colliding hopelessly beyond any known context, each unknown to the other, the sweat oozing from his pores warm and chill, down his forehead, the nape of

162

his neck, the gluey swamps of his armpits, drenching him. And the urge persisted to break into wild relieving mad laughter until the tears would come, and again only by a monstrous momentum of will was he able to choke it back inside him, rigidly ignoring the set, weirdly lit eyes, the erratic-sweeping cigar, the fingers now biting hurtfully once more into his flesh, and the numberless eyes, mouths, faces turning upon him, ripping aside his precious anonymity, exposing him, his panic, his hysteria, his lost little measure of self-knowledge, self-containment. A line, a passage dredged from nowhere, flashed through his mind like a siren of rescue: 'The counterfeit presentment of two brothers . . .'

His mind leaped beyond the trapped moment. The self-willed alienation of brothers, each cocooned within his own identity, a separation not even love could annihilate, yet brothers still under the mythical all-sensitive skin, seeking an enlargement of themselves, a response to the unspoken cry of isolation, an echo to the speechless plea for communion. He grasped in that moment that there was no such entity as a stranger, only some-one as yet unmet, as certain flowers or poems or countries are unfamiliar above the febrile surface of the senses, only to be rendered instantly, mysteriously, intimate and familiar in one moment of meeting, known at once to the deeper sensibility under the light inconsequential scattering of ordinary time-held existence. The swift lightning-stroke recognition of this stilled the panic in him, took away the barbed fear from his mind; a gradual lassitude pervaded him, the steely rigidity ebbed, and in its place came a certain melancholy awareness of all the loneliness and fear and of all the lost unrealised things that must prevail upon the earth.

Full of this new insight, flushed with this new hope and the elation of this assurance, he turned to face the stranger who was no longer such, words wise and welcoming ready to flow from him; but the seat was empty, the man had gone, the pungent wood-smoke after-smell of his cigar the only mark and testimony to his existence.

Everything now revolved around the imperative question-mark that hung in the air where the man had been, the inexorable why and wherefore buzzing in his bewildered mind like an inquisitive exploring wasp stinging him into

163

response. Who had that dark disturbing stranger been, marking him out for a transitory moment of solace from the hundreds of people surrounding them from some of whom he might have been given a larger measure of charity and understanding? Paths remote and alien crossing each other with such comic casualness and improbability, leaving such a deep imprint upon his brain, the brevity of the moment of meeting, the incalculable consequences of that moment.

He saw the slightly swaying curtains on the stage, the now quite ordinary people in the tiers of seats around him, at home in their own pockets of existence, free or imprisoned or both; the lights already beginning to dim again, a cough here and there, the innumerable rustlings of life all around; he observed all this, even the minutely moving calligraphy of bone upon his own fists, and he knew it had happened, it had all been real, an eternal moment back, that those remote and improbable paths had indeed coincided, that he had been indeed touched briefly by the flare of another separate life. And still the question-mark remained, the great imponderable why of the encounter. The cigar smoke had faded, had evaporated completely, erasing the only tangible evidence that the man had ever lived, a life gone, rubbed out, wafted into invisibility and nothingness. Yet their paths *had* crossed, briefly a bridge had been thrown between them linking their lives, for a moment spanning the stellar distance between, and it was this single isolated factor, this undeniable truth, which mattered and would endure infinitely beyond the encounter itself, it was this that rendered it at once absurd and strangely moving, and the cigar smoke now gone was not the end of it, was no longer even significant beside the force and importance of what had occurred so irrationally and indubitably a flickering of an eyelid ago. Someone had briefly, farcically entered his life, touched his mind with the raw rantings of his own, a shadow had taken on substance and spoken, a cry had been uttered, and he knew dread and wonder at the unguessed-of mystery of all that lived.

His mind fluttered raggedly back to the stage; a frame within a larger frame unfolding with startling dexterity before his entranced eyes, drawing his senses to heights of awe and fantasy that no chains of mind or body could hold down. Silently crying and shouting with the full-throated momentum of release, he knew he could soar above himself, in whatever perplexity or circumstance, harbouring those tremendous words in his heart, words that cleaved through him like a bright triumphant sword, with a sharp clean thrust of elation. Even as he knew that moment of affinity with the vari-coloured intricacies of language flaming up from the stage, he knew once more the magic and the bitter blessing of solitude, the cruel cherished certainty of loneliness shadowing each separate life within the reach of eye and perception of his mind, the utter and unerring conviction of his own distance from the lives of others beyond the wishing or the willing of it, a certainty more implacable than his own tormented desire to reach and be reached, touch and be touched, confront and challenge and encounter and be drawn beyond the doors of himself. Suspended between extremes, between the deep sea of involvement in the lives of others, and the deeper sea of isolation in his own, he could do nothing save look on, with mingled wonder and anger, locked in, barred, caged, indomitably looking outwards, enmeshed in a web that expanded subtly and as subtly tightened again with his every effort, his every struggle towards release. He heard the words and felt their majestic measure, their singing in the blue intricacies of poetry, strained towards them desperately, and failed, already caught in the whirlpool of descent back to the stone and wood and granite and smoke and smells and little futilities of ordinary time, caught in that other life of tar and turf ash and the swilling of dark brown beer.

It was as if, there in stark delineations upon the stage, in each rehearsed movement and gesture, in each impeccably enunciated syllable issuing from the mouths of the caricatured participants lording the imaginary cosmos of the stage, he were watching the disinterment of his own buried life, the exhumation and clinical dissection of a ghost down to the most finite facet and particle of its burned-out mortality. Fear crept along his marrow, gnawing into him, a busy insatiable worm, fear of total exposure to the merciless uncaring eyes of others, uncovering him in all the secret places where alone he could abide with himself in safety and peace, a certain slight precarious wisdom. He knew the danger of words, as well as their enthralment, how easily words could betray what he would not willingly lay open even to the most loving eyes in the world, scattering pieces of his most hidden life upon any wind. Language was a two-sided sword, wounding, lacerating him who brandished it just as it felled those he thought his enemies and thrilled and protected those he thought his lovers and friends. Words, like friendship, like love, could present two faces, one compassionate, tender, wise and caring, the other cruel, fickle, adjudicating upon one's nature, mistrusting the most naive gesture, laying bare one wound even as it healed and closed up another. He might have been the only person in the world, and for a moment he was; he knew this with a kind of satisfied dread. Then he heard the seat next to him creak, the merest pressure on his arm, a voice whispering above the rising clamour from the stage.

'I'm back, kiddo.'

He saw her slow smile in the eerie gloom, and for a while forgot all the strange sad frightening imponderable things he had been thinking. He sat back to watch the unending play come to a close.

At first, the scene that met their eyes seemed an almost complete replica of the last party he had been to at Jericho Pines. The atmosphere was the same, at once highly charged and jovial, restive, relaxed, humming with conversation, people standing in groups large and small, garrulous and intimate, overt, discreet, long tables holding an astounding assortment of drinks and food, sombre-clad menservants moving quietly and efficiently through the crowds dispensing instant cocktails, medieval flunkeys in modern dress, faceless men dissolving invisibly away as they went about their bacchanalian task. The massive crystal chandeliers suspended from the ceiling far above swayed imperceptibly, cascading light upon the massed gathering below, filling the aquarium-type room and spilling out on to the balconies and tiled terracotta porches flanking it. It all seemed an extension, an unbroken continuation of the previous festivities, as if that evening had never ended, had merged indivisibly into the present. Riley even imagined that the people themselves were not only the same, as they probably were to a larger or lesser extent, but that they seemed hardly to have moved from the same positions or changed their very postures and gestures, figures caught in animated suspension, friezes and frescoes hanging in a timeless continuum owning no yesterday or tomorrow, only the blurred present that now held them. The sensation was weird and unsettling, like walking through a mausoleum alive with loud-talking congenial back-slapping beaming hard-drinking ghosts setting up a ceaseless clamour, exuding animal heat, all the palpable physical furore and excitement of a crowd.

'Another of Jay's discreet happenings,' said Abbie, having to speak loudly to be heard, although she was right beside him, her hand on his elbow in cautionary guidance. 'I have the feeling we've been here before, don't you?'

'I feel like I never left,' he rejoined, looking for some place to sit down as people smilingly moved aside, opening up little avenues for them to pass through.

Having finally found a couch that was, unbelievably, un-occupied, by an open window, they sat down. Out of nowhere one of the ubiquitous expressionless flunkeys stood before them with a loaded tray of drinks, which Abbie quickly requested that he leave with them to save her from having to get up and excuse her way through the swarm each time their glasses required refilling. The man, with impassive mien, placed the tray carefully between them on the couch and withdrew as innocuously as he had appeared, an efficient well-trained zombie.

'I hope Laurie got here,' said Abbie, starting to look around. 'No hope of spotting her in this polite mêlée. You know,' she said to him, picking up a drink and sipping it. 'I don't know why I keep coming to these soirées of Jay and Sue's—great people, but they've absolutely no sense of proportion. Seems they invite half of New York City to their little At Homes. Everybody talks to everybody else and nobody knows who the hell anyone is. Seems the only thing to do is drink—'

'Which isn't a bad motivation for coming,' he interjected, lifting his own glass. 'Not that it matters, but what exactly is it anyway?' He peered at the drink before tasting it.

She laughed. 'I don't know, but there's ninety-proof booze in there somewhere!'

He had never seen Abbie in a dress before (she had changed after the theatre), and it was a strange transformation; she looked different, in what way he could not say, it seemed to cast her into a new role, almost a new personality, as if she herself changed with the changing of her clothes, subtly, distinctly. Hers was now a new, a different beauty, no longer hoydenish or piquant as in her black jeans and sneakers, but assured, aware of her own appeal, a little unsure still to the eye that knew her, but triumphant. The dress had changed her in the time it took her to slip on, into a charming kind of regal imperious tomboy, new to the part but adapting to it quickly. He was amusedly aware of the glances that men were giving her, darting them at her like arrows fired in hope, the speculatively raised eyebrow, the pensive chewing of the lower lip, the unconscious predatory probing of the tongue as they surveyed her, her slimness, the dark cloud of her hair falling thick on her shoulders, her long exquisite legs and eloquent hands now holding the glass as reverently as though it were the holy grail. Nothing escaped his ferret-sharp eyes, and he wondered what thoughts, images, frenzies moved behind these gleaming faces beaming across at her like so many imperative beacons across an amber expanse of alcohol. Men, for example, from the svelte wilds of suburbia parading in their executive suits and city eye, putting up with the hitherto seen-it-all-before boredom of it. So he sat and watched these humans indulge in their desperately casual dumb-show, not a trace of honest redeeming lust in their eyes; as they looked over the bare shoulders of their wives at Abbie, he saw in their eyes only sick-puppy longing, guarded interest, a pathetic kind of little-boy-lostness, especially from the older more paternal-looking men chewing on corpulent cigars and wiping their glistening foreheads with immaculate white handkerchiefs, brushing back bushy eyebrows with a tongue-licked finger.

Abbie seemed totally oblivious of those rapt secretive eyes turning in her direction, and Riley in his fanciful way could imagine how they looked upon them, light and shadow, hope and the taciturn negation of hope sitting side by side, faun and satyr, his own sallow saturnine countenance glimmering darkly in the shade of her radiance, his crutches slung across the arm of the couch. He swallowed the last burning drops of his drink and picked up another automatically, never taking his eyes from the faces swimming endlessly in front of them, fascinated as always by the intricate interplay of expressions that moved across these faces like the shadow of clouds over desolate deserted landscapes. These eyes did not ogle, their lidded timidity would not allow so brave a display of the male peacock; they merely blinked in remote impossible longing, instantly shuttered if found out.

'Isn't this all very strange to you, Riley?' asked Abbie. 'I suppose you'll put it into your next book—I suppose you'll put us all into your book, including me?'

'What do you think?'

'It scares me a bit,' she said, musing. 'It would scare me to have even my portrait painted, afraid of what I might see. I don't have many photographs of myself, you know, just a few high-school snaps. I don't like looking at myself. I'm a coward. So what would it be if I should one day pick up your book and find myself between the covers?'

'Depend on how I saw you, wouldn't it?'

'That's what scares me—how you see me,' said Abbie, feigning a shudder, then she looked at him, her eyes searching his face. 'How do you see me, Riley?' She turned away quickly. 'That was a stupid thing to ask. Forget it, please.'

'You'll just have to wait for the next thrilling instalment,' he said, deliberately flippant.

She paused. 'When can I see it—the manuscript? I'm not intelligent like Laurie, you wouldn't want to come to me for criticism or anything like that, but I *would* like to read it.' She looked at him uncertainly. 'You're not angry at me for asking you, are you?'

'Angry? Why should I be angry? I'm flattered that you want to see it.'

'Then I can?'

He smiled. 'Any time.'

She smiled too, in some excitement, and reaching over squeezed his hand tightly.

'Aha!' boomed a voice they both knew, looking up to see Jay Simon coming towards them with a rather bedraggled young man in tow. As if caught out in something tremendously clandestine and illicit, Abbie drew her hand back quickly. 'Even above this racket do I hear the trumpets blow and the cymbals clash? Ah, I remember, I remember!' Jay said with a gusty sigh, winking hugely. 'And to think I brought you two together!'

'Beneath that Wall Street exterior there beats the soul of a male version of Mrs Henry Wood,' said Abbie coolly.

Jay laughed uproariously, hastily grabbing his handkerchief and pressing it to his mouth to suppress his spluttering, and wiping his eyes.

'Beautiful, beautiful!' he managed to say at last when the tides of his mirth had somewhat subsided. 'Riley, you're a lucky guy to have captured such a witty companion. You writers certainly seem to mesmerise the gentler sex, and when you're a poet too—' Jay spread his hands out in abject deprecation. 'Well, what chance has a poor plain family man like me got?' He seemed to remember the young man beside him, throwing a fraternal arm around his shoulders and pulling him forward. 'Speaking of writers—tonight's modest indulgence is in honour of the latest addition to our proud list of up-and-coming authors destined for fame and immortality—it's my great pleasure to introduce you good folks to Manny Mendell!'

Jay made the introduction as if from a stage or rostrum, all that was lacking was a microphone or, better still, a megaphone to complete the theatrical trimmings, and Manny Mendell, like a circus animal hearing the master's whip crack, came or rather rushed forward and, completely ignoring Abbie, grabbed Riley's free hand in both his own huge ones and proceeded to pump it up and down with powerful enthusiasm, meanwhile gushing forth a seemingly endless flow of talk that at times almost bordered on the incoherent and unintelligible.

'Am I glad to see you! Welcome to the States! Believe me, I'm one of your fans. That book of yours was *so* good—listen, I never put it down once, no sir, not once, till the very last line! What a vocabulary you have! You made my head spin! Jay here has been ranting and raving about you non-stop ever since they brought the book out. Listen, do you think I could see the new script, huh? Yeah? Might pick up a few hints, huh? How do you manage it? Let me in on the secret, huh? Do you have a routine, work regular hours each day, or are you one of these guys that jump up in the middle of the night and grab pencil and paper before the idea goes out of your head? Listen, I once read something about Thoreau or was it Thornton Wilder taking a hot bath just before sitting down to write, said it opened up their pores and they could think more freely. Myself, well, I take a nice stiff drink of hot chocolate—I swear by it! Nothing added, mind you. I've heard of *your* habits of work and maybe they work for you, but me—well, me, well, listen . . .'

Riley could only stare blankly, hardly knowing a word the young man was uttering and wishing to God he would let go of his imprisoned hand, which ached with the constant pumping up and down and the crunching pressure of Mendell's hard spatulate fingers wringing his own. While the murderous hand-shaking and the monologue were going on, Riley caught a glimpse of Jay positively beaming in the background, rocking back and forth on the balls of his feet, like a proud doting father who had brought two long-lost sons together at last after endless years of searching and heartscald, modestly taking a back seat at this supreme moment of brotherly reunion. Abbie was looking on with an alarmed expression, a bemused spectator watching a weird impromptu performance take place before her eyes.

Music suddenly blared forth, jazz music, blues, cacophonous, deafening, pulsating, mercifully overlapping the shattering cascade of Manny Mendell's unrelenting soliloquy. Somewhere in the tangled mazes of sound a heavy-handed piano pounded out a vague recurring theme that was supposedly meant to be melancholy, couples were gyrating with varying degrees of urgency and lassitude to the disjointed tempo, the bellies of fat men and women wobbling like soft mounds poised precariously on cliff-edges, the smooth hips of young women moving silkily, sensuously as if drugged, or moving in a sort of trance with bland faces glowing and upturned to the rainbow showers of light falling from the chandeliers, a distinct undeniable refined carnality permeating the very air hazy-blue with cigar and cigarette smoke, the faces on the further fringes of the room swimming like remote reflections seen through clouded water.

He noted with surprise and not a little admiration that Mendell still continued to talk, unheard as he was, his mouth opening and shutting like an animated ventriloquist's dummy, speaking to nobody in particular, turning his face magnanim-ously to whoever happened to be passing within range of his verbal fusillade and clamping a large brotherly hand on any shoulder which came within reach of his boundless amity, standing there with a changeless all-encompassing smile on his heavy-browed broad-nosed rather coarse face, a benign bloated cherub very carefully and cautiously unkempt, his violently red shirt wide open to his navel, revealing a muscular sweat-glistening torso covered over with gross black hair, his neck rising like an oak trunk surging into the massive ceaselessly turning head. Manny Mendell was probably over twenty years of age, perhaps two or three years over, but he behaved with the tireless exuberance of a schoolboy suddenly let loose in a room full of older densely academic imbecilic citizens upon whom he pounced with smacking lips and loud claps and cries of unnerving gusto, engulfing all around with amiable voracity, a human whirlpool sucking in everything within touch or sight, insatiably seeking out new victims as fodder for his unquench-able social appetites. His appearance was more that of an evangelical cowboy or crusading stevedore than the conven-tional idealised version of a literary animal; he did not merely meet people, he ploughed into them, bull-like, snorting with frantic friendliness, burying them under the sheer weight of his good will and enormous desire to please, and be not only liked but loved and coveted and sought after, an over-grown precocious puppy romping uproariously about licking faces and hands at every turn, wanting to be cuddled but above all wanting to cuddle.

There came a brief lull in the pervading bedlam, the throng seemed to be drifting outwards on to the terraces and into the gardens, leaving a little space in which Riley and Abbie found themselves temporarily islanded. The tray of drinks had been unobtrusively replenished, Manny Mendell had drifted along with the tide of the congregation, and Abbie looked at him, smiling in a sort of dazed fashion.

'I'm tongue-tied,' she said, spreading out her hands in puzzlement.

'I'm glad somebody is,' Riley replied with unusual fervour, drinking half his glass. 'I don't believe he's real. I think Jay must have invented him.'

'That may be truer than you think, Riley,' said Abbie, musing. 'The Frankenstein syndrome brought up to date pro-ducing a friendly version of the monster, but damn monstrous just the same. My God, imagine being on a desert island with *him*! Or even,' she went on, her eyes widening, 'being cornered by him in Times Square! He's a walking gramophone plugged in all the time—I bet he not only talks in his sleep but recites Paradise Lost and the Gettysburg Address!'

'Who is he?' Riley asked her. 'Have you met him before or heard of him?'

Abbie shook her head. 'He's a new horse in the Simon stables,' she said. 'And unbroken, it would seem, though maybe Jay intends to keep him that way. I must admit he creates a certain impression—like being hit over the head with a battering ram. I wonder what sort of thing he's written? Hardly a treatise on silence—hardly the Trappist monk type, our Mr Mendell. Even the name sounds unlikely—do you think it's an alias or something?'

'I think *he* is an alias or something,' Riley decided, keeping a wary eye out for the return of the animated talking wonder as for the oncoming approach of a tornado. 'He's like something that was created by somebody with a perverted sense of humour.'

'Oh, come now,' Abbie remonstrated smilingly. 'Don't be too harsh. Under all that mouth he's probably a shy bashful small-town kid trying to disguise a dreadful stammer.'

'I'd prefer the stammer.'

'I think he's rather cute,' Abbie reflected, 'in a paralysing sort of way. Cuddlesome, like a big untamed untameable bear.' She gave Riley a deliberately archful look. 'I think I'd like to cuddle him myself.'

'Ask Jay to fix it for you.'

'Dammit,' Abbie said, brows together. 'Why can't you be jealous? I could quite easily have one hell of a torrid affair with him, you know. Or with Jay, for that matter.'

'I'm sure you quite easily could,' he agreed, his nonchalance sounding genuine as his gaze went round the immense room, seeking out a certain face.

'Except that I like Sue so much,' Abbie went on, trying to sound soulful. 'I wonder what kind of lover Jay would be?'

'Extremely efficient and economic, I should think,' Riley opined. 'Not an iota of superfluous energy wasted, like his publicity campaigns.'

'It might be fun to try—'

'I don't think you'd have to try very hard.'

'Except that he's like a father to me, if that doesn't sound too corny.'

'That shouldn't impede you,' he said easily. 'Merely a Freudian slip. Most girls have them.'

'That's only in adolescence,' she replied, and added with surprising vehemence, 'and anyway I think it's bullshit. I never wanted to go to beddy-by-bys with my father, or anyone else's father. Anyway, my Pop died before I could tell the difference between him and my mother, so I never had the opportunity to indulge in such carnal fantasies. Maybe that means I was denied a normal childhood, would you say?'

He shrugged. 'I couldn't exactly set myself up as a judge of what is normal and what is not.' He continued to search with his eyes.

'I wish you'd be at least normally jealous,' Abbie said rather peevishly. 'And I wish you'd stop looking for her like a lost pup. I'm sure she's here somewhere. Don't despair—she'll get your scent sooner or later.' She finished her drink abruptly and stood up. 'I'm going to pick up a man,' she said, leaving him and moving towards the crowd, not looking back.

He was acutely aware of the void her absence left; already she had vanished, swallowed up greedily by the restless mass of people, and he felt alone and unheeded in a sea of strangers.

What was it, he thought, that made it so virtually impossible for him to respond openly to others, that so sealed him off that he was almost literally a prisoner of himself? Something in him cried out to speak and be heard, something in him raged mutely against the choking constraint that threw such an implacable distance between him and other people, yet conversely something in him remained indomitably withdrawn, a mocking spectator looking on everything from an unscalable height with a cold detached gaze, deriding more fiercely than anything else the very need he felt to participate in the life going on around him, a thing that kept him apart and chained to the pitiably small rock that was himself. He had no poetic illusions about communication; he felt he had little if anything to communicate, though he would always have pretensions, he would always amuse and occupy himself with the idea that he had something of importance to say to others. No, he did not delude himself in that area at least, he did not

174

want to open the dam and be drowned in the intimate lives of others, but he did want a little outside freedom, he did want to lose himself, if only briefly, in the lived experience of another human being, to scale the walls and escape from himself for a while, to become happily lost and taste just for once the sharp sweet savour of total self-abandonment.

'I think I'm going mad,' he heard himself thinking aloud.

'Aren't we all?' a voice he vaguely recognised echoed. 'I'm afraid it isn't fashionable any more.'

He lifted up his eyes and saw the man standing in front of him, tall, angular, clothes hanging on him as though on a scarecrow, the same crucified look of resignation and melancholic weariness on the lean saturnine face, the same blunt-nosed blue pencil sticking like a snout from the breast pocket of his seedy jacket, the cigarette drooping from the corner of his mournful mouth as he looked down at Riley with sad wistful speculation. Jake Pellmann. The name sprang to his mind with surprising ease. It seemed an incredible period of time had passed since he had last met him, yet Pellmann looked exactly, uncannily the same, a taller version of Chaplin in the same inimitable garb, baggy trousers flopping about his ankles, his jacket draped about him limply as if his frame had unaccountably shrunk. Jake smiled.

'I see you remember me,' said Jake, sitting down on the couch on the far side of the tray. 'I'm flattered, friend, though in this business it's sometimes a blessing to remain a nonentity. May I proceed to bore you for ten minutes or so?' Jake picked up a glass from the tray, sniffing it delicately. 'I see we are well fortified, always one of the better features of Jay's little soirées. Your very obedient servant, my friend,' Jake intoned, raising the glass to his lips after having carefully removed the ubiquitous cigarette and tilted it very precisely on the edge of the tray.

'Good luck,' rejoined Riley. 'Glad to see you again.'

Jake closed his eyes as if in inner contemplation as he drank. 'A very excellent blend of whatever obnoxious potion it is,' he said. He opened his eyes and regarded Riley meditatively for a moment. 'I think you really are glad to see me. Extraordinary. Why are you glad to see me—do you know? You don't have to answer my ridiculous questions if you don't want to—'

'But I do,' said Riley, quite definite. 'I'm glad to see you again because I liked your company the first time and I'm sure I will like it now.'

Jake considered. 'Hmm. Good enough reason as any for being bored,' he finally judged. 'I decided to come over out of this mad motley and tell you that I finally got around to reading both your novel and your volume of poems the other night, all alone in my for once womanless bed. Not that my having read your stuff will have any enormously beneficial affect on you—'

'It might have,' said Riley, settling back to enjoy what he was sure would follow.

Jake lazily raised a laconic eyebrow. 'Really? You don't give much away, do you? You don't want my opinion of your work, do you? To which you will no doubt reply "I might do," cagey Celtic bastard that you are. By the way, notice how I invariably end each sentence with a question-mark to which of course there is no answer.' Jake had by now finished his drink and picked up another so quickly it seemed the glass had never left his hand. 'Notice also—in fact, nota bene, to show off my abominable Latin which I picked up from one of these do-it-yourself books I bought for a dollar fifty somewhere in the Bronx—where was I?' Jake looked genuinely puzzled.

'You were asking me to notice something,' prompted Riley.

'Nothing unusual,' replied Jake, sighing as if he meant it. 'I'm always asking people to notice things. I act as if I'm writing plays the whole time, pointing things out to people, saying, "Look here, see this, don't forget that." I see everything as taking place on a stage. Which is as it should be for a writer of plays, don't you think? What was it I was asking you to notice?' Jake picked up his cigarette, inhaling deeply, keeping the smoke in his mouth quite a time, letting it out in an almost sensuous way, reluctantly, like someone reaching the close of an orgasm. 'I would say you're a poet above anything else,' said Jake, as if he had never left off. 'Would you say that?'

'I would hope so, yes,' answered Riley, when he was obviously expected or rather allowed to, as Jake pertinently paused.

'Your poems move me to mad mirth and practically simultaneous tears,' Jake continued, now holding glass and cigarette in either hand. 'And both the mirth and the tears are therapeutic in a society becoming increasingly emotionless with their gorgeous blend of irresponsible Irish satire and profound sadness. The tears behind the smile, the smile behind the tears.' Jake paused again. 'Jesus, that sounds terrible. I'm beginning to sound like Julie Andrews. Please don't hesitate to stop me short with a quick salubrious insulting remark whenever I become too unbearably nauseous,' Jake solemnly entreated. 'Good for my soul. I'm not going to ask you where I was, because it's coming back to me now.' He closed his eyes, kept them closed for some moments as he spoke before opening them slowly. 'Poetry and verse. Butter and margarine. Fine brandy and bootleg gin. A woman of pleasure and a pox-ridden courtesan down on her luck. The holy sword Excalibur and a butcher's knife dripping with cows' blood and excrement. A horse like Northern Dancer with all the grace of Pavlova, and a poor jaded flea-bitten bollocksed mare between the shafts of a milk-dray stumbling half-blind down the dark early-morning streets of Harlem or the Bowery . . .' Riley could almost hear the requisite dots following upon Jake's deep pause. Jake looked straight at him. 'That's the difference, the unbridgeable difference between poetry and verse. One is such a thing, the other another, and never the twain shall meet. Hark ye to the voice of Solomon.'

Jake looked down into his glass as if in search of some fathomless mystical significance in its depths, before taking another long draught. 'That novel of yours is something else again. It's good and it's lousy, sometimes almost great and quite often appalling. The contrasts are irresistible, good and bad. I think you're going to be a marvellous writer once you've stopped shitting yellow.' Jake stopped. 'Jesus, that sounds so patronising. I don't strike a good figure as Moses on the Mount. Why don't you slip in a smart insulting repartee or something? You shouldn't let me get away with things just because I'm older and more famous and successful than you,' Jake said, sounding genuinely reproachful. 'Do you realise I haven't stopped talking for at least five minutes?'

'Longer,' Riley corrected, enjoying himself. 'You haven't stopped at all since you sat down here.'

Jake smiled a slow mandarin smile. 'I am duly chastised,' he said. 'If I wrote as fast as I talk I'd never be idle or want for a dime. But you've only yourself to blame—you should stop me.

People just sit back and let me ramble on—it's terrible, and shows a distinct lack of initiative and gall on their part. You don't strike me as being a guy without gall,' Jake remarked, suspicion in his voice, giving Riley a shrewd look.

'I just don't have much to say for myself,' said Riley.

'Whereas some bastards have too much, huh?' probed Jake. He put down his now empty glass and raised his fingertips to his nose, smelling them fastidiously, nostrils almost quivering. 'A terrible thing happened to me when I first got inoculated. They used a gramophone needle instead of a surgical one. I talk every broad out of my bedroom. Some of them swear I even talk while I'm screwing them. Must put a tape-recorder under the bed the next time to prove or disprove that theory though to be honest I even listen to myself talking in my sleep. I think I was talking a dozen to the minute while still in my mother's womb. The Pellmann nature abhors a vacuum, quite definitely. What are you writing about now? Your name *is* Riley, isn't it?'

'My name is Riley, and I'm working on a novel about New England as seen through Irish eyes, not always smiling.'

Jake Pellmann laughed or more aptly chuckled quietly for about half a minute. 'That's good, that's bloody good,' he said, absolutely composed again. 'And what do you know about New England?'

Riley picked up a fresh drink. 'Nothing,' he returned. 'Nothing at all. I'm writing a novel, not a tourist's guidebook. And you said yourself I had gall.'

'A sterling quality,' Jake said, nodding. 'A sterling quality indeed. Do you think it is possible to write about some place that you don't know very well? Yes,' said Jake in reply to himself, again nodding his head. 'Yes, I suppose it is. I suppose that's what art, real art, is all about—leaping over so many geographical and mental boundaries, brushing aside immaterial things like chauvinism and inherited environmental knowledge. Do you think I could write a play about Ireland?' Jake blinked at him benignly. 'Do you think I could even write a play?'

'I haven't seen or read any of your plays,' Riley admitted, 'but I am told from usually reliable sources that you write some very good plays. And as for writing one about Ireland—well, you could always *set* it in Ireland, provided you too possess that sterling quality, gall.'

Jake mused. 'A musical maybe, full of leprechauns and fairies and crocks of gold and endearing alcoholic assassins, like Finian's Rainbow, that load of unadulterated shit. But a play . . . no, never a play. I am chauvinistic in the sense that I can only write very slight plays about frail impecunious people from Brooklyn or Queens or the Bronx, usually in the throes of newly bedded bliss putting up a brave fight against the nasty little bureaucrats who hire and employ them. I suppose you could say I romanticise the semi-poverty of the ambiguous middle class, and I suppose I do, but Jesus, if there has to be poverty in the world why not make it *sound* romantic at least? If we must have paupers let us make them romantic. I know you've been poor, and so have I,' said Jake earnestly, 'so I know I'm not speaking to one of those bastards who sucked champagne instead of milk from their mother's tits and who are always sounding off about the nobility of the working man. What do you think of poverty?' Jake leaned forward as if in intent anticipation.

'I hate it as much as you do,' said Riley. 'But not as much as I hate the poverty of the rich. That is real poverty.'

'Don't go all metaphysical on me,' said Jake, wagging his forefinger. 'You mean the born rich, the inherited rich, or guys like me and you who got their bread the hard way? Wealth can either be a hereditary disease or an acquired one, and both can be malignant. You speak now about the poverty of the mind—the poverty of imagination? That too can be either hereditary or picked up through infection—through environmental pressures, as my psychoanalyst would say, who is incidentally quite imaginative, believe it or not.' Putting down glass and cigarette, Jake placed both hands on his kneecaps and inhaled deeply, as if on the seafront. 'I think there's nothing better than a good discussion with a kindred soul—keeps the blood circulating and the adrenalin up. Would you be offended if I invited you along sometime to see one of my plays? There's usually one or other of them running on or off Broadway—'

'I'd be delighted,' Riley responded, 'thank you.'

'Don't be premature with your gratitude, my boy,' warned Jake. 'I write some lousy stuff most of the time, more suited to the goggle-box than the stage, full of trivial domestic situations and plots contrived over periods of idle nose-picking while I wrestle with my idiotic Id.' Jake retrieved his glass and drank, his stringy windpipe jerking spasmodically up and down. 'I'll find out which of the least imbecilic of my playlets is running lately and give you a buzz—okay?'

'You're very honest with yourself,' Riley told him, feeling a surge of admiration for this lovable lost mongrel of a man.

'Don't let that fool you either,' Jake replied solemnly. 'It's easy to be honest when you've nothing to hide, like an incurable habit of chasing cats up and down fire escapes. If I was really honest I wouldn't write at all, I'd spend my time sitting on my arse on the veranda looking at the newest hoarding on the rear wall of the delicatessen across the street and drinking myself to death—which of course I do anyway, the writing lark being just another of my frantic foibles. My so-called honesty as you call it is just a very thin, very ragged cloak I put on from time to time to keep warm. Most of the time I slouch about wearing the heavy woollen clothes of self-delusion. Incidentally, I don't really go chasing cats up and down fire escapes, which I admit is a great pity as it would make me a more interesting person.'

Just as the partial exodus had started a few moments before, so the room seemed to be filling up again, the guests, refreshed with cool night air, were flocking back in amiable droves to the music and the heat and the hot bustling proximity of bodies.

'Return of the cannibals,' came Jake Pellmann's sonorous voice. He finished off his perennial umpteenth drink and stood up. 'I will go hence and be duly devoured—a ritual sacrifice, you know.' Jake was silent for a moment, gravely contemplating nothing, rubbing his chin ruminatively. 'I wonder will the walls of this particular little Jericho come tumbling down some fine day? Thank you, friend, for the pleasure of boring you and for the convivial libations you so generously and charitably shared with this wandering refugee from David's beautiful if beleaguered land.' Jake smiled in rueful melancholy, bowing ceremoniously from the waist, turned, and wandered absently away into the tobacco-blue depths of the crowd, an amiable tramp happily without directions.

Riley caught sight of Abbie, looking disconsolate, stranded in a little group of people, a tall thirtyish-looking man at her side pouring an endless stream of words into her unheeding ear as she stood gazing with thoughtful downcast eyes. Laurie still had not appeared, and he wondered about that. She was usually so punctual. The small isolation he had enjoyed began to be encroached upon and eaten up, and random bits of talk from the entrenched pockets of conversation filtered through to him lightly touching his mind.

'. . . Last play of his a complete disaster, taken off after a week, and even at that it ran too long . . .'

A laughing voice raised in agreement. 'Oh terrible. Obviously losing his flair, if he ever had one. Wife trouble, you know—'

'I would say self-abuse, more likely.'

A sly ill-restrained snigger. 'You mean . . .?'

'Of course! Living on his own like that—what else? . . .'

Voices full of the leathery aroma of libraries.

'. . . A dainty poet was Herrick, a fussy old maid of a poet, worrying over his verses like an old woman doing needle-point embroidery—'

'I'm a Donne man myself. Ask not for whom . . .'

The scented patter of female gossiping gliding past in satiny ripples lisping in delicious martini intimacy, casually vicious.

'You don't say! Not Melanie Blair—'

'I'm telling you. She's a good actress, sure, star dressing-room and all that, but she sleeps with her understudy, sure as hell, a greenhorn kid—Shirley something—'

Uncertainty creeping in alloyed with wavering loyalty wanting desperately to be ousted. 'Well—even if it's true—'

'Hell, Miriam, I'm not old-fashioned, a lay is a lay, but that sort of thing—well, it isn't natural, is it? . . .'

Whiff of exaggerated sea-saltiness blowing over him from city voices assuming the gruffness of young-old-middle-aged mariners.

'. . . So we sailed into the teeth of it, no other choice, rode with wind and tide, tossing like a cork, waves bursting over the sides—what else could we do?'

'. . . See you and Sally-Jean down at the yacht-haven Saturday noon, Mort, might try and sail out as far as the Island—'

'And stay overnight in Horseshoe Cove? Bring the habachi and have the girls cook us some steaks—'

181

'I'll see to the booze—the forecast's excellent for the whole weekend . . .'

The tinkle of glass, the slurping of tongues, waves swelling and receding around him, surging, diminishing, loud, distant, falling within sight and hearing with a soft sibilant sighing, a cackling laugh breaking like surf upon the fringes of his mind.

Perhaps for the first time in his life, certainly with an unblurred perception he had not experienced until now, Riley became increasingly aware of the fact that he was getting progressively drunk. It was an intensely intriguing happening; it was as if he had switched roles with Abbie and it was he who was now behind the camera taking pictures from every conceivable angle practically without moving a muscle, his eyelids acting as a shutter, clicking open and shut, the succession of images being instantaneously received and registered, each superimposed upon his brain as upon a thin susceptible layer of film, some of these images a little fuzzy round the edges, but clear and sharp at the centre, each detail sensitively defined whether of face or body or texture of clothing or facet of inanimate object passing incidentally through the perpetually mobile lens of his sight; his brain was both observation tower and darkroom, taking random snapshots and developing the proofs in one unbroken process, some cleanly delineated in stark black and white against a densely dark backdrop, others highly coloured in violent sunbursts of multi-mingling shades changing and interchanging bewilderingly as this veritable inner aurora borealis mounted and spread through his mind rainbowing every thought it contained, every tincture of material, every inflection of voice and sound that came sweeping in upon him from the wide seething ocean of living energy ceaselessly pulsating around him on all sides.

And something stranger still; he not only heard the words issuing from innumerable mouths, the words themselves became visible as well as audible, not merely sounds but separate illustrated entities within their own frames, oblong, triangular, elliptical, circular, myriad shapes and sizes all perfectly projected and perceived by him before being superseded by others with hardly the infinite shade of a second between. There was no easy diminishing of consciousness now, no languid sailing away on porpoise waves gentling his mind in soft twilight harbours where no rude alarms intruded or gave cause for panic; there was now instead a clamour of swift awareness mounting to an intolerable pitch, yet pervaded throughout by a fine delicious calmness that made him at once painfully vulnerable to every sensation filtering into his brain, and at the same time impregnable to the lesser denizens of panic that habitually invaded his thoughts. Had anyone asked him right then to describe his exact state of mind and body, it would have been immensely beyond his power to do so; his very veins acted as eyes, as antennae sensitive to the merest stirring, every word-thought-image resting like flavour upon his tongue exquisitely tasted, relished and absorbed. It was like being in a darkened swarming picturehouse, except that instead of looking at the screen in the ordinary fashion, the screen was behind his own eyes upon which were thrown unending reels of images with astonishing rapidity forming an intricate montage mounting and disintegrating and reshaping with the speed of an eyelid blinking. It was like sitting on the very edge of a precipice falling sheer to the sea hundreds of miles below, and looking around oneself calmly, keenly observing the separate and massed features of the scenery with the unerring eye of a hawk. It was like all these things, and many others as diverse and varied, and yet it was like none of these things at all, and what he was now knowing and feeling, what he was now being, he had known and felt and been before, somewhere in another skin, and it was all absolutely new and unknown and mysterious to him and induced no surprise whatever.

He played with the mere fact of his inebriation as a child with a toy, rolling it about like a bright coloured ball, bouncing it off the walls, from one end of the room to the other, watching it fly through the air, flashing through space, zooming past things precariously, whirling round in a spiral, caroming brilliantly through the dazzled universe, a fiery-edged meteorite skimming the tips of other planets in its headlong horrendous career. He knew the pain and ecstasy of colour, the delicious agony of texture, the torment and tremulous delight of sound, the singular shapes, the curious curvings of things, the fathomless depths of shadows paling to infinity, everything issuing its own identity, asserting its own existence uniquely and with either arrogance or composure, pride or modesty, everything a

declaration, a statement in itself, proclaiming its oneness where
before all had been submerged in a sludge of sameness. The
throwing open of so many windows pouring in such a primal
flood of light was dazzling, blinding in its translucence, and like
a bat lured from woods deep and dark out into the open, his
mind ran here and there banging into things, hurting itself at
every turn, bruising and scarring itself, yet he possessed a
certain excruciating serenity he had not known before such as
must have prevailed upon the first morning of creation, a sense
of peace and wonder too exquisite to be caught in words or even
framed in thought. He knew this moment could not last, as the
fresh nubile morning grows into perplexing mendacious day and
then secretive night, and it did not matter, for he was knowing
and living it now, and it would never pass from him no matter
how many countless days and nights might unfold for him
beyond tomorrow.

Someone came and sat down beside him. He was aware only
of whiteness, cool, smooth, meticulous, materialising without
fuss or explanation, part of the elaborate mosaic disassembling
and constantly recreating itself in his head. He found himself
singularly fascinated by the subdued sunset glitter of a ring on
a very slim finger; it seemed to burn slowly into his brain,
growing into a rainbow spanning a wide dark river glinting
with polished fire. It held all his mind over the dark rush of
centuries, burning, mesmerising, telling him something from
the other side of the sky. The waves sighed and broke inside him,
leaving their timeless imprint, ebbing reluctantly away,
trickling in and out between the sand-dunes, leaving their story
in wet perishable hieroglyphics. The ring burned. A wing rose
darkly on the left-hand corner of his patterned mind, blotting
out much of the light, a fluttering wing waving aloft its black
rebellion, the bitter black heart of the bird adorning its wing
like a badge, indomitable, silencing the little foolish cry of
innocence that trembled like a leaf on his strangely moving lips.
The burning ring searing his malleable mind. Rainbow over
impassable river luring him into its flames. Come and be eaten,
be burnt alive here in my consuming cleansing flames. Cast out
fear and dread and suspicion of the night and all the mean
preponderances of the lonely mind and step into my welcoming
flames. The ring and the rainbow and the river glowed brutally,

drowning his immobilised thoughts in a molten expanse of fire. He did not know if the hand which the burning ring adorned held morning or night and he dreaded that it would open and reveal its secret to him. Cower and conceal in darkness the hidden face of the coward nourishing himself with lies and self-deceit wrapped in bright paper. A long thin splinter of flame pierced his mind, but he felt no pain, only surprise at the peculiar beauty of the flame. He swooned towards the flame with sensuous fervour as if to the breasts and thighs of a lover opening to receive him into love's voracious mouth. The rainbow burst asunder, flinging showers of cruelly magnificent light outwards igniting the whole world, and the river shrank to the dimension of a black thread and then it was a tiny blue vein on a round alabaster breast rising above the brim of a multi-coloured quilt washed over with dawn. And still the ring burned defiant, defying him with its existence. The light shot through everything, incandescent, contemptuous of secrecy, merciless, implacable in its hunt after its own obscure creation. The ring moved, upwards, towards him . . .

'Sorry for being so late,' she said. 'The chauffeur couldn't get the damn car started.' She looked at him concernedly, a little suspiciously, holding her ringed hand indecisively in mid air. 'Hope you haven't been left too much alone. Are you all right?'

He found himself speaking with elaborate clarity. 'I'm fine.' He stopped and looked very intently at her. 'I think, you know, I do think I am becoming quite, quite drunk, in a sort of religious, almost spiritual way, and it is fascinating.'

Laurie's eyes widened and her hand finally touched his own. 'I don't want to spoil things for you, Riley—'

'You won't,' he said serenely. 'You can't. There are some things even you cannot touch.'

He saw but did not feel the hurt in her eyes. 'That was a rather cruel thing to say,' Laurie whispered, withdrawing her hand. Her eyes dropped to the many empty glasses on the tray, then moved to his face again. 'To get drunk or not is your own business—'

'Yes, it is,' he agreed amicably. 'I never imagined it could be such a metaphysical experience—'

'That is surprising,' she said icily. 'Reading your first book and now this new one, one gets the impression that drink was not altogether foreign to your background—' She stopped, biting her lip. 'I'm sorry—'

He looked at her cheerfully, his mood buoyant, exuberant, happily objective. 'Don't be,' he said. 'You're right. I grew up weaned on the stuff. It substituted mother's milk. I saw my father and then my brothers throw it up regularly, whoosh!' He made a sudden lurching movement, clutching his stomach grinning slyly up at her. 'Which struck me as a terrible waste—'

'Don't, Riley—'

'It's all right, Laurie, I do assure you,' Riley said, the colours still dancing in his mind, pulsating behind his eyes, picking up another still-full glass and regarding it as if it were the mythical philosopher's stone. 'I took to it as a duck to water. But I drank for all the wrong reasons, you see. I was conditioned to it, conditioned to the inevitable mediocrity of it all.' He leaned back, drawing the glass to his lips, barely touching it, letting it play round the tip of his tongue. 'The dull ritualistic piss-up of Saturday nights, so many Saturday nights starting with the clean smell of my father's shaving-soap and boot-polish, and ending with the swish of his leather belt and the stale after-smell of whiskey on his breath as he roundly cursed the lot of us. . . .' Riley drank suddenly, urgently, clutching the glass. 'Notice how fast I am talking, an unusual phenomenon for me—'

Laurie's gaze was a study in pain. 'Riley, there's something I must say, something I must tell you—you see, Don—'

'My book's a lousy book,' he said quite serenely. 'I am a pygmy Narcissus endlessly gawking at himself in a golden pond of whiskey—boring, boring. And the writing itself . . . all that morbid introspection, all that dull self-searching, heap upon heap! Like stumbling through a forest at night, thinking you see a light ahead, following it desperately, only to fall once more into another soggy swamphole of overladen prose.' Riley contemplated his glass as if trying to draw some message, some answer from it. 'They don't fool me, you know—Jay and Martin, nor you, for that matter.' He spoke without rancour, without emotion, softly, as if to himself, lifting his gaze to the heavy tobacco-blue haze of the great room. 'It should qualify for a prize as the dullest book of the year—it would win that race pulling up.'

'Don't talk like this, please,' pleaded Laurie, her face swimming into view like a petal on dark water.

'It will sell, of course,' he continued, as if he had not heard. 'It will fill our separate coffers. Which will make me very happy, having been thoroughly disenchanted with poverty and believing wholeheartedly in the glittering whoredom of wealth and success. But let's not add insult to injury, let's not start talking about talent or dangle the bright red carrot of genius in front of me as if I were a donkey wearing blinkers, egging me a step further on the path of self-illusion. My mirror may be cracked, oh yes, but I can still see quite clearly—darkly, perhaps, as through a glass, but without serious distortions.'

'God, you *do* enjoy playing Scott Fitzgerald, don't you!' said Laurie, exasperated. 'Though maybe Dylan Thomas would be a more suitable prototype to your damned Celtic ego. Don't you realise that such pseudo-tragic literary postures are hopelessly outdated and rather comic, not to say boring?'

He brought his eyes to focus upon her, innocent, ingenuous. 'But of course,' he told her, tilting his head sideways. 'I know it very well. It is the Zeldas and the Caitlins, the Beatrices of this world who don't recognise their true roles. They realise they play a purely secondary role, more often destructive than supporting, which of course enrages them and makes them even more tyrannical and possessive. It isn't the role that's important —it's the quality of the playing.' He was happily gone, riding out the swift flowing tide of his spectacular intuitiveness that gave him at that moment supreme certainty of his own truth and his own failures. He dwelt marooned in a comic vision of himself, noting with acerbic humour the wilting blossoms that now scarred the fanciful garden of promise into which he had strayed like a wilful wayward child, slowly losing his way among the dense undergrowth, choking in the impenetrable foliage that had lain hidden under the glitter of morning. As long as the morning still shone, even though its glow be less, he told himself, and lost the paper-thin smoke-trail of thought.

He did not try to pursue it, content to let it vanish in the tenuous twists of other tangled themes that were rising like clouds of incense before him. Now something, some fragment of word or shape, of fact or dream, would shine through the clouds like a piece of clean bright porcelain, delicate as a Chinese vase, and he would savour it avidly, absorbing each detail, turning it over in his mind, seeing the obverse side of the coin; and then these things swam away, darkened, dwindled down the narrowing stream through which they came filtering in to him. Perception was opening inside him with the delicious slowness of petals under the green mercies of the seasons. He heard the hooves of impatient stallions pounding upon another shore, and the sound came distantly to him like thunder far on the other side of the horizon, and below the more softly insistent echo of a woman singing in some forgotten shadow of the sky, down the jagged steppes of the sky behind the wind at the far end of a cloud, lamenting the over-ripe corruption at the core of the bright apple, love and desire grown sickly rich with decay and the ever-quick worms fat and slovenly on an abundant harvest of doubt and indecision. And the eyes of the woman were known to him, full of the dark loneliness of earth, the bitter mystery of love and the pain at the end of it, full of the desolateness of the empty ground where the carnival had been and the lost music still echoing in the acrid air. The eyes of the woman were the blank windows of a sepulchre and her lids the black shroud that blinded them to any last joy that might remain in the world, and her hair like a long dark night held the secret odour of dread and desire that no touch of morning could ever find and plunder.

There sounded a metallic switch in his mind, and he found again the concerned face of Laurie, clearing out of obscurity, and he looked with rare distance at her, as if her face were some sculpture he could look at for hours at a time in the marble remoteness of a gallery.

'I'm trying to tell you, Riley,' Laurie was saying, leaning towards him, both urgent and fretful. 'Please listen. It's rather unpleasant. Don doesn't usually drink much, as you know, but he's rather tight just now and in a very odd mood. Not aggressive, exactly, but—well, I'm worried. He has this ridiculous idea—if he says anything to you, please understand . . .'

He realised she was speaking, he almost formed the words in his mind, watching her lips move, but there was no connection, no link between them and himself, he felt enormously unstirred by her words, merely watching her lips move, intrigued by that very fact and that alone, and he took in the whole swelling

188

scene about him in the same way, like watching figures flickering on a huge lighted screen back through celluloid ages to the silent movie, for now all sound had gone from his mind and he caught only the movement, either slow or fluid, like dancers in a dream ballet, seen through green gauzy water, or jerky, automatic, puppet-like, manipulated by string in the hidden hands of a cunning puppeteer concealed somewhere high up in the swirling shadows of the domed ceiling. Sunburst after sunburst rose from the floor in blinding intricacies of colour, so many miniature mushroom clouds, showering death with a pall of beauty, masking faces looking into death out of life with bizarre demonic magnificent violence, splendour flung from the brush of a mad Dutchman scattering his own tormented visions of intolerable loveliness on to inadequate rectangles of canvas like heart's blood, as he was soon to scatter his brains upon the dewy grass of the quiet asylum in a last savage triumph of rage and blasted love, the bullet singing its way into that honeycomb of magic behind his fanatical eye. Vincent, a name unbearably innocent, fragile, crushable, tasting of white blue-lined milk jugs on bright childhood mornings and the smell of glowing haystacks heaped high in burning fields under puffy filigree clouds gliding over the fierce seeking eyes sunstruck with light. The self-same bullet of deliverance sang now through Riley's mind, exploding with Beethovian majesty, a star disintegrating, a universe engulfed in arson, livid fingers and tongues of flame flaring across his retina, convulsions of colours catherine-wheeling crazily into black infinities, reds, yellows, mauves, greens, blues, hurtful, bruising, slapping hard against the sight, tearing the soul out of its long unknowing limbo, caught transfixed in the cold blaze of moonlight drenching midnight fields. A curse that twisted and trembled into a prayer came to Riley's lips, un-uttered, and he cried inside himself for the things he saw and the things he would never see and for all the words that danced inside his head sweet and jangled and the words he would never catch, flying like wild cranes away from him upon impromptu winds, and cried and laughed too inside himself for the one poem he would never write in all the days he might know and the one thing he might love above all else that would remain forever sealed and beyond him in a place he would never find.

His eyes stung and smarted as though mustard had been flung into his face, he saw everything through a haze of remote delicious pain as a woman's fingertips touching most intimate parts of him, begging both for the touch to cease and for it never to stop, knowing at once a sweet surfeit of pleasure that itself bordered on pain, and an insatiable lust for the torment to continue though it drove him insane. A strange cinder-black burnt-cork smell assailed his nostrils from out of nowhere, and all the colours blurred into a dull bronzed evening glow over a gnarled pock-marked landscape pitted with open sores of famished earth and ragged bare-limbed lads burrowing down into that earth, scavenging for clinkers that would fire many a cold neighbourhood grate and buy two hours of illusion down in the flea-littered picturehouse snug from bitter November winds whipping viciously around corners slashing at skinny legs. Absurdly that land where it was always November and that time where it was always evening came back to him then in a dark swift onrush of fiercely beating wings overshadowing his mind to the exclusion of all else, the gluttonous over-fed albatross zooming in from the forever reachable past, darkening this room now and everything in it, reducing it to the crabbed dimensions of a birdcage, a low-ceilinged box of a room with one cracked pane of window that was never opened out on to the eight-foot plot of dying earth ugly with rocks and starved cats and strewn with half-buried bedsteads and rust-red mattresses worm-swarming that once before the morning bells ceased pealing groaned under the stale relentless bounce and pressure of desperate love in some forgotten wet-tongued moment of blighted ecstasy shattered by the all-too-soon curious convulsion and the flat-fisted groping in the dark for the whiskey bottle. A bird hobbled lame and maimed beneath that one-eyed window, flapping its one unbroken wing up at him in sharp-eyed defiance, its queer little black body wriggling in the snow a last defiant affirmation, a thin high-voiced squeaking celebration of life, leaving its tiny arrow-splayed footprints in the frost-bitten earth, hobbling away with dignity into the shadow of the meagre stunted bushes that had died in infancy. And a boy's bedizened broken-toothed face came to him grinning unkillably over a heritage of fenced-in backyards, cheek torn by the disjointed knuckle of an afternoon enemy, his turquoise eyes flashing famously with devilment and the lure that lay behind certain wild garden hedges beckoning the injudicious over into perfidy lying on the liquorice-sweet tongue of a twelve-year-old siren with wheat yellow tresses and cracked fingernails clasping the gleaming three penny piece zealously in clammy palm as she tolled out the thirty-second wonder in the tall weedy grass under the cold November eye glittering in the sky piercing the sullen clouds, a thin shield for the unwise.

In the heavy sweat-sodden smoke-laden heat that now enveloped him, he felt the cold tongue-lick of the snow falling on him out of that other time, melting the moment it touched his burning skin, melting into his veins, and he shivered, back under a brooding cloud telling him things, of coming doom in the long parched grass that never caught the benison of sunlight. A vast starless void spread before him, as if indeed Jericho's hallowed walls had come at last tumbling down, and the house stood crouching before him on its haunches like a wizened old beggar, the mantle of snow on the roof forming a fleecy shawl over its humped shoulders. Its eight dead eyes stared back at him, four below, four above, unshuttered, like those of a corpse, the black hall door ajar like a mouth hanging half-open and slack, the thick weeds climbing up the front like a raw scurvy beard infested with vermin slithering about in the dead nightshine of the sky. He felt the heart within him hang heavy as a block of ice. A street lamp threw its yellow blade of light across the frozen footpath, climbing brokenly over the low uneven garden wall like a luminous snake transmogrified in its slimy path. Down the arctic wastes of the street an accordion was dervishing about with an improbable Mexican tune, accompanied by the metallic clapping of hands and the hobnailed belting of boots caught up in a ritualistic fire dance over broken beer crates and mangled corned-beef sandwiches. A young girl face bent down with a lonely abandoned air walked wearily down the street, her wind-driven skirt pressed inwards against her thin thighs, wobbling like a newborn filly upon her spindle-heeled shoes, a half-moon of a scarf over her dark defeated head on her mournful way home from midnight mass; she did not even look up when a yellow-furred mangy-ribbed ugly-snouted mongrel skulked from behind a hedge and snapped viciously at her bony ankles mud-splattered from the slushy snow at the kerbside.

As if he had never left it, he saw the fading black and red squared linoleum on the kitchen floor cracked and snarled at the edges, saw the dark shadow of a bellicose rat slithering over the feet-smooth time-worn surface from the turf-smelling coalhouse under the stairs to scuffle its way into the jagged hole in the wooden skirting, its wriggling corkscrew of a tail the last to disappear out of sight. The face of the time-scarred clock that never kept time grinned down from the wall, caught in a square of moonlight that gave back its mocking grimace contemptuous of the death-rattle of hours. And the undimmed red glow throwing the face of a music-hall hard-done-by Christ into relief on the wall above the fireplace, deliberately debilitated, a pain-crazed face, neurotically driven, mad as any Saturday-night countenance caught transfixed in the yellow-lit door of a tavern, uplifted to the night sky in marvellously amateurish resignation, and holding up the two carefully pierced, perfectly holed palms in perpetual admonition, a few pristine scarlet drops of blood dripping delicately down the feminine wrists.

'My God, you haven't heard a word I've been saying!'

Laurie's words bobbed along on the surface of his mind like cork on a fast-flowing stream, driven into little hollows of shelter by the convoluted swirl of the current. He found her face a thing of singular mystery, a map he could never quite follow, a code he could never quite decipher, and he looked at her with such intensity that she cried out petulantly, 'Why do you stare at me like that?'

He hiccuped a little and rubbed his suddenly dry mouth with the back of his wrist, vaguely apologetic.

'I don't know,' he told her, drawing his brows together as if caught in the middle of a profound metaphysical argument. 'I honestly don't know. I don't think it's just because you're beautiful. Did I ever say that to you before—about you being beautiful?' He shook his head, perplexed. 'I don't think I ever did, come to think of it, which is a dreadful sin of omission, I admit. Well, you are beautiful, of course, but that isn't the reason why I'm staring at you. No, there's something else, nothing much to do with the fact that you're beautiful. Help me find it, Laurie, help me know what it is.' His hand hovered indecisively over the array of empty glasses, as a hawk over a barren plain, finally finding a full one and lifting it to his lips.

'Riley, please listen,' urged Laurie, inclining her face towards him in desperate intimacy. 'Don's acting very much out of character tonight, making wild accusations, and I'm very upset —I don't know what's got into him—'

'The truth, maybe.'

He saw his own words bouncing up and down before his eyes like firecrackers, and like a child hugely intrigued he sat back to play with them.

'What do you mean?' Laurie's voice was both angry and unsure.

'Maybe it's the truth that's got into Don,' he said, or rather heard himself saying, since only a small inconsequential portion of his mind spoke and the rest was one attentive hearing organ listening intently to each syllable above and below the sounds. 'It has a way of injecting itself into our bloodstream sooner or later no matter how we try to immunise ourselves against it. It's usually accompanied at times by a high fever and a nervous twitch, but in the end is usually salutary.' He saw quite clearly Laurie looking at him, incredulity covering her face like a gauze, and derived a certain perverse pleasure from the effect his words were having on her, dismay and anger chasing each other across her face like clouds casting shadows on a summer afternoon hillside where all was normally serene. He knew he should stop talking, but his words carried him along as of their own volition insistently.

'I've been dabbling with the truth on and off for some years —it's a dangerous game, for once in it's hard to get out, and once started it's impossible to stop.' He revelled in the patent pomposity with which he spoke, grinning inwardly at himself, invisibly smirking at the spectacle of himself which he was grimly assembling as the alcohol raced like liquid fire through him, its euphoric fumes spreading to the remotest outposts of his mind, igniting places that had until then been dark and impenetrable; the more pompous, absurd, grotesquely arrogant he was the greater zest he experienced from the exercise. 'Like a good woman, truth is hard to come by, and—to extend the simile further—like a woman, it has many faces. A morning face, an afternoon face, the mysterious semi-hidden face it assumes at night before the light goes out, and—ah, yes, the most peculiar of all—the face it wears in the dark, hardest of all to find, but best of all if you find it, because the face that comes out of the night is free from all deception and slyness . . .' He looked at her cunningly over his glass. 'No—don't tell me I'm being pedantic—of course I am, but you couldn't say it with the same conviction as I could myself.'

The music, hidden as it was, seemed to grow louder, more shrill in volume, seemed to envelop and fill every space like waves washing over everything, vibrant with a harsh undulating syncopation that riveted itself on the walls and bounced back into the crowd massing on the floor. His mind was drunk as much on fantasy as on alcohol, the one feeding the other in like kind, each more volatile and insatiable as the moments snarled at the heels of each other, leapfrogging over time. And the music grew louder, louder, always threatening and never reaching a crescendo, quivering on one sustained implacable note, dizzying him with the cloying after-sickness of exhilaration, with a stomach-churning surfeit of pleasure, like one too long at a feast, a bejewelled bacchanalia.

'What is it, Riley?' Laurie was asking him, forgetting her private worry in her concern for him. 'You look like Saul struck blind on his way to Damascus. Is it just the booze?'

He looked at her, feeling his face, his whole body glowing as if he were an incandescent vase.

'Yes, that's right,' he answered with the chirpiness of a bright-eyed sparrow, almost chortling with glee. 'That's it precisely—just the booze.'

She sighed, tiredly brushing back her hair from her face. 'What a time you picked to get sloshed,' she said morosely. 'I've never seen Don in such a weird state. He keeps quoting the most banal lines of romantic poetry and flinging them at me like darts, throwing them at me like accusations—'

'Whatever could he be trying to say?' Riley interrupted, almost lisping, hearing the ridiculous leprechaun trill in his voice, the puckish frivolity gambolling over into inane heather-ripe mirth above the pealing of distant Sunday bells and a creaking crone praying and cursing softly in the green shadow of a hedge.

Laurie gave him a look of wounded trust. 'That's all I want

now—a stage-Irishman,' she said bitterly. 'I thought you'd want to help—I haven't had to face this kind of thing before, and you're the only one who could possibly understand. But you're drunk—you're both drunk, the pair of you, and I'm caught in the crossfire, as always.'

'Speak not to me in riddles, good madam,' Riley said, enunciating elaborately. 'It scatters my poor wits, breaks them like eggs upon a hard stone floor. As for being caught in crossfire —as far as I know not a single shot has been fired yet—not a solitary volley.'

'You're drunk,' she repeated, not condemning, merely matter of factly.

He nodded his head several times. 'That is by no means a profound observation,' he replied, squinting at the dwindling drink in his glass. 'I admit it with a cheerful openness of heart. I think I'm truly drunk for the first time in my short young life, and I am enjoying the experience to the point of exquisite lunacy. I feel like an anchorite in the desert suddenly stumbling upon a cache of wine buried in the sand. I feel as Thomas De Quincey must have felt when taking his first snortful of opium. I'm not merely experimenting, you see—I feel I *am* a whole new experiment, not just the vessel containing the nectar, but the nectar itself, drowning everything in golden fiery sweetness—'

'You're not drowning *me* in any sweetness,' said Laurie, looking over at the crowd with remote hurt eyes. 'You're drunk, that's all.'

'No,' he patiently explained as teacher to pupil, 'not *just* drunk. That is *not* all. That would be nothing, merely an exercise in monotony, like shaving or brushing your teeth or eating just to stop from being hungry. Might just as well say that Francis of Assisi or Goethe or Beethoven were *merely* inspired or that Gauguin or van Gogh merely saw colours the way they did because they were insane. What I am experiencing now, the thing that is happening to me now, at this precise moment, is as spiritual, as mystical, as anything that ever happened to any of the people I've just mentioned, as much beyond the scope of comprehension as the metamorphosis at Cana where with an elegant lift of his virginal hand the Messiah changed water into wine—' Riley paused with tremendous meaningfulness, with sly significance, looking at her sideways out of half-lidded eyes like a conjurer doing a trick. 'The evidence is overwhelming, isn't it—the fact that I am not *just* drunk? If it was just that, would I be talking like this? Could I see things as clearly as I do now? Explain that away with your cool New England logic.' He ended on a note of smug triumph, with a courtroom flourish.

'I am duly impressed and chastised, good master,' Laurie answered with mock ceremony. She scanned the tray of glasses hopefully, looking for a full one. 'I could just about do with a drink myself—just listening to all your talk makes my throat dry.' Her quest proved successful. and she took a grateful sip. 'As for my cool New England logic—it tells me something distinctly unpleasant is about to interrupt this high-faluting discussion. Over here, dear,' she called out, and looking up Riley discerned Don making an erratic path towards where they sat, large and loping like an amiable if shortsighted bear, making instant apologies in his deep Southern voice to people he brushed against as he made his way towards them, be-spectacled, hair slightly dishevelled, a look both bemused and vaguely combative on his face, holding a half-full glass of drink at a precarious angle in his hand. Don was wearing a dark suit and tie rather loosened and askew, giving him a rather im-probable rakish look. His clothes always managed to hang loosely on his large-boned awkward frame, the cuffs never quite reaching his wrists, the ends of his trousers dangling an irritating inch or two above his ankles though he dressed with impeccable taste and decorum. It was simply that he was a very large man.

'Greetings!' Don boomed, coming to a halt in front of them, creased eyes going from one to the other of them, amused and quizzical behind the thick lenses. 'A full and lively gathering inside Jericho's marble walls tonight to pay homage to our Parnassian friend here! How does it feel to be a living legend, Riley?' Don was smiling down at him, amiable as ever, but there were tight rigid lines about his mouth and his fingers gripped rather than held the glass.

'I'm sure Riley doesn't want to even listen to such a silly question, dear,' Laurie broke in, half rising.

'Don't go, honey,' said Don, putting a friendly though firm hand on her shoulder and making her sit down again. 'If it was a silly question I'm sorry and I'm sure Riley will be magnanimous enough to pardon me, but I asked in all seriousness. How *does* it feel like to be a celebrity?' repeated Don, turning his face fully to Riley, expectant and demanding at once.

'Am I a celebrity?' parried Riley, seeing the man in front of him as huge and of Brobdignagian proportions towering above him, wavering oddly back and forth, first remote, indefinite, then menacingly near, smiling the same perplexed bemused smile as if forever striving to put a giant jigsaw puzzle into place and both baffled and resentful that superior intellect had so far failed.

Don's smile widened, though there was a note of irritation in his voice. 'Come, false modesty ill becomes you. You're much too shrewd and intelligent to play the modesty game! As Churchill said of Attlee: "Clem's a very modest man, having much to be modest about." You hardly fit into that category!'

'It can be a dangerous thing,' said Riley, squeezing his eyelids hard against the pupils, 'putting people into categories.'

'Oh, I disagree,' Don announced, standing arms akimbo, one hip jutting out at an arrogant angle. 'I think we all belong to certain kennels, bulldog, Alsatian, Pekinese, Yorkshire terrier or Kerry blue as the case may be. We all belong to homo sapiens, sure, but we're each a different class of animal, and a bulldog doesn't stop being a bulldog by putting it in a kennel marked dachshund, the same applying to any other species of animals using any method of transposition.'

Riley roused himself wearily for the battle. 'Then surely that argument cancels out your upposition about categories and reduces the usefulness of kennels to point nil?'

'On the contrary,' insisted Don, still smiling, but his eyes quite hard and steely. 'We must categorise people and things, otherwise all would be chaos, but that doesn't mean a particular category has necessarily got to remain fixed and static. We can move from one category to another if we are nimble and ingenious and ambitious enough, and it can be for good or for bad, like everything else in human nature. One of the things I admire in a man is to move from a small into a larger category, and that is also what I admire in you, friend Riley.'

Don turned to Laurie. 'You admire that in him too, don't you, honey? Why, sure you do! She sees so much more to

197

admire in you than my own poor uneducated eye can see—isn't that true, honey?'

Laurie turned a martyred face up to him, long slim fingers resting the glass in her lap. 'You're asking the most absurd questions tonight, Don. There's no sense or meaning to them at all. I'm tired,' she said, her shoulders lifting in a sigh, putting her glass down on the tray. 'I think I want to go now.'

'And methinks the lady doth protest too much,' Don retaliated blandly, throwing back his head and heroically tossing his drink down his throat like a reckless sailor aboard a blazing ship predictably doomed, just barely suppressing a convulsive coughing spasm as he re-surfaced. 'I'm enjoying myself, darling —why can't I enjoy myself once every decade or so? Is it such a great sacrifice for you to see me enjoying myself? That's something I'd very much like to know.'

Laurie again sighed, almost an exact facsimile of the sigh she had given a moment ago, a sigh of tangible weariness. 'You're not enjoying yourself, Don,' she said. 'You're just drunk, that's all. Like our friend Riley here,' she added, giving Riley a sad lip-drooping look of betrayed trust, of confidence prostituted for the gross aggrandisements of lesser mortals. 'You two are so alike, you know, so full of the potential to please people and be charitable and witty at the same time, both of you entirely without malice, to be sure, but so lacking in maturity, in real depth of emotion—both of you, really so *shallow*.' Laurie fell back, leaning her head upon the sofa, letting her arm trail over the side, as if surrendering herself to the monstrous injustice of it all. 'Yes,' she mused, staring upwards, 'and so full of imagined wrongs.'

'We are sat upon in judgment, it seems,' said Don, shrugging his shoulders and holding up both hands in resignation. He turned to a passing waiter and politely and with irresistible courtesy relieved him of a handsomely overladen tray. 'If we are to be acrimonious and soul-searching,' he said, putting the tray down on the floor, 'let it be with a hey and a ho and a hey nonny no.' He handed a glass to both of them, Riley inevitably accepting, and Laurie who fretfully declined, saying she had a headache. 'To truth and respect in all our dealings with each and every one,' moved Don, raising the glass to his mouth, his broad forehead beginning to glisten.

'Please, Don, let us all go after this one,' Laurie pleaded. 'It's a long drive back—'

'Indeed it is, indeed it is,' said Don sonorously, declaiming. 'A long way back to where we first started out. Ah.' Don closed his eyes and turned his face upwards to the swimming smoke and lights:

'I have forgot much, Cynara! gone with the wind,
Flung roses, roses riotously, with the throng,
Dancing, to put thy pale, lost lilies out of mind;
But I was desolate and sick of an old passion,
Yea, all the time, because the dance was long:
I have been faithful to thee, Cynara! in my fashion . . .'

Don opened his eyes and looked at Laurie with a faint look of mystified enquiry on his face, repeating the last line of the poem with histrionic melancholy. 'I have been faithful to thee, Cynara!' He paused, letting out the remaining words with a whimsical sigh, 'In my fashion . . .'

Riley caught the tentative thinly disguised agonised inflection hovering on the last line, the very last sentence.

'You're lousy at recitation, darling,' Laurie said laconically. 'Why don't you finish your drink and we can all go home?'

'As I told you dear, I'm enjoying myself,' said Don, surprised, as if marvelling that she should doubt him in this affirmation of his enjoyment. 'And it doesn't matter a sweet damn if I'm drunk or not.' He smiled, a strangely youthful ingenuous smile, at Riley. 'I'm beginning even at my advanced age to understand why the bottle should hold such a special lure for you, Riley—do you think I'm too old to yield to such temptation?' he asked with sly intentness.

Once more Riley heard himself parading out the facile cliché, as if the Wildean ghost was bending over him whispering into his ear with silver and claret tongue. 'One is never too old to yield to temptation. It is when you no longer recognise it that you know you're too old for anything except death.'

Don heaved a lugubrious sigh, shaking his head. 'Now why can't I think of clever things like that to say? It's very frustrating, you know, to be closeted in such close proximity with a genius over a period of months. What must it be to be married to one? I'm sure it would be either a question of suicide or murder, possibly both. Aren't you lucky to be married to an ordinary mediocre clot like me, honey?' Don added to Laurie. 'Seems that sailing is all that I'm good at, and even there I have to have your invaluable assistance, whether I want it or not.' He gave her a smile of such jaded self-doubting it cancelled out any hint of offence.

'You get by very well, dear,' Laurie rejoined.

'Oh sure,' concurred Don, swilling his drink around in his glass before swallowing it down with hardly a trace of volcanic disturbance this time, though his eyes did bulge a little. 'No mortgage, steady job, respectable salary, two cars in the garage, a bank balance that's always just that lucky few bucks out of the red, our own tub, even if it doesn't quite measure up to America's Cup standards, two well-mannered well-scrubbed little kids, a wife who is beautiful, as well as dutiful . . . Sure, I get by, the personification of the American Dream. After all,' continued Don, stooping a bit stertorously to pick up another drink, the light gleaming on the small bald clearing that was beginning to form in the middle of his head, 'it isn't every young guy that's nominated Man Most Likely to Succeed— that's what they voted me when I was at Beloit, you know,' he said to Riley, standing back a little distance from them, striking a Napoleonic stance, his self-derision patent. 'I used to say that with a pronounced swagger once upon a time, usually at some of these soulless social functions, much to my wife's discomfort—it distresses her to remember that anyone in their right senses could ever have chosen me as one most likely to succeed, or that I was considered in my callow youth as that bright young boy from Beloit—'

'This masochistic display is beginning to pall, my dear,' Laurie put in with veiled wrath. 'I'm sure Riley hasn't the foggiest idea what you're talking about, or whether Beloit is a reformatory or an automobile plant—'

Don's eyes glittered brightly behind the spectacles. 'But surely, even he in his dark dense Celtic twilight must have heard of Beloit? All the civilised world knows of Beloit! The cultural flower-garden of Wisconsin, comparable to the Alexandria of Illinois, the Athens of Atticus, South Carolina, where young

MacDonald Franklin Waldo Emerson first saw the pristine light of day in a riverside cabin loud with the music of mosquitoes and the burned smell of baked beans over a primus stove! Why,' asserted Don, craning his head forward and managing to resemble an intent eagle ready to pounce on any scurvy jackal that happened to be lurking close by, 'they even wrote a limerick about me,' and without preamble he dived right into it:

'There once was a young man named Don
And sweet Laurie his eye was fixed on.

Don gave a rather hollow guffaw and went on, slightly shamefaced, 'Sorry, I can't remember the rest of it, but Laurie always maintained there were carnal undertones in that, but then she always did have a very virginal mind, which I believe she has managed to keep intact up to now.' He turned his suddenly predatory head towards her. 'Isn't that true, sweet-heart—you still have a virginal mind, don't you, despite the debauched influence of our friend the Wild Gael here?' Don again eyed them both with a rather desperate amity, like someone attempting to cross a narrow mountain ledge and perilously unsure of his footing.

'What comes next in your social repertoire, dear,' Laurie asked, 'in your calendar of social advancement against inconceivable odds? How the boy from the backwoods of South Carolina worked the railroad, erected telegraph poles, dug ditches, swung pick and shovel till his hands were raw and bleeding, working his brave solitary passage through college with honours and finally winning the fair hand of Professor Kingston's brainy but over-indulged daughter—now there's a success story from the brave New World if ever there was one!' Laurie, face suddenly hard, mouth compressed, picked up a full glass from the tray at her feet. 'I can almost hear the violin strings throbbing heart-brokenly in the background, and as the lights come up there isn't a dry eye in the cinema.'

Riley, from the distance at which he found himself from them and from everyone else in that loud echoing immense auditorium of a room, felt the interplay of some totally intimate and exclusive dialogue pass between these two people, the half-playful, half-intentional flicking of a cat's paw swishing the air between them, no intonation of distrust, no inflection of regret or disillusion, rather a vague impression of things unsaid, remote amorphous images and intimations out of their shared past that time had fleshed if only with dust and the thinnest semblance of reality, engaged in a game only they could play, knowing the recognised rules and intricate dictates of that game, not so much shadow-boxing as moving through the subtle steps of a shadow dance perfected through time and time's long pauses allowing them both to adapt themselves to the changing rhythm of the dance. It was the sense of exclusiveness that most made itself felt; Riley knew himself then to be outside these two, a stranger briefly, transparently known over a ribbon-thin stretch of time already spinning itself out like tyre tracks disappearing invisibly over a rapidly receding skyline. It was as if he did not exist for either of them now as they parried forward and back with knowing eye and trenchant tongue, and the imaginary distances that in his facile self-deceiving way he had created between these two vanished completely; they were now both on ground he could never know, inaccessible to any foolish aspiration of trespass or transgression on his part, and in the long tired closing and opening of an eye they had become blurred participants in the larger cosmos of shadows that moved and merged everywhere around him, distinguishable only by his slight knowledge of them both, and that too might obscurely leave his presence like the last fitful flicker of a candle yielding to the blandishments of night. The thought of his own appalling simplicity struck him with great impact; he had dared so much, and yet so very little, he had shouted out loud, his embattled defiance, his fantastic hope, his belief in something beyond what could be held solidly in one's palm, and in the end of it all, it seemed, only his own echo came back to him, lonely, bitter, derisive.

Then Don, tiring of the secret game, turned and looked at him with peculiar melancholy, speaking half to himself:

'Down, down, down into the darkness of the grave
gently they go, the beautiful, the tender, the kind,
quietly they go, the intelligent, the witty, the brave,
I know. But I do not approve. And I am not resigned . . .'

'Is that going to be so with you, Riley?' asked Don with a long sigh. 'Are you, too, going to feed the roses before your time? Yes,' he went on, his mournfulness evaporating, nodding his head with emphatic exasperation, 'I bet you'd even have the arrogance to die young—you couldn't resist such a great publicity stunt like that!'

'Don, that is uncalled for!' said Laurie sharply. 'You're being deliberately insulting.'

'Oh, come now, let's be honest,' Don insisted, lifting his hand reprovingly. 'I'm sure Riley would be the first to acknowledge he is first and foremost the egotist par excellence, the opportunist supreme, his own best publicity agent—there isn't a Doubting Thomas bone in his body as far as his own opinion of himself is concerned! I say this in all good humour,' explained Don in a grave tone, 'though also in all honesty. I've been very quiet these last few months, but little escapes my eye, and I've been watching you very closely since you moved in with us as our guest.' Don paused and took a quick swallow of his drink as if anxious not to let go of his present train of thought. 'I know my dear wife is darting looks of anger and warning at me, and tomorrow I shall probably regret what I'm saying now—'

'Don—for God's sake—' protested Laurie.

Don held his hand higher still like a speaker calling for order. 'I'm going to say it just the same,' he said, his mouth set determinedly. He gave Riley his full attention, creating the impression that he was pondering deeply, though he spoke with a speed that was unusual in him. 'I like you, Riley—do you accept that? I like you a lot,' he affirmed as Riley half opened his mouth in reply. 'And I've a feeling you like me, but that's beside the point—'

'Would you mind explaining what that point is, please?' Laurie interrupted, her voice controlled though flint-edged.

Don gave her a quick glance, quizzical. 'I should have thought it would be Riley here who'd have asked me that,' he said, 'but he seems instead to be listening intently, for which I give him full credit—'

Riley heard rather than listened, looking intently at the glass in Don's hand moving jerkily up and down, giving off glittering tangents of multifarious light shooting off into space like comets' tails flaring furiously in the jangled void.

'I'm very much aware how dull a figure I must strike beside such a volatile, tempestuous bohemian young man like yourself,' Don said with a hint of rising oratory. 'No, don't interrupt,' he told Riley, who had not the slightest intention of doing so, still fascinated by the magical glass in Don's hand which was now the focus of everything. 'I'm an exact carbon-copy of every commuter you'd meet every morning and evening on the trains into and out of New York—dull, respectable, neatly dressed, carrying the ubiquitous briefcase, a constant look of harassment and resignation on their faces. I haven't a flair for anything that demands imagination, except sailing and growing tomatoes, which don't exactly call for Promethean feats of the intellect. I'm a fairly efficient mariner, and my tomatoes are at least edible, but that stretches my ingenuity to its very limits. That bright young boy from Beloit sure lost some of his promise along the way to man's estate!' Don looked thoughtfully into his drink.

Laurie moved restlessly. 'As an exercise in self-analysis I'm sure all this is immensely interesting,' she said, 'but as a topic of convivial conversation I find it quite boring, and I can see Riley has lost all touch with your tortuous exposition. Why don't we all go home?'

Don smiled faintly down at her. 'You do us both an injustice, honey,' he rebuked mildly. 'Our friend here is hearing every word I say—don't be taken in by that look of poetic withdrawal, and I am being quite succinct without being downright rude—'

'Your idea of tactfulness eludes me,' Laurie said. 'To my mind tact consists of something rather more than making vague hints and veiled innuendoes.'

'Ah, but you speak with a clear unclouded mind undimmed by the juice of the grape,' Don countered almost waggishly. 'You have an unfair advantage over both of us, so you must dispense charity with clarity, or the other way round if you like. I can only speak the truth as I see it, and if I see it as a kind of blur, forgive me, but at least I am not totally oblivious of it.' Don spoke with a strange self-satisfied air.

'You're talking like an Indian guru,' said Laurie. 'What is this marvellous gift of perception the gods have bestowed upon you all of a sudden—what is this truth of yours, Don?'

Don turned his eerily shining face to her. 'You mean it hasn't yet become apparent to you?'

'It might help if I knew what it was that's supposed to be apparent,' she said patiently. 'The only thing that's apparent to me just now is that you're even more drunk than Riley.'

'That may or may not be true,' Don acceded easily, 'and it's unimportant anyway, because it doesn't prevent me from apprehending the truth no matter how imperfectly—'

Laurie made an impatient little movement with her clenched fist upon her knee. 'For God's sake,' she almost cried out, 'stop saying "the truth, the truth" like some damned mystic struck by a sudden bolt of revelation!'

'Not exactly sudden,' replied Don, musing. 'More a gradual process of revelation culminating in an irrefutable truth. I think Riley knows what I'm saying,' he said softly.

Laurie looked at Riley intently. 'Do you?'

The lights still danced and expanded and mushroomed all around him, and he was intensely conscious of them both staring at him and that part of his mind that saw and heard them was clear and deep and calm as a pond at sunset.

'I think Don might think that I do.'

'That only adds to the mystery,' said Laurie unhappily. 'Why should either of you prevaricate in such a silly way? It's just childish.'

'There are none so blind, etcetera,' spoke Don, pursing his lips into a tight aperture and letting the drink trickle thinly on to his tongue. 'It seems I find myself in the ironic position of being the first to bring you the glad tidings—well, so be it. All the world's a stage and this is my first dramatic little part. Don't you know, Laurie, fine perceptive female creature that you are—don't you know that Riley here is very deeply in love with you, and has been all summer?'

Riley found himself hearing Don's words quite clearly, found himself observing Don intently, the bright covering of sweat gleaming on his cheeks and forehead, the reflecting glitter of his spectacles flashing with each turning and moving of that large granite-hewn head, the dry compressed mouth deeply lined through years of stern self-drive, the scraggy brows, even the tiny tufts of hair sprouting from the tight winged nostrils and rather large ears; it was as though he were transferring each detail of the man's countenance to memory, engraving its very facet upon his mind, though the actual words that Don spoke left him detached, unstirring, rooted in himself, as though invested with the strange power to remain remote and outside the swirl and pull of what was happening at that or any other given point in time. He felt no smack of surprise, no jolt of unexpectedness, hearing Don's words; what he did feel was this curious intentness in looking on, in watching, observing the minutiae of the abiding moment in which all these things were evolving and emerging like separate blooms out of the thick surrounding foliage of events growing and existing in other parts of the room. It had become obvious to him, as his own mind cleared, that Don was strangely excited, and only contained that excitement by considerable effort of will working in the taut muscles of his face and hands.

He caught the sharp quick intake of Laurie's breath, and in turn looked at her. He could not tell if her colour had changed in any way, she seemed the same as a moment ago, only her eyes were wider now, the pupils dark and distended as she stared up at her husband, her cheeks shadowed, her faint green eye-shadow barely visible, yet lending her face a strangely garish unreal look, like a face in a painting, caught in a stage spotlight, almost disembodied from the rest of her, pushing up out of darkness: her lips were oddly stark, like a thin dark shadow painted on to her face. It was a face one might meet in a disturbed dream about to fade indistinguishably away at any moment, settling upon one's subconsciousness like a breath ineffably felt.

'Don,' she said, speaking very quietly, 'don't say anything you will afterwards bitterly regret.'

It was Don's turn to look baffled. 'Regret?' he echoed, 'Regret? Why should I regret what I've just said? It is the truth, but that's no reason for not speaking it, is it? Why should it either astonish or anger you—what's so strange or disturbing about Riley falling in love with you, or any other man, come to think of it? You're damn pretty, out-and-out beautiful, in fact, and Riley here—well, for one thing he's a poet, isn't he, and they're such an impressionable bunch, falling in and out of love at the drop of a stanza or metre. In fact,' went on Don, smiling from one to the other, 'I'd have been disappointed if he hadn't fallen for you! Whips up my ego real good to have men love you from afar and to know I'm the one who finally cajoled you into the corral!'

'You might,' said Laurie in the same voice, 'you just might consider Riley's feelings, even if you think mine are of no account.'

'Oh come, honey,' said Don with an attempt at heartiness, but looking confused. 'Riley's no sensitive plant—he's not going to wilt away and die of shame—are you, Riley?' Don asked, still smiling that fixed readily amiable smile, putting his broad-fingered hand on Riley's shoulder in a friendly squeeze. 'Women are so damn sensitive about these things. There'd be no fun in the world if we men were to be all that intense—eh?'

'I guess you're right at that, Don,' said Riley slowly, pleased to discover his glass was still half-full and looking over the rim of it at one of the bright silver buttons shining in Don's waist-coat. 'I guess you're right at that.'

'It's one thing to be intense,' said Laurie, breathing rather hard, 'and it's quite another to be insensitive—which is just what you've been, Don, with a vengeance. I apparently do not matter, but you should certainly apologise to Riley—don't you see what an impossible position you've put him in?'

'How—what position?' Don said, almost stammering.

'As a guest in our house—what else?' Laurie retorted.

'I don't see—' began Don, furtive, perplexed.

'No, you don't, do you?' Laurie went on, her eyes sharp needle-points of anger, her cheeks quite visibly flushed now. 'You didn't stop to think, did you—to think how your stupid words and behaviour will affect the whole atmosphere at home from now on, how difficult it's going to be to maintain an ordinary uncomplicated relationship between all three of us now that you've given vent to those infantile fantasies of yours?' She turned to Riley entreatingly, her eyes faltering somewhat. 'Please don't let this upset or change anything—we all speak out of turn at times—'

Don's face reddened. 'Now look here, Laurie,' he said harshly, 'I don't want my wife to do any apologising for me—if there's any to be done I'm quite capable of doing it myself.' He addressed Riley direct. 'My friend, do you feel offended in any way by anything I have said? If you do, I'd be obliged if you

207

were to say so, but I would also like to know why you're offended.'

Riley, realising he was expected to answer, found it extraordinarily difficult to say anything, and quickly emptied his glass. 'I—er—well, no—offended? Who—me? Oh, no, I don't think so—no, of course not,' he finally managed to say in an affirmative manner. 'It's nothing—nothing at all—' He blinked rapidly up at Don. 'Wasn't that Edna St Vincent Millay you quoted just now, and before that Dowson—Edmond or is it Ernest Dowson?'

Laurie looked quickly at him, wounded, as if he had failed her somehow, betrayed her in some very grievous way; she seemed crestfallen, and looked from one to the other of the two men with an air of hopelessness and goaded pain.

Don threw back his head and almost bellowed. 'There—what did I tell you, sweetheart?' he said delightedly. 'Didn't I tell you he'd understand? You were just being touchy, that's all. Takes us men to have a sense of proportion. Don't look so woebegone, darling!' he said, kissing Laurie on the forehead and putting an arm around her in an awkward, strangely touching gesture of protection and reassurance, nudging his cheek against hers. 'We both love you—isn't that so, Riley? Don't you know, don't you feel that we both love you, honey?' Laurie stiffened and strained away from him. 'You're not still mad at me, honey, are you?'

'No, Don,' she said, lowering her eyes wearily, 'I'm not mad at you. I'm not mad at anyone anymore.'

'Have a drink, sweetie—'

'Yes,' she said, sounding a bit reckless, 'yes, I think I will—a large one. Why don't we all get drunk? I mean, it's a long way to Tipperary, isn't it?' she added on a note of absolute irrelevancy as she took Don's own glass and swung it in a high wide arc before lifting it to her lips.

Again, the same sense of precious delicious isolation came upon Riley, descending like an invisible sheath between him and everyone and everything else. He beheld Laurie with a vague pang of regret and remorse, seeing her colour heighten and her eyes peculiarly glow as she drank with a kind of grim hysterical gaiety and determination, giving her attention now almost totally to Don, laughing too loudly and readily at his wisecracks, tossing her head back carelessly, quickly joining others in random conversation, nodding avidly in agreement or smilingly dissenting, waving her hands in front of her giddily, a strange transient lustre about her, a certain quivering glow that might go out at any moment like drapes being suddenly drawn over a lighted window. But it was impossible for him now to dwell overly long upon her or anything else in that room; or to notice that they had moved off together, his arm around her shoulder, towards the door. He felt marvellously insubstantial, transparent, rootless, free of anything that would hold him in any one place, free of ordinary ties, affinities, recognitions; he did not feel committed to a single thing, thought, emotion, his mind passed lightly over all things like a wind, hardly touching, going where it pleased, where it wanted to go in its serene idleness, a clean bright receptacle for every sound, taste, touch, scent, movement, for all the tentative innumerable shades of sensation abroad in the room.

Everything drew him to a sensuous conclusion, poised precariously on the thin edge of a tremendous climax unlike anything he had previously known, guiding him with sure intimate fingers to the verge of his own cognition. The rainbowed shafts of light flashed like frenzied asterisks in front of his eyes, the music mounted to a peculiar triumph, rushing through him like water, like air, like sunlight, streaming joyously through him, rendering him concussed with the force of his ecstatic response. He visioned himself then, mesmerised, monkey-like, goblin-like, staring with mad shining eyes into the very solar core of that blinding impossible light, his veins incandescent as glow-worms singing their way through him, alone and insignificant in all that galaxy of nerve, noise and furore, curiously expectant, waiting for something, knowing if he did not concentrate all of himself on the expectancy, the waiting, it would pass him in a single solitary beat of a pulse.

And then, somehow, absurdly yet predictably, he was outside in the night, on a balcony or veranda, a poppy-field of stars overhead, a plain of moist glistening grass below, the black and silver silhouettes of trees against the sky, the breeze passing lightly over his face, and someone close beside him.

'You sort of passed out, I think,' she said. She bent to peer at her luminous wrist-watch. 'Almost two.' A pause. 'How do you feel, kiddo?' The windows behind still blazed, yellow rectangles of noise and babel music, a blurred throng of shapes and shadows crossing and re-crossing, the hyena noises of people, a demented beehive of clamour, opulence, a thousand trees madly shaking their arms, banging their palms against a thousand shuttered panes. The row and commotion inside his head began to roar again, began to grind and pound with a grim incessant savage rhythm, and he held his temples imploringly.

'Are you okay?' she asked, her voice a little frightened.

He heard himself talk. 'Yes, I'm okay.'

A little silence slumbered between them, and he thought he heard the moon whisper something, but it might have been a bird meditating on some distant branch, or she may have been speaking quietly for a while before he heard her words.

'Let me take you back,' said Abbie, her fingers cool on his hand. 'My car is just down the driveway.'

'Yes,' he said, letting her help him to his feet.

They went down some moon-washed steps on to a silvery beach of gravel, her arm entwined with his, the frail scent of her hair making him want to cry out brokenly like a spent exhausted child full of a nameless need.

VII

Only gradually did it become apparent that summer was merging very finely into autumn. The mornings were still bright and the birds still gave promise, the evenings still took a long time to yawn away into night; it was something in between, somewhere in the slow hours of the afternoon that something was taking place, a shadow lengthening across the narrow street, creeping across the room, the dressing-table overflowing with scent bottles, combs, tubes of cream, jars of lotion, clips, hair bands and other paraphernalia of feminine cosmetic mystique, a subtly moving shadow filling the room more each day, dulling the reflections in the mirror.

Earlier now the street lights would be switched on, invisible against the day. The solitary tree that could be seen from the window was daily shedding its leaves, a crinkling yellow confetti spreading in the gutters, a tired querulous breeze lifting them listlessly over the cobblestones like a convalescent child bored with its playthings. Looking up one such day from the typewriter, reaching for a fresh sheet of foolscap, his eye idly wandered to that tree, gnarled and twisted as if with palsy, rooted in concrete, still gallantly growing in the dank shade of an alleyway between an impecunious coffee shop and a disused Methodist mission hall, and with a shock of sad recognition Riley knew that the long torpid summer was at last wearing the last of her finery, a gracious lady putting the last of her make-up on, making the best of her fading charms in a final farewell.

The same would be happening in city parks and wooded ways, the leaves piling up in thick mounds at the foot of trees, the bark cracked and withering, peeling in dry scales, sap gone, the grass arid and brittle, stiff-veined, snapping like burnt matches under the heedless feet of children gambolling in their summer-long sojourn away from the classroom, too young to observe the seasonal signs of passing into shorter more sombre days. The signs would be there, too, he reflected, in the quiet leafy avenues of Randalswood, the strangely haunting smell of burning leaves and wood-smoke, the people down on the beach would be fewer and quieter, the sea would have a graver look on it, a dull bronzed leaden look, and only an occasional sailing boat would dip languidly on the horizon.

He guessed that with the last of summer Midge would go for long pensive strolls in the quieter parts of the town, Cricket lumbering sleepily after her, sniffing the hard dry earth, ears touching the ground, and maybe she would gather a hail of marigolds on the way home to put in her blue-papered room, her sun-brown sandalled feet scratched and dusty.

The days seemed to brush past him with faster pulse, the leaves to fall and swirl with greater momentum. In the Square the pigeons were as numerous and arrogant as ever, strutting boldly around the feet of the gnarled bony-fisted old men forever moving stone pieces on stone chessboards, oblivious to any change taking place in the trees overhead. It was strange to wake near dawn in that room above the narrow street and hear the first nervous twittering of birds in the stillness, strange to imagine that they could still sing and be heard above the perennial din and ferment of human entanglement, the squeal of traffic, the wail of trombone or clarinet from the dark belly of clubs that never closed, the staccato beat of bongo drums, the jangled jibing of steel guitars plucked in twanging themes of melancholy. He was grateful for the other music heard most clearly and sweetly at dawn.

He seemed to wake earlier, trying to keep still, sometimes wishing he was alone, by himself in his own bed, no matter where, not to have to think of anyone at all beside him. It was agony at times, holding himself rigid, coiled up in an intense stillness, eyes burning from want of sleep, hearing her quiet breathing next to him in the dark. He would twitch convulsively as her hand or shoulder or leg touched him, stirring in her sleep, and draw stealthily away to the far side of the bed as to a refuge; he ached from forcing himself to remain in certain unobtrusive positions, damp with sweat, perhaps drawn up in a foetal stance, chin touching bony kneecaps, arms vice-like over legs, brutally willing his body into iron-clad obedience. She would sometimes turn, half awake, and ask in a sleep-hushed voice if he was all right, if he was comfortable or wanted anything, and tumble back into easy slumber again before he could croak a mumbled assurance in reply. The sheer unfamiliarity of sharing a bed night-long with someone grew inside him like a baleful neurosis, turning what should have been a pleasure and luxury into a nightly marathon of nervous endurance and physical ill-ease. She slept so soundly, it seemed once she closed her eyes she sailed blissfully away into oblivion, leaving him wide awake and restless, painfully alert in every bone and muscle to the innumerable creaking sounds of night, ruefully contrasting all that he had heard and read about carnal love in the great poems and novels of every age with what he was now feeling, the furtive movement timed with the cunning of a thief to the last hypersensitive second, the maddening betrayal of the mattress creaking beneath him as he strove stoically to edge a further inch away from the girl sleeping sublimely beside him, the linen clinging damply to his stiff aching limbs, flinching as she groped with her fingers, murmuring wordlessly, her throat thick with sleep. The night thronged with the poetical lies of centuries, the perfumed untruths of millions of lovers unwilling to admit even to themselves the harsher truth that the ache and pain of love was not exclusively of the heart, but more of the mundane muscle and sinew, the claustrophobia outwitting the euphoria in the end.

Sometimes, when he wanted to work at night, she would sleep in the tiny boxroom at the back, which held a bunk-bed, only a drape covering the doorway between, and he was guiltily aware of the loud banging of the typewriter keys, knowing she might have to rise early to meet a special assignment and leave long before he had stumbled awake, having written himself into exhaustion and feeling doubly ashamed at having had the bed all to himself. He would sit around all day in a kind of musing torpor, hardly glancing out the window, now and then making desultory notes in a school jotter on ideas for the next chapter, making frequent forays into the brandy that always seemed to be on hand, waiting for her return from work in the evening, incredibly chirpy, coming into the untidy cluttered-up room like a fresh sea breeze, animated and vivacious, hugging him happily and asking what sort of day he had had, if he had thought about her at all or had been too busy on the novel to indulge in such unprofitable fantasies. At such times her liveliness was unanswerable; it swept through the room, blowing away whatever grey cobwebs the long day might have gathered, wildly exciting him, yet often leaving him bewildered, resentful, long schooled in lonely hours pounding the typewriter into metallic creaking revolt, only in the pauses and interstices thinking of her and anticipating with a quick lurch of pleasure the hour when she would come back to him from the tremendous bedevilled bedlam of the city, overladen with groceries and the usual battery of cameras slung around her shoulders and neck.

She never again asked to read what he had written. Instead, she would stand wistfully at a little distance, hands behind back, like a child looking at flowers which she longed to touch, timorous of making the request, waiting to be invited, eager, expectant, and having held out long enough he would tell her to pick up the bloody pages and read, while he stretched the tired length of himself out on the couch and drank the remainder of the brandy, meanwhile observing with sly comfort the tell-tale shape of the new bottle she had picked up in the liquor store across the street, the grocery bags sagging on the table. After reading it, she would start getting supper ready, making inconsequential conversation, relating small incidents of her working day, what she had done, and where, the people she had met; after supper, she would lapse into a pensive mood, carefully turning things over in her mind, face dreamy, eyes large, unfocused, fingers idly touching a button in her blouse. When she did begin it was again with the almost gauche uncertainty and hesitancy of a young girl wanting to ask and find out things, things that puzzled and intrigued her to the point of wifely or at any rate sisterly concern, patiently waiting to be told things, given answers, explained to, enlightened. It would have been comfortably easy to conclude that she was merely being meretricious for effect, playing the urchin-type ingénue, appealing to the more tender feelings of the protective male, aiming at the peacock pride in him; she was, after all, quite a worldly woman in every sense, not at all a virginal novice newly released from a nunnery, but perfectly capable, assured, intelligent, wise, self-mocking, no panting female waiting and willing to be devoured by male flattery, He did not know what she was or might seem to others; he only knew her as she was to him, and in that she was utterly devoid of pretence, the hard glitter of feminine beguilement and adroit sleight-of-eye coyness, the feline shrewdness camouflaged behind expertly simpering Botticelli lips, serene and bucolic inanity brazenly deriding the possibility of a man's sensibility and insight.

At times her naivety infuriated him, her puzzled confusion over certain sentences and paragraphs, diffused meanings, the chronology and interplay of events, she was at once more than willing to accept what he explained to her, deferring to what she deemed his better judgment, yet never letting subside a point of view that she earnestly held, returning with calm insistence and a grave half-smile upon her face to certain things in the script that continued to elude and harass her imagination. When she was at last satisfied, once these certain things were resolved in her mind at length, her eyes would give him thanks, at odd moments she would clap her hands together happily in a way simple and spontaneous. In contrast to the doubts ever swarming in his mind, those evenings with her in that room above the wakening night streets gave him a delicious mandarin feeling of wisdom, dissipated only when the brandy had gone and another new day had to be confronted alone.

He learned to recognise the sounds that each day brought, hardly pausing from the typewriter, so familiar did these become for him. A toilet being flushed, a door shutting with a strange definitive finality, stairs creaking, footsteps on the landing outside, a transistor blaring distantly, a hard masculine cough, the cat-like banshee meowing of an infant, a fine spray of enraged Italian maledictions from the basement, sourly answered in guttural bulldog German, a flash of brown fur in the scalded leaping of a dog out of a window followed by a boot thrown by unseen hand in vociferous exasperation, the crash of a bottle in the tiny concrete courtyard at the back of the building. And smells, too, some strange and exotic to his nostrils. Pungent, savoury, some smelling of the sea and remote magical lands he had encountered in books; peppers, spices, olives, cinnamon, cloves, clear and sharp, rancid, acrid, full of an alien acidity, making insulting sallies upon his sensitivities. He grew to know and identify these sounds and odours and sometimes try to create fantasies for each of them, to imagine the separate little worlds to which they each belonged, the chance or deliberate human acts, foibles, inclinations that delivered them each day, and how strange that he should be there to discover and know them.

It had always been so with him; he had never considered houses as merely square, oblong, variously shaped boxes inhabited by people, but as individual creatures in their own right, the walls, floors, carpets, furniture, every object they housed, all redolent with the known or unknown personality of their possessors, each quirk, liking, susceptibility of the persons living there expressed in varying shades, stamped on the choice of object, or conversely on the lack of it, whether it was in shape, colour, tone, in the way these things were arranged or, as it might be, studiously not arranged, a vase of flowers half in shadow against a window, rugs patterned or plain making meaningful angles and cross-angles on bare boards, a lampshade tilted slightly at an oblique or pronounced slant, sparse naked twigs in a jam-jar oddly eloquent against a pale lemon wall, even the manner in which a curtain was hung so that it swayed on a certain way . . . he saw all of these things as private statements, individual portrayals of aspects of the characters living in these houses, whether by chance or design, deliberate or accidental, forming a mosaic often as diverse and as complex as the minds spinning dreams, fantasies, aspirations and conspiracies large and small within these walls. Everything drew into itself something of the people living with it, so that a certain chair, a bed, a table, ashtray, cushion, even a single cup or glass, became strangely imbued with the uniqueness of somebody, became identifiable and almost synonymous with a certain person, and on entering a room the eye was unerringly drawn to the whereabouts of a particular object and the person associated in the mind with it and the multitudinous patterns of associations springing from it.

He remembered his delight in reading Dickens, of being literally transported into a room, smelling old leather, old volumes, home-made punch, high collars crisp and starched, feeling the warmth of loquacious log fires, the marvellous sense of being there in the midst of what the author was describing, seeing these things, the reflections in gleaming brass and copper pots, in dark mahogany headboards, the sheen of crisp fresh fruit clustered in a wooden bowl, each lovingly and meticulously painted, so that objects were not merely incidental, not merely used as background padding, but were felt as well as observed and suffused with a life of their own, integral to the story as the human characters portrayed in it. He would enter a room with Dickens and see everything in it as the writer saw it, and knowing the room became paramount to knowing the people in it, the flavour of the room rose up from the printed pages as compellingly and unforgettably as the mannerisms and incongruities of the characters themselves crowding in all their bountiful shapes and disguises through countless midnights making his own skeletal little room warm and magical against the cold cat-haunted night outside, filling it with the illusion of companionship.

This room did not have the solidity that Dickens imparted, lacked any sense of identification; everything seemed to be in a state of impermanency, with large wooden crates stacked high against the walls, some unopened, travel-bags still bulging with her personal belongings, random pieces of bric-à-brac stuck here and there to relieve the musty unlived-in bareness, comical little African and Oriental statues in smooth ivory and oak, beasts and hunters, high priests and demigods malevolently grinning and glowering from the mantelshelf over the huge empty firegrate, standing on the windowsill and on top of the crates as if to ward off evil spirits and invoke chivalrous ones, large blown-up prints taped to the walls, all in black and white and all her own work, faces and buildings, landscapes and skies, the seasons of the year and the more unpredictable seasons of the mind captured in one form or another at odd unprepared moments and in moods from the pensive and sublime to the violent and destructive, drawn from her travels through the kaleidoscopic labyrinths of her own country to some of the least over-exposed fragmented impressions of Europe. These photographs were of necessity spontaneous and unrehearsed, taken as the eye had lighted upon the scenes depicted, yet a curious link or rhythm ran through them, observed with professional objectivity, but each seeming to contain a deep unstressed undercurrent of sadness, sensual and non-intellectual; the majority of her faces were of old people not in themselves sad, but somehow expressing the sad inevitability of men and women in their groping to understand each other and escape out of their own isolation, pictures too of no possible value to anyone any more, yet retaining a validity of their own, an aesthetic dignity that defied the abuse of time; the riff-raff harvest of things washed up by the tides, a battered boot, laceholes staring like scalded eyeless sockets; a dead seagull, wings rigid, straight back, stark against sand, holding all the lost adventure of air and sea; simple human footprints shadowed in sunset, toes and heels deep-running with a day-long joy, pursued by a faint other-shade of another sorrier time . . . such had Abbie caught, more often in moments of self-indulgence, to please only herself, to fit her mood of quiet facile suicidal flirtation, and these uncannily linked with the things she had been feeling at these moments, becoming statements of her mind and spirit. He saw that Abbie, too, had her own special way of looking into a mirror, her own way of finding things not for the casual eye, not for the world's seeing. These black and white statements on the walls were her own affirmations, not of life, nothing so pretentious, but of bits and pieces of herself as she happened to discover at lightning-flash moments, and as such were beautiful, if only because of their self-revealing honesty.

The camera was her palette, as the typewriter was his; she did not arrive at conclusions, she did not pursue them, for she saw nothing conclusive about sea and sky, wind and sand, cities, deserts, trees, children playing, old people dreaming; she saw nothing conclusive about any of these things, nor about love, which she plainly saw as ephemeral, ineffable, a seasonal thing, which made it, in her wistful questing eyes, all the more precious and remarkable, a constant phenomenon which any ordinary unremarkable day might wash up like the lost things on the shore. In these pictures Abbie was speaking to herself, making overtures of understanding with herself, engrossed as any artist in the intense solitude of his vision; that final taut pressure of the index finger upon the shutter, presaging the ultimate whirr of a caught instant, was merely the finite climax to an infinite sequence of observations, searchings, discoveries teeming in a lonely corner of the day or night, a dream minted from the same coinage as that springing to life in her mind, from somewhere in herself that she was forever finding and losing, a book opened at random upon a page she had not read before. Each picture said what she had meant it to say, while at the same time creating the impression of being subtly incomplete, inconclusive, and necessarily so, as if she had deliberately left many things unsaid, not as yet having found a tongue eloquent enough for the saying.

He spent many hours, temporarily resisting the typewriter, looking at these photographs haphazardly stuck on the walls of that sweetly paranoiac room, when she was absent, finding out small fragile things about her, guessing her moods when she took them, imagining her fantasies alone at dawn or sunset on a deserted New England shore or fey and restless and more than a little reckless in the dark night swarm of New York with its million pitiless eyes and gorged mouths everywhere engulfing her. These prints took the place of books, for whatever books she had were still wrapped and strapped in the crates, except for a few scattered around: novels of obviously Gothic nature, time-licked and well-fingered, giving off a secretive closed bedroom smell that somehow reminded him of candle-wax. Once, coming upon a red leather-bound edition of The Ingoldsby Legends at the musty bottom of a drawer, he was instantly reminded of a pot of bright yellow mustard, for no reason that he could remotely think of; looking down at that volume he could see quite vividly the mustard pot standing in a slanting streak of sunlight against a checkered backdrop, positively glowing, and for hours afterwards the image stayed in his mind before quietly glimmering away.

'I'm just a small-town hick with a camera,' was one of Abbie's favourite descriptions of herself, said not with any solemn self-deprecation but a nonchalant throwing up of her hands and a shrug of her shoulders—an impish piece of clowning, like so many of her gestures. Yet it never deceived him, for with her somewhat zany outpourings, her love for the fickle and extravagant, went a grace and unobtrusive wisdom that travelled far beyond the trivial and capricious, a way of looking out at the world beyond the current trend, the fashionable trinkets and tinsel of the passing pageantry of modes and manners. She may indeed have been as perilously unsure of herself as he was of himself, as much a victim and prey of her own passions and drives, and he instinctively knew that she could not be otherwise, yet she possessed and retained a range of discernment and rationality that he could never gain, a sense of balance, of perspective, of knowing herself to be quietly capable of coping with whatever large or small events, challenges, disasters that she might encounter through the course of any day. A thing, a creature of exquisite paradox she might be, and that delighted him, but she was also a steady light, an unwavering flame, unafraid to explore dark areas, squaring up to life with all the exuberance of a delicate yet pugnacious greyhound, eager for the fray, rippling with finely tuned strength, measuring with cool eye the distance between herself and the thing to be challenged, poised and agile, a smoothly oiled spring that could coil and uncoil itself with deft feline dexterity and readiness. She constantly reminded him of a gazelle on the edge of a wood, intent, inquisitive, ready to leap ahead into the clearing, graceful and joyous, seeing everything with dark delighted eyes, rounding on some unmet mystery of herself with insatiable pleasure, and if he by chance happened to lead her to such a mystery her pleasure and surprise surpassed anything that had gone before, opening up for both of them new things to speculate on and enthuse over, like children being presented with unexpected gifts.

They had both been grotesquely awkward when he had first moved in with her two months or so ago. On the surface they treated each other with tremendous aplomb, with a blasé sense of fun, facile and familiar, making every copybook gesture, saying easy undemanding things, as if they were two characters in a smart inconsequential novel, or playing out a meticulously scripted part aware all the time of the cameras whirling above them, careful not to shatter the prevailing make-believe cosiness that cocooned them with an injudicious word or movement. Underneath this thin sheen of assurance, both were violently flung about like trees caught in a sudden summer storm, almost pulled from their roots, shaken by forces outside themselves and nearly beyond the capacity of either to comprehend. It seemed that neither of them had had a prelude to anything remotely akin to all that they were feeling and experiencing then; they were totally unrehearsed, unprepared for each other, finding startlingly little common ground, groping towards each other like blind people, a terrible hollowness behind the fevered too-rapid flow of words which they flung between them desperately, a bridge hastily erected and doomed to collapse, having nothing stronger than a faint unformed hope to sustain it. She did not go out to work at all at first, perhaps thinking they would get to know each other better merely by being together uninterruptedly, which of course they failed to do; they merely succeeded in getting in each other's way, crossing paths too soon, in too great a hurry to adjust, to fit into the other's moods, fancies, whimsicalities. They jumped fences impetuously when they should have measured them carefully before attempting the take-off; in their eagerness they bumped into each other and came crashing down, often sore and shaken, to stare puzzled and pained across the littered distance between them, wondering what had brought the fall. So they would help each other up and set out again across the tricky terrain to reach one another, a little more cautiously each time, tentatively probing, advancing at a more measured pace, circling warily, learning to distinguish the real signs from those camouflaged and put up in haste. It was a tortuous process, almost a war of attrition, both of them having to exert themselves to the limits for every inch of understanding gained; often they would sit together, the room darkening with evening, hardly speaking, and the silence was not one of companionable knowledge, but nervous and strained, full of baited apprehension, little traitor thoughts that moved almost visibly between them, scurrying surreptitiously from one to the other, and she would lower the book or magazine she obviously was not reading, and look over at him with eyes that were hurt and baffled, and quickly he would dash from one meaningless pause to the next, not wanting to meet her eyes, not wanting to disclose himself as bewildered and lost as herself.

'How about going out tonight?' she might ask him brightly, standing irresolutely by the window, hands swinging behind her back.

'Oh, I don't think so,' would come his usual stock reply, clearing his throat. 'I'm trying to finish this damn chapter, you see, as soon as I can, for I've a great idea for the next . . .'

She would nod casually and turn away, leaning upon the windowsill, looking down at the comings and goings in the street and then across the sloping humpbacked rooftops to the silhouettes of buildings in the city haze beyond reddening in the sunset, her face and hair lit by it. She would remain so for quite some time, hardly stirring, and from behind in the room he would watch her, seeing how the fine outer strands of her hair seemed like blazing silk aureoling her head, the evening radiance enveloping her. She was very lovely then, and his fingers struck the keys of the typewriter blindly, his head swimming with her.

'How about a drink, kiddo?' she would propose at length, stretching herself, the movement that accentuated the shape of her neat firm breasts. She would bring out the bottle and they would drink and fence about a little, waiting for the old fallacious magic to work, and warmed by the brandy once more they would lower unknowing shields and talk a great deal about nothing in particular and laugh and exchange memories that neither of them wanted especially to hear or remember.

One such night had started almost exactly the same; he had been in a particularly fertile mood and had worked steadily all the afternoon and evening, finishing a chapter and instantly starting upon the next, only during brief pauses taking a quick quaff from the brandy bottle and, thus renewed and stimulated, plunging back again into print, his fingers a pale blue over the keyboard. Usually, he found it difficult to concentrate on writing when the day outside was alive with all the bright rustling and green airiness of summer; his mind would wander down the sunny spaces of the street and glimpse broad hillsides of blazing gorse and heather, and it seemed a crime of ingratitude, an obscenity almost, to remain shut up behind curtains, in a room full of chill semi-gloom, a lively restlessness eating inside him. He would chafe against the self-imposed régime that chained him to a cranking heap of iron that served merely to squirt out his turgid words like drops of sour milk from a grossly swollen udder. This day, though, he felt good; he was safe and immune from the blandishments of August beyond the window, sweating freely but almost unaware of it, in full cry of word and image, caught up once more in that furious breakneck chase, the brandy bottle beside him, almost an unremembered companion.

Abbie, in contrast to his own rather hysterical liveliness and nervous spontaneity, appeared tired and uncommonly dejected when she returned home that evening. It transpired an unexpected trip down to Boston accounted for her dispirited air; it had been a rush job, a special assignment which she could not reasonably refuse, and both the journey there and back and the extra time and work she had to get through in the small private dark-room she had in a drugstore downtown had combined to sap even her energy and leave her tired and a little on edge. She set out to cook something for him, telling him she had already eaten, but he did not relish the idea of food very much, so he left the typewriter resolutely and they sat together by the glowing window, he on a bubbling boil of words and she quite happy to hear them, resting her head against the side of the window frame, regarding him attentively.

He talked a great deal, about a motley of things, but returning again and again to the novel, telling her his quiet secret hopes for it, his frantic enthusiasm too often swamped by his glowering despair at judging it, the ecstatic possibility of writing that fabulously inconspicuous yet magical little three-letter word 'end' on the final page at a point in time he could still only wistfully imagine.

And then his talk became a torrent, like someone under hallucination, like someone dreaming aloud or drunk, half in love with everything in the world, with life, with death, all the sad foolish angry demented people in the world demanding morsels of immortality from the scraps of phantom talents, his mind quick and lavish on the high wind of his bombast, soaring, impatient at mundane stops and hindrances of speech, alive with images, shapes flashing and darkening before his eyes, gathering in the whirlpool centre of his brain and rushing out of his mouth. It did not matter that she listened, he was too feverishly engrossed in the words he was spinning to step aside and consider such a trivial thing, but she was listening, not taking her eyes from his face, as if she could see the things he now talked about and described; she sat like someone watching a film as a succession of pictures crowded and turned before her in a bewildering montage of colour and movement. The room sang and swam with his words, as though he were verbally reiterating all the thousands of words he had splashed upon hundreds of sheets of paper through a hail and haze of midnights, leaping from him now like a staccato stream of bullets.

He spoke with incredible quicksilver élan of sad improbable things, reaching out and touching the edge of things only half dreamed about in odd slippery rushes and shallows of time; of books fat and slender that still came back to him a newer and friendlier ghost, special friendships that had dwindled and grown less special as his mind grew sharper talons and ripped away all the comfortable and diverting masks from faces that were lamentably less candid than he had imagined, old wounds and hurts exhumed and dissected now in the amber-warm bravery of safe distances, the heart almost forgetting its many previous dyings in the remote soft lowering of eyes, the animal comfort and reassurance of bodies huddled together under a single fiercely fought-for blanket and a thin knife-edge glint of starlight piercing a slit in the faded cardinal-red curtain hurting his sleepless eyes with a hint of icy splendour, his mind drawn back over the shoals of memories dipping to catch a bright elusive school swimming swiftly under the murky surfaces of ordinary thought. He sat, face lit by the homeward-moving sun melting behind the broken landscape of rooftops and chimneys, his eyes mad, fanatical, gone on a voyage of their own, seeing other walls and beyond them, hearing in his voice the far echo of many another voice that had spoken to him of things he dared only contemplate in silence, things he assumed were somewhere in the world only as he assumed that he would one day die and pass out of it, and Abbie, sitting across from him, her face half in shadow, listening grave as a child to such tumbling turbulent talk from a craggy Celtic mount.

He stopped abruptly, as he would often do when rushing downstream on a flow of words machine-gunning from the typewriter, dazed, still hearing the crash of syllables tripping themselves up in his head, shooting behind his eyes, out of his skull. They were both silent now, Abbie with a look on her face like someone deafened by the noise of a carnival, waiting for the chairoplanes to stop whirling, the roller-coaster to slow down;

then she leaned forward and filled his glass. She held the bottle up to the light, shaking it slightly, knitting her brows in annoyance.

'Damn—we're out of plasma.' She got to her feet and slipped a scarf round her head. 'I'll nip down to Vino's on the corner.' She smiled back at him from the door. 'Don't fly off on those wings of yours.'

When she went he shook his head angrily, cursing himself for his sudden garrulous outburst, berating himself for bombarding her with such a weight of words, bludgeoning her as with a hammer; and also illogically blaming her for having listened like any ordinary docile household creature, letting him ramble on and gabble away, not interrupting once. He had acted like an idiot babbling animatedly away to himself in a padded cell, Narcissus-held in a pool of words, in an act of obscene self-attention, stripping himself verbally naked, caught up in a grotesque-comic gnomic jig to the crack of his own dervish-driven words, his tongue galloping away like a hare over-charged with adrenalin, chased by innumerable hounds. It was as if some nameless force had taken possession of him, bending him to its will, making him as helpless as a ventriloquist's dummy, jerked this way and that by one strident word after another tossed upon any chance shift and wind of thought that happened to sweep through his mind. He had made a parody of himself, a hapless sap of a harlequin strutting about on his own little makeshift stage in preposterous poses playing to an imaginary gallery of fellow fools rollicking with imbecilic glee. It seemed his life would go on being what it was, a long unending lesson unlearned, a ragged mocking rhythm that he would always limp after, trying frantically to step in tune and failing repeatedly, forever having his nose rubbed in the sawdust and tar. Turning to pick up his glass, he caught his reflection in the mirror of the wardrobe door that had swung open, saw his face blazing there like an angry cloud, hair lifting in forks of defiance, the pale intense blue eyes spitting out at the world and at the same time laughing derisively back at him. He flung back his head and emptied the glass without stopping.

Sensing his change of mood on her return, Abbie took off her scarf, shaking out her hair, and unwrapped the bottle. After refilling the glasses, she took a sip of hers, then sat cross-legged on the floor beside the portable record-player that lay on top of some unopened suitcases in a corner, rummaging through mounds of LPs to find the ones she wanted. After a little search, she drew a record from the pile and put it on; the needle scratched raggedly and stuck in a groove; she lifted it up delicately and put it down into its proper place. There came the sound of a guitar being plucked with a gentle, insistent, worrisome rhythm, slow, dreamy, meandering; then a man's voice, rusty, sandpapery, lifting above the plaintive guitar, words mumbling, lachrymose, as if he were trying to tell himself why he was feeling sad, scorned by his woman, hard done by, querulous with the world; the words struggled through, became clearer, defeating the singer's melancholy.

> Since my baby up and left me
> ain't nothin' to do but cry,
> since my baby up and left me
> ain't nothin' to do but cry.
> Well, if she don't come back and love me
> guess I'll just drink my drink and die.

He looked down at the narrow street below, beginning to darken with evening, to fill with people, neon signs flickering, taverns, cafés, night clubs advertising their wares, selling their wiles, promises of Nirvana, respite from daytime dilemmas, merrymaking till dawn; people moving in pairs, in tight convivial groups, laughing, chatting in intimate clusters, calling out and waving to friends, musicians, most of them seeming to be middle-aged and fat, in flamboyant garb, gaudy printed shirts open to the navel, patchwork trousers and straw hats, cigars stuck in their mouths, strolling to their one-night stands; people in love or on the breathless fringe of it, lovers of opposite or of the one gender, young men and women, young girls together, young men, holding hands, faces turned in to each other, some kissing in quick little bird-like flurries of affection, fingers fondling an arm, shoulder, haunch, buttock in coy familiar interplay; the raucous bark of a taxicab horn, the bleat of a police whistle somewhere, the first tentative squeaks and rumblings of night music that would last until dawn, when the street sparrows took over.

Inside the room, the melancholy man still sang.

My ever-lovin' woman says I'm just a man of straw,
yes, that ever-lovin' woman says I'm just a man of straw.
Well, if I can't satisfy that woman
guess I'll pack my old guitar and go to war.

From the shrill sounds it was emitting, the guitar was galloping into war, the enemy obviously the fingers that were plonking its heartstrings so harshly, the woebegone words forming the battleground over which it shrieked with such discordant disarray, flinging fusillades of vengeance in all directions. Through the banal and jerking beat, however, the voice held something, a coarse undulating defiance, mixed with the almost inarticulate pleading of a grown man for the love of his scornful mate; the simplicity of both rhythm and words, raw, unpolished, gratingly tender, swept away critical finickiness, and even as he winced fastidiously, Riley felt himself respond grudgingly, unwillingly, to the unashamed, unpretentious pathos of the song, the self-indulgent melancholy, the blues ingratiating itself, strong and clear as any line of poetry, as undeniable, a sad, recurring echo of near-comic carnality that ran through the crude uncouth theme. It seemed to say that the music of the blues did not belong endemically to the hot sultry climes of the Deep South; its voice was one of lament, of loss, and was heard and spoken everywhere, the poetry of dingy one-night hotel rooms, dank soulless alleyways, murky bars that never closed, filled with desolate desiccated people who never seemed to sleep, yet whose eyes never seemed to open save to squint at the remains in the penultimate bottle of bought oblivion, hopefully spinning it out until morning; the cellar music of people slouching in nocturnal procession through the clouded nowhere of their lives.

Abbie stirred as the record grated slowly to its finish. 'Makes me sad, that man,' she said, lifting the record off the revolving dial. 'His songs remind me of things, warm, beautiful, good things, coming to an end. I play him when I feel sad.' She turned the record over in her hands. 'Mind if I play the other side?'

'Go ahead,' he nodded, seeing how the little luminous green light from the player glowed in the deepening dusk of the room. 'Are you feeling sad now?'

She put the record on, squatting with her back to him. 'A little,' she said, stooping over, again guiding the needle into the right groove. 'You see, I know you're not in love with me.'

Her voice was calm, matter-of-fact, neutral almost, as she watched the slow swing of the needle, making sure it did not stick.

'You love me in a way, I know,' she went on, as the music started. 'Else you wouldn't be here. But I love my kid brother too. It's different from being in love.' She glanced at him quickly over her shoulder, smiling. 'Don't worry, kiddo. It's all right. I'm not going all intense on you.' She made a criss-cross sign over her left breast. 'I promise.'

She moved over on her behind, palms downward on the floor, until she was sitting facing him. She put the new bottle between them, reaching for his glass. Sitting in the chair, he looked down at her, seeing the fine dark level line of her brows, the slight uptilted angle of her nose, the small firm cleft in her chin.

'Happy days,' she toasted cheerfully. She rested the glass on her knee. 'Remember those young people of yesteryear, the ones who used to put flowers in their hair, beautiful young Messiah types, barefoot and meek? I wish I could be like that, preaching perfect love without possession, just wanting to give, not bothering about taking. Alas,' she said, sighing with mock intensity, 'I lack the true bohemian spirit—I find it damn hard to love and ask for nothing in return. Must be cosy to be able to do that—no hassle, no sweat, no hang-ups. Just a nice warm ever-loving feeling all over.'

It had grown dark outside; from over the way the neon light above Vino's liquor store flashed on and off, dancing garishly on the wall, playing on her face, giving it a weird unreal pallor. In the softer parts of the blues from the record-player, he could hear the electric hum of the city. He held his glass up to the window, seeing how the light flashed and broke in its amber depths, tiny bubbles bursting in minute brilliance, infinitesimal galaxies exploding as he shook the liquid to and fro with a slight turn of the wrist. The sky was very clear, a few early stars out and about, the moon coyly lifting a pale shoulder over the rooftops. Lights blazed suddenly in a top window of the house opposite; shadowy figures moving behind the yellow blinds, a man and woman coming together, arms reaching, hands groping, then abrupt darkness again. The record had reached its end and was once more making scraping noises, a shrill falsetto screech as the needle struck a certain point in the groove.

'Would you like Sibelius now—Finlandia?' said Abbie, putting her glass on the windowsill. 'Or perhaps the Pathétique?' She gave a quick laugh. 'Sorry—I'm getting maudlin now. Mustn't get maudlin.'

She put on some more records, different in style, old well-loved, well-played 45s from her high-school days, reminiscent of first dates, local hops, clean-shaven pink-chinned callow youths, girlish confidences and jealousies, Valentine cards wrapped in blue string from the unknown admirer with the pimples who sat across the aisle from her in class. Again, as with the photographs, she was revealing another side of her, shy, expectant of ordinary contentments, coveting the ordinary fulfilments of life, her head full of wishing, still believing in the good homely understood things that waited for her round the next corner. Her face was still very much that of a young girl, that other girl who used to spend her pocket-money on these adolescent hit records she was now playing, these simple nostalgic tunes of a day already out of vogue in the relentless onward stampede of the newest trend; it was still a hopeful young face, pert, piquant, not hidden or subtle in its changing expressions, instantly mirroring her moods, her thrill in things that fired her, day-to-day perplexities, contentions, challenges met with a defiant jut of her jaw and a brighter flash of eye. She was someone who would age very well, he thought, someone who would grow old without noticing it, without showing or feeling it, save for a little gasp of surprise a moment before the petals closed. She would always smell of lavender and leather, he thought with a slow invisible smile.

After the records had been put away, they sat staring out the window at the panoramic spread of the city glowing beyond the humming little habitats of Greenwich itself. His mind was clear, sharp-edged, perceptive. He would wait for the moon to rise higher, drift clear of the clouds floating like thick salmon in the sky; he would say things to the moon, converse with her with that silver eloquence that belonged uniquely to the night; he would wait for that moon.

The moon on this night was tardy and languid in its rising; it lay drowsing on the edge of the sky like a drugged sleeper. He waited, fondling his glass, aware of Abbie only by the smoke of her cigarette trailing grey-blue and snake-like from the oyster-shell ashtray on the rug beside her. Like eager centurions, the stars came to surround the moon, brandishing their slim silver spears, heralding her ascent, silver trumpets ablaze and blaring down the long teeming spaces of the night. He saw as through a finely coloured cloud, the fleecy contours of the clouds following their mistress as at last she rose slowly, rising higher, an imperious queen in a refined tantrum struggling to be free of such minnows as they trailed ignominiously after her. He waited. Slowly he felt the moon's cold tongue lick his cheek, slide into his mind sinuously, creep quietly along its shadowed canals. The cigarette-smoke trailed into his nostrils, disturbing, intruding, unwelcome.

Abbie lifted her glass, emptied it, looked obliquely up at him, the green-and-amber glow of the neon light streaking across her face. 'Au revoir, Riley,' she said in a whisper. 'Good night.' He felt the barest touch of her lips on his forehead, ineffable as the moonlight itself, and she had gone.

The moonlight crackled like ice, blinding, bringing each shadow alive, mobile, delicately sinister, full of brooding and subtle menace. It held him in idolatry, enveloped him in a gleaming cocoon, sealing his senses to whatever else might be abroad in the night; he no longer heard the night sounds of the house as it settled down to sleep, doors opening and closing discreetly, the hollow flush of drains, the metallic click of light-switches being snapped off. These things no longer intruded, were no longer even flickering on the edge of his consciousness; he sat by the open window, listening to the moon sibilantly whispering to him, attentive as any beguiled lover, willingly succumbing to such sly witchcraft, knowing the danger in the lure that was now pulling him with such irresistible siren music, yet surrendering himself wholly to the moon, slipping into the dance with her, the mad demented dance of deliverance from the meaner little dyings of every day.

His mind went off on a spin, lurching out towards where the moon danced in the middle of the sky, impossibly distant, yet as near and known as the back of his hand. He sat in the chair by the window, rigid, hands gripping the sides, hearing now inside himself the same low humming noise that had filled the moonlight a moment before, a long deep intake of breath moving him on an unending upward spiral, without pause, swirling like fumes of insane incense in the cells of his brain; he sat, witless and lost, the moonlight sweeping through him as though he were made of glass, and still in all the wildness and clamour of that satanic dance his thoughts lay quiet as leaves on the dry bed of a ditch harboured and safe from the wind, hardly stirring. The music of the dance thundered on around him, mad and besotted, loud with loquacious lust, silver-sandalled, forgetful of earth in every sweep of starry limb, every dying echo of ribald gaiety, nudging him into merciful unreason that fell in a fine shower upon his spirit. Witless and lost he sat, the night shielding him, the moon pouring her silver caskets of wine into him, dancing famous and free behind his spellbound eyes. The stars, like minor supporting players, retreated into the background, waiting in the wings for the cue that would never come, Salome having the stage to herself, consumed with her own captivation, reaching for his soul with her glittering talons.

Abruptly, the face in the sky became distorted and ugly with pain as the clouds stretched forth their arms, striking in fury like gnarled twisted branches of trees, drawing smears of dark blood across it in black bedizened murder, revenging the slight that the moon had cast upon them as she rose in the dance; she sank beneath the marauding horde of clouds, smothering, drowning in a deep dark pond, her death-rattle filling the night, her dance ended grotesquely, her siren call turned to a low sobbing wail that fell to steely silence down the broken promontories of the sky. The moon died in the very shudder of her ecstasy and triumph.

Riley stared into the blackness that was left, stunned by such a monumental carnage, then through a viscous opening in the vast obscuring wall of cloud, a dazzling stretch of strand came shining, spinning far out over the horizon, and beyond lay deep dense turquoise water, brightly burning like the eyes of a woman in a fixed stare of desire. A wet trail of footprints zigzagged up from the edge of the shore, breaking the creamy smoothness of sand; he saw these footprints quite clearly, and they had the same slight shock of vague regret and mysteriousness at discovering, in a place otherwise utterly deserted, signs, traces, remnants of human presence, of someone having been there and leaving behind them a small inconsequential testimony of their existence, a token of their having been on earth. These tell-tale footprints, scrambling towards nowhere, told him things of other lives, sad, wistful, foreshadowed things; buried little intimacies, conclusions that were never reached, dreams followed and never found, tongues thick with the honey of lies, tripping over in the heat of love lest the bright moment should pass and no love gained, promises hotly made and never kept, broken as lightly as twigs, smooth reasons given for deceit and accepted with a bland indifferent closing of eyes, the loosening of fingers that once held fabled lures, dropping limply away from past fantasies, a quiet word that ended a life's long hope, spoken on a butterfly afternoon heavy with wine and the hot stones of the earth, and a hawk static in the stillness shimmering overhead, wings barely stirring, casting a shadow, waiting.

The magical strip of lonely strand in the sky merged at the drooping and lifting of an eyelid with the garish light-splashed street below the window, and the moon, not entirely vanquished, left a lingering scent of her behind in the room. It lay white and still, upon the bed, a fine dark fern-like cloud hovering above it, a long white flame perfectly coiled upon the sheet, breathing quietly, watching him, and as the moon had drawn him before, he found himself rising from the window, his mind clear and full of light, rising and moving calmly towards the flame, the white cool flame lying upon the bed, moving towards where Abbie lay, waiting.

And he waited too, drawn to the edge of a high cloud, waited even as he went forward into the flame, brave and foolhardy, entered into the cool deep heart of the flame quietly singing and crying, moving into its soft voluptuous scouring depths with a splendid sense of dying, and in there all was reverence and dusk and silence as in a chapel at evening, full of hollow re-echoings of past worshippers, the candletips of past penitents flaring in the sepulchral gloom above the set, severely serene faces of half-glimpsed half-mad saints and young virgins raising alabaster palms in dewy supplication; in there all was incense and beeswax, cool sequestered aisles and side-chapels mysterious, inviting, full of a strange repose, fold upon fold of new peacefulness opening up for him, receiving him with a profound lethargic generosity, opening and softly closing veil after veil, lifting secret lattices into lost forlorn desires, drawing him deeper into the flame, brushing past him like a light early evening breeze over a white lake with the long unknown promise of night sweeping underneath it.

And he waited, hardly breathing, for the thing to happen, the thing he had no name for, the thing that lay coiled inside the flame, folded inwards like the deep red heart of a rose, waiting for the petals to burst asunder, to shoot outwards buoyant and bountiful, for the flood of scent to gush forward from the sweet blushing pods prodded into wakefulness; the incense rose strong in his nostrils, a musky smell, lying on his senses with a certain insubstantial heaviness, a raincloud passing low over his mind, dark and swollen with secret pollen, passing over him with slow meaningful oddly menacing intent, and the faint taste of grape on his tongue slowly beginning to ooze its rich blood, a precious birth in no unseemly haste to begin, pulsating under a petal, and his ears hearing the distant sea-lion roar of the waves drawing ever closer with a slow imperceptible imperturbable pace, a rhymed rhythm that grew in volume with measured momentum, deliberate as the thrust of grass through earth. It was as if the moon had never died, flooding through him again, cold and new and young, destructive and fantastic, indomitable in her ice-calm loveliness, offering him everything the night had ever held, every hidden hoard of nameless riches, all kinds of largesse, every shade and tone of lust, every charm, jewel, emblem, artifice, condiment, every glittering vanity to taunt and tantalise; the moon offered all, save herself, ever beyond his keeping, unreachable as true beauty shall ever remain, touching his servile senses and blinding him with her cold fire, but forever untouchable and inaccessible to the dust and dross of himself. He halted, captive as ever, again drawn on an upward-turning spiral of breath, and stared into nothing and nowhere with vast incomprehension, waiting with the same fanatic intentness, waiting for the least sound or faintest fall of leaf, as in the silence of a wood at the dark intense edge of dawn, waiting for a single sound to startle the world into light.

A faint almost unfelt flame began to lick along his marrow, a sharp furry tongue of flame, insistent, tentative, needle-pointed, arrowing its way along his spine, dying down, flaring, subsiding, each time glowing brighter, gem-like, more intense, imperative, but slow, purposeful, precise; it fanned out unhurriedly, forking through him, touching with its hard hot tongue secret sensitive areas new to such exquisite probing, exposing, opening up, infiltrating. He looked at this flame with immense surprise and curiosity as it grew in him, his thoughts gathering and buzzing around it like a swarm of inquisitive insatiable fireflies irresistibly drawn to its light, seeing it make its flarepath-way throughout him, lengthening and pursuing its own way independent of him, a hard metallic glow now heightening, looming, igniting more and more of him as it spread busily, touching him strangely, uniquely, biting deep; it widened, broke, became a river coursing bright and broad in him, molten, flowing swift and deep, rushing and thinning abruptly to a dark furious channelled inlet, gathered to a boiling pitch of walled-in intensity, threatening, treacherous, thundering in his head, sweeping him up, tossing him into a storm-cloud that sucked him in and seemed never to let him go, whirling him endlessly about in its tight airless fury.

A moaning sound came from somewhere inside the flame that he knew now held him in its cold brilliant mercy. It lasted but a moment, then he lay in a strange ease, stretched to the length of himself, locked in the long curving flame that anointed his limbs in an abundance of charity, moving over him with cool sisterly compassion, kissing his rapt staring eyes, his set unyielding mouth, his bird-thin chest, downward to the soft hidden hollow of his navel, hard brittle tip of tongue licking and burrowing industriously along the marble fold of his hip into his groin, small cold ferret teeth nibbling at his inept acquiescent flesh, and long slab-cold arms holding him in a rainbow, jealous of the moon never leaving his eyes and the silver poison of it sliding about in his brain.

He rose abruptly on a high swell, weightless, to come down softly upon the shore, and it was no longer cold, no longer dispassionately solicitous; it was burning to the touch, moving restlessly underneath him, covering him with his heat, drawing him down into itself, creeping along his limbs, over his thin taut buttocks, under his armpits, its heat searing into him, bringing no false ease any longer, no illusory lassitude, but a pulse-leaping urgency, a tremendous haste, a blaze of sudden knowledge that surged from him with the swiftness of impetuous steeds; the soft shore parted under him into a deep haven opening to receive him in a homecoming that seemed never to have ended.

Yet, like a merciless surveyor standing at an unbridgable distance, he looked on at this frantic involvement, this abandonment of limbs tossing upon the sheets, as if intently watching some outside performance, something separate and unattached to himself, noting carefully each groping, spasmodic movement, each wild gyration that brought the two participants nearer the edge of that total eclipse of the senses towards which they pulled each other, as though embroiled in deadly combat, a sophisticated exercise of attrition quite void of felicity or mutual concern. It was as if a live vital current had gone through him and been drawn out, leaving him blighted, nerveless, enervated, capable of a certain implacable detachment in the very midst of such upheaval; he felt her fingers touching, guiding, stroking into response, felt her come with tremulous impatience nearer the onrush of her release, yet when it came, that release, that ecstasy was quite exclusive from him, it was an intensely private thing that cast him almost literally away from her, making him more than ever a spectator, someone who merely happened to be there in that same moment with her, never sharing the moment, never knowing the insideness of her bliss and hardly touched by it, save only as one is touched by a passing summer wind hot with sand and the pungent brine of distant waves. Nothing lived for him in that ultimate moment, the flame had turned cold again, cold as the tongue of the moon that had given him the mocking patronising kiss of deceit; he felt the pain of his own latecoming release merely with a slight surprise, an irrelevant postscript to what had gone before, a thin trickle of brief comfort seeping unwillingly from his body in a tired display of male bravado, an anaemic after-thought of imagined joy fizzling damply out in a dank cavern of his brain. Nothing lived or had relevance for him in that moment, except the peculiar shape of the remotely swaying curtains, the bright circular gleam of the oyster-shell ashtray burning in a square of moonlight on the floor, a frail ring of smoke still rising from it, and her arms limply falling away from him.

The pillow felt deathly chill against the back of his neck when he lay back down again, down from the height he had too briefly climbed, but full of a relief he had not known a moment ago, back inside himself once again, in bleak but sure possession of himself, again filled with an intense desire to be alone, wrapped invisibly against even the tenderest intrusion, in the swarm or the stillness of his own thoughts whether they assailed or consoled him. This, then, was the only truth he had as yet come upon, his undeniable wish to be alone, and it was becoming fiercer than any gravitational pull others might hold for him, stronger than any fanciful longing for the company of others, for the wise or foolish words of other people, for the slavish reassurance of their fidelity and understanding which he had frantically tried and finally failed to convince himself he sought and needed; to be prepared to know and yet be free of others might well be the only triumph, as it might also well be the only tragedy, worth knowing, if out of it came the acceptance of others as well as of oneself.

He had played with the idea of wanting to be understood; it had been an intriguing and at moments an ingenious game, full of certain set rules demanding skill and perseverance and a quick willingness to deceive everyone involved in the game at their covert behest, something that inevitably meant the deceiving of oneself, and he had not so much lost the game as given it up in despair of ever learning to play it well enough to win. The understanding of others was not abhorrent so much as irrelevant to him; he had never really taken other people into consideration, he had never really thought deeply about them, and had mostly seen them as somewhat unreal and insubstantial figures moving around him, each locked within their separate identity, making gestures meaningful only to themselves, gestures that only incidentally might make some slight sense or achieve some tenuous contact with others, but gestures that remained intrinsically self-meaningful and rooted in the life-long journey into oneself. He saw others precisely as he saw himself, in the irremovable uniform of one's skin, a cap, a glove of which one might take off, a button or pocket of which one might open, but out of the whole of which it was impossible to step without risk of mortal injury or the more horrible process of slow disintegration as one became fragmented and swallowed up in the lives of others. He reflected with some amused dismay that he had almost certainly never said a meaningful or significant thing to anyone in his life, had never spoken once out of total forgetfulness of himself or taken part in an act that had not eventually led back to himself to his own pride or disgust. And he was not fooled by this inexorable and intolerable narcissistic obsession that stained and coloured his every thought; it was a demon he knew quite intimately, a monster that drew breath every moment he himself did, one with himself, with his brain, blood, bone, that lived in the shadow of his fear and in the occasional shining of his hope; it was not something that lived furtively inside him, creeping out at dark unguarded moments, but a live thing that was with him at all times, waking and sleeping, dwelling behind his eyes, in his mind, in his guts, hovering behind every word spoken or written; he himself was his demon, and his demon himself.

The lugubrious truth of it made him smile balefully in the moon-splashed darkness now, made him remember all the things that he had not said to people, the single word or sentence that might have strung together some chain of meaning for someone, that might have brought brief welcome on a day of failed promise, that might have given reason to even the most irretrievably lost cause, all of these words not merely held back, but simply unsaid because unthought-of, unvisited in his mind. He could not even tell himself that he was lonely; he could no longer use that deception on himself, for if indeed he was ever lonely he was aware of it only in a vague peripheral way, as a slight ache, a slight self-indulgent burp, parading his loneliness like a poet trotting out bright and dark images, grandiloquently commiserating with himself and his splendid solitude, finding much pride in that he was lonelier than anyone else on earth, lonely and misunderstood, an original misfit, finding solace only from the determination that he would make a good and fabulous thing out of his loneliness, fill it with truth like any ardent anchorite fasting himself into glory.

Himself was his demon, his demon himself. It might have been a line from a particularly atrocious poem, one of his own half-baked arid pieces of inspired mediocrity culled from the thick gluey soup of indigestible thought that lay on his mind and which he somehow rather daringly managed to pass off as intelligence. No, he could not tell himself he was lonely; it could even be that he had never been really lonely in his life, not with that awful bite of total separation that made one physically sick and each new day brought its apportioned quota of nausea. Like everything else with which he surrounded himself, his loneliness sprang merely from self-indulgence, from a desire for ostentation even as he hid behind a mask; it was so with his writing, all those unscalable mountains of words he had set out to climb and conquer, the endless spate of words filling endless pages, pyramid after pyramid, festooning his life with words like sickening strangulating foliage, choking whatever small life they might once have held and sustained, erecting a bamboo maze of words from behind which he peeped fearfully out at life like a moribund half-blind creature jerking quickly back into the shadows whenever too much light penetrated. He had built himself a snare in which he was slowly strangling, and this positive genius for self-destruction had spilled over into the ordinary avenues of his existence, bringing with it this curse for emotionless scrutiny and analysis that spread like gangrene through the most intimate encounters and relationships that he had come to know, spoiling the wine even as he put it to his lips. His kind of deliberate isolation was not brave; it was shoddy, scornful, arrogant, pretentious, wilful, and ultimately an act of the utmost cowardice.

Her fingers on his shoulder startled him a little, bringing back the room, the faintly swaying curtain, the gleaming ashtray, the slight ferny feel of her hair on the pillow next to him.

'Riley,' she whispered, her voice seeming to come from inside his head, softly as an oiled lock-spring. It seemed as though he had been asleep for many hours, asleep in an ocean of moonlight flowing over and beneath him, the touch of her fingers waking him at last. The room and everything in it had now an unfamiliar feel, almost alien, like passing out in a drunken or epileptic seizure and waking up somewhere completely unknown, high walls soaring off into nowhere, windows full of hard hurtful light, sheets that lie upon the skin like cold chains. He lay without saying anything for some moments, almost without thinking, absurdly trying to recall where he had been, where the night had gone without him, how many nights had passed, had slipped obscurely and obliquely by like a shawled veiled woman on a clandestine rendezvous with a lover under a dark arbour of cloud; he felt like some victim of amnesia, some voyager not knowing his own name stumbling ashore after crossing uncharted continents and seas, feeling the sharp savage stones under his feet, the claws of the wind cutting across his cheeks, drawing blood. He drew breath, sucking air into his lungs and chest, praying it would not stop half way; mercifully it did not, the numbness in him began to dissolve. Her words dropped dully into his mind.

'You cried out her name,' said Abbie, very softly, her fingers lying like thin slivers of ice on him. 'In the very last moment of all, you cried out her name.'

He lay there beside her, greatly puzzled, thrown into a new enigma, thinking how strange it all was, for he had not thought about Laurie at all for several days now, not a solitary thought, as if he had finally written the last chapter of his book and could not remember a single line of it.

The twisted tree on the other side of the street, seldom escaping from the shadowy clutches of the alleyway, appeared to be bearing some kind of strange improbable fruit, little yellowish clusters of blossom that were in some places greyish-dull, as if the senile thing was developing dandruff. It splashed these signs of second childhood proudly against its permanent background of wastrel gloom, proclaiming with dignity and a touching eloquence that life was not ashamed to visit such broken impoverished unregarded things as itself, that it was still capable of hanging out its own faded finery in defiant celebration of itself, its past beauty, or what substituted for beauty in that place of stone and semi-daylight, now congealed into hardihood, but the seasonal sap not entirely gone from its withered veins. Seeing the ragged little tatters of colour blooming against the sombre wall of the alleyway like matches flaring in a curtained room, Riley felt a sort of reverence for the mystery of all growing and decaying things: there was something unkillable about life that constantly defied and delighted the mind and made curious music in the most obdurate heart.

It did not make him feel any sanctimonious humility or arrive at any profound conclusions about his own smallness and insignificance in comparison to nature, which he preferred not to spell with a capital letter; rather, watching that old underprivileged tree from the front window of Abbie's two-roomed quarters, as it struggled with difficult birth in old age, he felt part of that unique process, part of that growth of life in such marvellous defiance of the forces that would strangle it; it made him see, hear, touch, taste and smell the growth of things in the world, and more especially those things that had to fight to survive and attain dignity, deformed diseased dilapidated undefeated things growing tenaciously and with odd beautiful perversity in noisome condemned forgotten back places of living, shunned by fingers that might otherwise have cared, trampled underfoot by men and beasts alike, half alive, yet refusing to die wholly, clinging to whatever meagre morsel of earth that sustained them, glimmering through the dark that was always theirs.

It fascinated him, that tree, pushing up out of its concrete bed, bent over like a palsied old woman, head bare in all weathers, lifting up its cracked dried hands not in entreaty but in glee, not in search of alms, but offering instead its own pathetic yet proud evidence of promise; he would often look up, baffled and furious as he sought for and fought for words to match his teeming racing thoughts, and his anger would evaporate at the brave spectacle on the other side of the street, the tree contemptuous of the stupid asphalt that held her imprisoned, flinging her few specks of blossom into the air gaily, frolicking with death, almost croaking in its face, an indomitable old woman lifting her skirts in the dance, determined to have her fling, to bow out with her threadbare shawl flung high and a few faithful lingering flowers in her hair. He would gaze at it for a long time, its very shabbiness delighting and cheering him, and the tree would give him something of its own spirit, forcing new light into his mind, and murmuring thanks as to an old and trusted friend, captive as he was, yet free, he would return to the typewriter renewed and ready for the battle once more.

That particular battle, too, was nearing its end; he was working on the chapter before the last, and he approached the end of his book not with the sense of overwhelming relief that he had assured himself he would feel, but with a strange foreboding, confused and irresolute, like stepping from a ship he had come to know well into an unfamiliar land, with no clear signs as to his whereabouts or guidelines to the future landscape. He could not remember now when he had not been working on the book—when it had not claimed his mind completely, when he had not woken each day with it looming like a predatory eagle over him and fallen finally to bed with it at night drunk with pride and satisfaction or weak with the despair of knowing he had failed to compose a single articulate paragraph throughout the preceding hours, that he had sat slumped in apathy or rigid with villainous anger when the words would not come, when they had reared back like strong-willed recalcitrant thoroughbreds on their leash and refused to come charging at his command, answering his insolence with their own. The book had gone through a bewildering succession of moods: from compliant mistress to tantalising whore, from cheerful companion to deceitful friend, from brave resilient comrade-in-arms to implacable enemy, from someone with cool wine and honeyed raisins in her hands to a sharp-fanged night-bitch who shredded his skin in a fury of insatiable demand, howling down the night at him, mocking his impotency, his feeble efforts to please her.

It was a farewell that he was strangely reluctant to make, like someone who, having grown accustomed to the rack, would not be able to walk upright without it. It would leave him without a feeling of guts in his belly, it would leave him useless as a scarecrow shaken by the merest wind keeping watch over an empty field, robbing the day of significance and turning the night into a thing of febrile fulminations, making life as appetising as a bowl of cold porridge. He had lived with it for so long, in such turbulent coexistence, not to have it there any longer would be like becoming wifeless, being bereft of someone who had held everything together, someone forever urging him on almost past his own endurance, seeing in him the better things he had not yet discovered or shown, exerting a precarious tyranny over him, infuriating, dictatorial, intensely vindicated and all-knowing. He felt only a sense of impending bereavement, almost of amputation, as if he were losing a physical part of himself that would leave him permanently dismembered, with a great gaping hole somewhere, like a window left unshut letting in a cold biting draught. To think of there being other books inside him waiting to be written was immensely unthinkable; it was like telling a newly widowed man that there were other wives waiting to be wooed and wedded, more tempestuous, passionate, intriguing, challenging. It was as if the book, far from being finished and put aside by him, was in fact abandoning and discarding him, jilting him like an inconstant lover, leaving him to contemplate life without her with fear, indecision and helpless lost hunger.

It was something other than summer that was coming to an end, then, and something other than the book itself, which seemed to have taken a little lifetime to write, but which he concluded, when he thought about it, had taken in fact less than two years from the unremembered, unremarkable day when he had put the first sentence to paper in that other time under a greyer factory-smoke sky, to where he now found himself beside the open window in that hump-backed claustrophobic room in Greenwich Village, on an afternoon like all the others, the sun still going strongly like a boxer finding an extra spurt of stamina before the final round, the nasal accents that were still strange-sounding to his ears coming from the street below, the ancient tree of classless origin at the mouth of the gloomy alleyway tossing its sparse spangle of blossom on the heavy sulphurous city breeze. An entire chapter in his life was drawing to a close, and he did not yet understand the real significance of it, could not discern its portents or evaluate what it might mean or how it might shape whatever other chapters might follow, if the colour and shade of it might permanently touch the remainder of his days. It was all too alive and immediate now to be coolly looked at and examined with anything save a distinctly jaundiced eye; he was too close to the eye of the microscope, the objects were too near, in too great proximity, and everything loomed larger than whatever future life they might hold and retain, like passing through a hall of magical mirrors where every shape assumed alarming proportions and gave back distorted horrendous reflections dwarfing the slight transient reality of the moment.

He approached the future with the peculiar indescribable sadness that somehow attaches itself to railway stations, airports, docks and other places of leavetaking, already forming weak ineffectual farewells in his mind, already seeing himself make the usual inane gestures, stunted at their very birth, having the penultimate drink, talking about stupendously irrelevant things, all the while eyes drawn implacably to clocks and watches, hounded hellishly by a vague indefinable and largely absurd sense of impending doom, words miserably failing to describe the heart's furore, lost in the very ordinariness of love, the precious commonplaceness of loving so rarely met in all the great love-poems and majestic novels of love, the sheer hard-working fabric of people loving the best in each other, rubbing shoulders with the little adversities of living together, wanting always to stay as one, and wishing many millions of times to be apart, busy with one's own quite separate self and life, thinking it treachery to own such thoughts, yet knowing such thoughts to be there inside one as real as one's guts. So he approached the end of his little lifetime of a book, its end and the end of something as yet indefinable in his mind, some alchemy that was quite removed from people, from both Laurie and Abbie or anyone else that had entered his life on that strange side of time, a parting from something within himself, which he alone would in time come to recognise, both a lack and a gain, though he could not tell now how much or how much less of either. He was as certain of this unnameable ending as he was that one day he would die, and it was as equally quiet and undramatic, yet as final and inescapable, as much of a definition and a conclusion as the room in which he now sat. There were so few real points of impact in life, he thought idly, putting a new sheet of paper into the typewriter, one made very little real impact on others, either by what one did, or said, or dreamed. In all the thousands of words he had spewed forth in an orgy of mental vomiting, he wondered if a single particle of himself had escaped in the deluge. He doubted it, and that doubt made him smile at the labour of self-love so uselessly lost. Life, he lugubriously concluded on that quite ordinary afternoon, moved relentlessly towards one terrible or magical little word that stared people in the face every hour of their existence under sun or moon, in love or forever out of it: end. He looked up and saw, appropriately enough, that the sunset had begun. The feeling of farewell deepened.

At times, in the evening, sitting across from him, ironing maybe, or valiantly trying to sew the heel of one of his socks, or with a magazine lying spread out but unread on her lap, Abbie would gaze at him in silence, her face puzzled, confused and concerned, as if always on the point of asking him a question, balancing the need to ask against his possible reluctance or inability to answer; something in her look spoke also of her own uncertainty as to what exactly she wanted to know, what words she could use in the asking. He sensed this urge in her, this need to ask him something, and he would become terribly restless, distracted to the point of irritation, his always precarious tide of thoughts thrown about, his forever mercurial concentration pulled in quite an opposite direction by a very different current. He always worked better when alone; in that sense he missed Randalswood, missed its green leafy isolation, its undisturbed, ordered hours, the long spaces of the day and night when he could be alone, the activity of family life elsewhere in the house hardly obtruding, hardly even existent when he would be alone in the quiet bedroom over the lawn facing the beach and the sleepy-lidded ocean. There, it had always seemed absolutely natural for him to work at night and have the broad sunny day for the quiet hours on the beach; his hours had been very neatly demarcated and divided up, save for the unusually convivial yet neighbourly quiet weekend. He had not felt any sense of guilt or remorse then, working through the night hours, no fear that others would be disturbed by his own owl-like energy and the click-clack of the typewriter, that sweet outrageous sound; there had been an exclusiveness about his room, a delicious sense of seclusion, cocooned there behind the heavy drapes, the heavy carpeting muffling most sounds, like working behind soundproofed walls. Here, above the narrow cobblestones, it was so weirdly different; footsteps everywhere, late into the night, making a clamour of morning itself, both inside and outside the house, and even in the occasional stillness there brooded the suggestion of the city, never sleeping, making even the windless summer night restless with slow ceaseless humming, the insidious invading droning coming from an unquiet beehive, having something of the ocean in it, the subtle rise and fall of human waves, human breathing, lifting, subsiding, stirring in animal unison, the metropolis coiled in the night like a huge many-headed monster that never quite lapsed into oblivion.

Here he felt obliged to work by day, for even when she went into the little boxroom he knew that Abbie must hear the iron clanging of the typewriter through the thin anaemic walls, a sound that neither exhaustion nor brandy could quite subdue, and the knowledge of her lying tired in there, listless and awake came down like a sluice-gate between the run of his thoughts and the worrisome sense of disturbing her hard-earned sleep, blocking his mind in midstream, slowing it down to a thin careful controlled trickle, so that he tried to strike the typing keys less violently, trying almost to caress them so as to make them spring lightly on to the paper, an endeavour defeated before it began, for the printing would not impress itself sufficiently upon the page, coming out merely as weak pallid squiggles, and he would have to push the carriage of the machine several spaces back and begin over again, hitting the keys with unnecessary vigour out of anger, frustration and ill-mannered recklessness. And he would pause more and more often to lift the brandy bottle to his lips, attempting to blur the edges of his conscience at the thought of her behind the cardboard walls, jerked from slumber by the stupid clamour of him writing his wild idiotic fantasies down on paper, trying to dull with brandy his concern and guilt at having woken her through a superfluous excess of energy, arrogantly assuming it all to be in the cause of creativity, these questing pathetic gropings of his hooded hounded consciousness.

So he tried instead to work through the day, when she was at work, trying to shut out the noise of the street and the city below, the ceaseless thuds and bangs of the house, trying to ignore the hard sunshine spilling into the room, mocking his attempts at seclusion. He felt like a nocturnal creature brutally ousted from the safe cosy darkness of his lair, flying blinded and in panic here and there, scorched and blistered by the hot searing daylight, a helpless eyeless bat-like thing crashing into things at every turn, crying in weak futile rage, flying aimlessly about the cage-like room fearful of the terrible devouring light of ordinary day. Mostly these were arid hours when seldom a single thought would come cleanly to him, hot, perspiring, horribly on edge, his nerves a shrill screaming uproar inside him, flinging the page from the typewriter, mangling it into shreds, throwing it into the little plastic blue wastebasket that Abbie had provided, throwing it anywhere, putting a new sheet in, staring at it malevolently as if it were an implacable foe, an adversary that must be destroyed, drumming his clenched fists upon his knees, dashing a wrist across his burning eyes, pushing back his chair with a squealing sound, groping for his crutches, hoisting himself to his feet and stumbling towards the small nutbrown cabinet in search of another bottle of amber comfort. There would follow a quiet hour of marvellous calm, sitting side-buttocked on the windowsill looking down into the street and laughing almost audibly at the passing scene, having sometimes to stifle a mad urge to lift his fingers and beckon someone, anyone, up from the street to share his brittle hour of madness and indifference, but no eyes lifted, no eyes saw him and his wild dark sunset face at the window, the bottle flashing in his hand, and the moment of solitary elation would pass, and there would only be the stunted blighted broken tree to nod wanly back at him, perhaps the only thing which knew something of his own voiceless defiance, understood a single throb of the force that made him propel himself forward and not lie still and acquiescent even when it would perhaps have been wise and propitious to do so.

Abbie sat one evening, a little shaded in a far corner of the room, curled up in the one large armchair, absently rubbing her fingernails with an emery stick, looking at him often with the same puzzled expression, a glass of brandy almost untouched on the floor beside her. There was a coiled subdued restlessness about her that affected him strangely, he was acutely aware of her eyes behind him, staring with child wonder over the fingernails that she was absently smoothing, and he banged the keyboard with such nervous impatience that some petals trembled and fell from the roses that she had put in a bowl on the sill, drooping with a faint unheard little moan to the floor to lie curled forlornly on the carpet under the window.

During one of his many deliberate and pretentious pauses she spoke, tentative, unsure, clearing her throat a little.

'How is it going—your work?'

He acted casually, as if he had not quite heard. 'What? Oh, that. I don't know, I don't think about it much.' He stopped, flicking the switch, and the machine went dead. 'I'm just filling up the pages, that's all. It's a relief getting to the end of each page. A long agony, getting each page filled up. Like crossing several little deserts time after time.'

'Is that all?' she said, surprised, a little shocked.

'Sometimes I think that's all.'

'But it isn't really?' she said, wanting to be reassured.

'Yes,' he said with tremendous gravity, staring sorrowfully down at the several mushroom clusters of pages on the floor around him, 'sometimes it really is all.'

'But that's awful!' she exclaimed, fumbling for her drink, taking a hasty sip. 'I don't ask you much about it, because you never seem to want to tell me, but—don't you believe in what you're doing?'

'Oh, I believe in it, all right,' he told her with heavy sardonic irony, 'as much as I believe in anything.'

She did not immediately speak. 'That's what I really mean, I guess,' she said slowly. 'You don't believe in much, do you? What are you afraid of, Riley?'

'Afraid of?' he echoed hollowly, picking up his own glass from somewhere, dreading what might come, the things that might be said, the answers he could not give her, not knowing them himself.

'Afraid, yes,' she pursued, thoughtful now. 'Why are you afraid to give of yourself, to respond, if only in spite of yourself? Why do you hold back from people, even in the simplest things? What is it that makes you afraid to come out into an open space—what is it that you fear? Is it love—not only to be loved, but to be expected to love because you yourself are loved?' Abbie stopped a moment, smiling wryly though unabashed at her own forthright questioning. 'Forgive the sudden

247

inquisition, but I really would like to know just what it is that makes you tick—I'm afraid I am not very good at enigmas.'

'Is that how you see me—as an enigma?' he asked sourly, as if somehow offended, as though she had just placed him in a rather objectionable category of beings.

'I'm sorry, but how else am I to see you? You're not exactly an open-and-shut case, after all. I don't believe in getting to know people overnight, but I don't believe either that it should necessarily take a lifetime to get to know another person at least beyond calling each other Harry or Joe or Sally or whatever the case may be—' She smiled again rather desperately and took another quick sip. 'That might sound rather extreme to you, but it's not all that far off the mark, all things considered. I feel that I hardly know you one little bit, Riley. Please don't stop me speaking,' she added in the same breath, choking a little on her drink. 'Like you with the writing, I find it hard to stop talking when I get started, even though it's all hot air, but there really are some things I think I should like to know, things that I feel I am entitled to know, without coming on all heavy and demanding—' Abbie was talking quite rapidly, almost breathlessly, taking imaginary sips of her drink, for she was hardly touching it now except with her lips, her words and sentences tumbling over each other in her great anxiety to say what was in her mind, to get it said if only for her own sake, her own private ease of something that was sorely confounding her and which she obviously had been confronting personally for some time. 'Would you think it was very stupid of me if I was to ask you if you were happy?'

She asked it with a sort of reckless gaiety, cocking her head to one side, lifting one eloquent eyebrow, a funny doll-like look of enquiry on her face, a sad terrible coyness that she deliberately drew about her, playing a straw-headed marionette, all the more cruelly pathetic because the playing was so obvious. And she put such intentness into the pause as she waited for his answer, curled shell-wise in the chair, wearing as she did occasionally a skirt instead of the jeans, her good-looking legs in dark hose curled beneath her, a touchingly elaborate picture of comic wistfulness as if she was posing with a clear certain purpose in front of one of her own cameras, a caught

248

stillness in the very act and gesture of expectancy, waiting for his answer.

He drank quite slowly, drank until he had emptied his glass, this time missing the familiar spread of warmth in his guts, as if it was milk, moving his tongue around in his mouth, trying to catch a faint aftertaste of that glow, and finding none. He leaned forward, placing the glass carefully on the windowsill, the few lingering drops clinging to the sides catching the sunset, gleaming sharply, playing back upon the glass, casting a twin minute glitter upon his irises. He thought of all the rooms there in that single street, high, long, wide, cramped as this one, or empty, ringing or silent, full of the sun at this last point of its reign, already darkening with the odd threatening presence of night; of the people living or half-living in those rooms, going through the paces of their existence, bored, hoping, adventurous in the midst of the ordinary and routine, making a miniature Eden out of potted plants, heirs to strange separate legacies of goodwill, suspicion, optimism that found its greatest strength in the dark, despair throwing its shadow over every small stirring of hope; so many people in so many places, so many moods, so many cages, without keys, without adroit formulas for the living of each day, without romance and the lure of the unexpected, voyaging through the neon nights and days on a stationary journey, looking up one day to find only the sadness and futility of themselves staring back at them from eyes that once held all that the world had ever known of love, and trust, and quiet conviction in a future not bound by dull caution.

He looked at Abbie then, having so many of these things in her, so much of these people, prepared to fight for the right and the folly to believe, pugnacious and vulnerable, eyes steady and expectant under level brows, waiting for his answer with a calmness that excluded doubt, and suddenly he felt much older than she, incredibly beyond her age and the stubborn expectations of it, felt older, empty, dry as a leaf in October, as if he had lived a whole lifetime through the summer that was burning itself out in the stunted brave tree across the street, in the parks and avenues of the city, in the bramble lanes and heathery hillsides of the country, a whole lifetime encompassing everything he had been and imagined himself to be, reaching a full stop at that moment, in that room, the end of something quietly momentous which he had failed to understand, the end of desire before he had allowed himself to touch it and lose himself in it and be driven mad and happily demented by it, with no mental holds barred, no clever reservations put into cold storage to be used on the day of delusion, the day of disgruntled reckoning.

'It's a brave question to ask, Abbie,' he said, heedless of the moments that had lapsed, 'and I have no brave answer to give you.'

'But don't you *want* to be happy?' she asked, bewildered and refusing to be denied some positive reply. 'My God, Riley, don't you?'

'I don't know what I want,' he answered, tightening his thin knuckles and noticing how they whitened. 'When I know what I want, then perhaps I'll start to be happy.'

'You'll never be happy, Riley, if you won't let yourself be,' she then said, a considerable sadness in her voice. 'I'm not talking about us, about you and me—that never got off the ground, you wouldn't let it, but never mind—and I'm not talking about Laurie Emerson—I like her, and I still don't know how you feel about her, but I imagine it is much the same as it is with us. I'm talking about you, Riley, in what regard you hold yourself, from what angle you look at yourself.' She gazed at the drink in her hand for some moments before lifting it delicately to her lips and sipping, holding the liquid on her tongue a while before swallowing. 'I've read what you've been writing, and I don't understand many things in it, but from what I've read you seem to be making out that we are all prisoners of ourselves and none of us can find the key to escape. That's true, of course, but there are different keys to different locks, and no prisoner has ever escaped without trying, without looking around for the chance to slip out of his cell.'

He stooped and gathered up a handful of pages from the floor, letting them slip though his fingers with a sound of crisp leaves. 'You think this is a book of no hope, then?' he asked with a gentle edge of self-mockery. 'You think it is all night and no morning?' He let the last page drop back to the floor.

'I don't think you have reached morning yet,' she replied.

'When you do, I'd like to be there, but I guess I won't be, so won't you please tell me, wherever we both are?'

'I think you will know,' he said, 'perhaps before I know myself.'

Abbie smiled and raised her brows meditatively. 'Maybe, but let me know anyway, in case the telepathy isn't working that day.'

She uncurled herself from the chair and came across, swinging the bottle casually in her hand, refilling his glass. She sat on the sill, facing him, her faint smile holding something that he could not readily define, and he thought how very well she must know him.

'I'm happy the book is nearly over, kiddo,' she said, the setting sun full behind her casting a slight shadow upon her face, making her eyes seem darker, more luminous. 'I'm glad that this is one good thing that's come to an end.'

She went to the side of the room where the records were heaped, and knelt down. 'Do you mind?'

He shook his head and muttered something, finding it strangely difficult to form words.

He had the soft lightsome smell of turf in his nostrils, heard rain beating in a familiar tattoo upon stiff yellowing grass, upon the dark murky sluggish waters of festering canals, beating upon asphalt and windowpanes, stinging his skin like pine-needles, sweeping in twisted white sheets down thin deserted roads, streaming past flaring lamps like a hail of fire-flies; he heard the rusty clang of gates being kicked open, banging against the small stone garden wall, hobnailed boots upon the path, a bicycle thrown against the bushes, the hard querulous scraping and groping of the key in the front-door lock . . . the wind tore through his thin jersey high on the pithead, slapped his cheeks like the palms of a spiteful woman, bringing winter tears to his eyes, and he opened his mouth hungrily and sucked in great gulps of the bitter wind down deep into his lungs, feeling it cold and strong and life-giving inside him; the wild staring yellow eyes of little famished houses beamed balefully in the howling mouth of night, and hunched women hidden in shawls shoved their weary weight home through the black guts of the town, mumbling maledictions on their sodden men as they pushed black prams with wizened pukey little children grimly before them as if trying to wrench their own unwanted flesh away from them . . . a penny flung high into the air turning and turning over and flashing to earth like a fallen star, and the black snake of leather swishing and flailing thin bony cold-blue shins in a wide savage swathe and faces swimming in a frantic arc to see who had the poker gods favoured this time . . . the smell of faded old cleanly ironed linen and new bread and hot milk and the hot heavy sickly-sweet baby smell everywhere . . .

The sun had glided away, and he knew it would be turning the East River to fiery liquid bronze about then, and the Greenwich sky was very blue and tinged with palest turquoise at the edges, and Abbie was playing her favourite blues song, sitting on the floor beside the record-player, her arms twined round her knees, eyes closed, head drooping a little backward.

I've got nothin' left to give, man. I ain't got nothin'
left to sell,
no, I've got nothin' left to give, man, Lord I ain't
got nothin' left to sell,
since my honey-coloured woman, she up and said
farewell . . .

The needle had stuck in a groove once more, and the melancholy singer was unbearably repeating himself.

VIII

Already it was yesterday, and the sea seemed to hold another voice, one that spoke to him with a well-known tongue. It seemed to move differently, too, with a slower, more deliberate, purposeful movement gradually swelling to a fine familiar pitch, like a musical composition turning with marvellous precision to its preordained finale. He felt this cool completion communicate itself to him and grow surely inside him with a deep rhythm and flow, filling him, wine being poured into a vessel, spreading serenely over his senses. The sea was a new person now, no longer a stranger met on another shore under a vaguely alien sky, but someone intimately known, definite, definable, trusted, saying eloquent gentle things to his mind, muted, yet clear, concise, saying quiet inevitable things, in music rather than words, calming whatever lingering fever might remain in him, waving him homeward across time, across the many subtle and indomitable barriers which that other time had held for him, so that the waves held a new breath, a different meaning, lapping his mind on that last day as he sat at the great spacious windows overlooking the ocean, the waves like huge white sea-lions sporting on the drenched seaweed-coloured rocks far below, a distant commotion in his heart.

There were a few other couples in the long timber-built dining-room of the seafront hotel, eating Maine oysters, sipping wine, talking in easy whispers, taking no notice of him whatever as he sat at the table by the window overhanging the ocean, vaguely wondering what was delaying Laurie; she had left to get his manuscript from the car in order to read the final chapters over a light meal and a bottle of wine or two. The large red stationwagon was parked just a few yards from the front entrance, and it seemed she had been gone quite some time; no doubt the sunset had proved too great a lure and she had stopped to gaze out across the craggy headland to where sea and sky glittered, caught in the fierce conflagration of evening. He looked down with some amusement at the immaculate pair of stiff white cuffs that extended from the sleeves of his jacket, smiling a little as he felt the unfamiliar rub of the shirt collar against his throat, and fingered his neat sober tie with a slight sense of awkward surprise. The seafood lay uneasily in his stomach, as if still afloat, the rather insipid wine hardly aiding either his digestion or his appetite; he longed for the sterner stuff of brandy, but decided decorum dictated it was still too early in the evening to start on that particularly familiar journey. So he sat in his freshly laundered suit, shirt, collar and tie, sternly undrunk, sipping tasteless wine, listening to the ocean, knowing already it was yesterday.

Hardly a single firmly shaped thought obtruded into his mood of lethargic ambivalence; the things in the room were noted and passed over, assimilated easily into the context of the present without inner comment, hardly without relation to each other, so that each retained a singular identity observed in suspended isolation. Everything appeared to be made of a dull reddish wood; from ceiling to floor, a deep mahogany broken occasionally by a lighter grain of timber, giving back something of the setting sky, a dark rose hue settling like a patina over everything; the toilet doors had simple respective signs of His and Hers on them, and unlike the rest, were of plain milky wood. Whenever the doors of the huge kitchen swung open and shut he could see great gleaming enamel cauldrons emitting hissing clouds of steam, and white-smocked cooks wearing enormous cocked hats scurrying about like frantic rabbits; the smells that came sweeping out with the swinging back and forth of the doors were a mixture of brine and, most improbably, cabbage water tinged with other indefinable odours which his imagination played with idly. The waiters all seemed to have gigolo moustaches, large brown puppydog eyes and Mediterranean accents and mannerisms that went rather strangely in that setting of Maine and Vermont pinewood, the one reassuring and indigenous figure being a waitress with a voluptuously virginal presence and matching proportions who bent rather recklessly over tables serving and taking down orders, revealing beneath her trim abbreviated skirt a flash of bare white thigh above black hose.

He beheld this glimpse of a seemingly unstormed citadel with a curiously jaundiced eye, hearing the girl's horsey giggle that sounded more of an obese belly-laugh, and seeing the ostentatious tossing of her black mane of hair as she passed, the heat of the kitchen draining her skin of all outdoor liveliness. Whenever the waitress passed his table he somehow caught the odour, not of the sea, but of dark back-alleys smelling of rotten fish, the fetid stench of feline heat, and her yellowish liverish eyes sprayed him with a look of feline contempt despite the set plastic smile on her mouth. She, too, along with the wine, did nothing for his palate. The disconcerting sound of the piped music was almost mercifully drowned above the loud sighing of the waves, as was the drone of the air-conditioning, the fans whirring noiselessly high up on the walls. He poked the soggy pieces of shrimp on his plate indifferently with his fork, glowering rather balefully at the wine still largely untouched in his glass; he had the sensation of being at a Neptunian funeral feast and eating the remains of murdered guests. He put aside fork and plate and leaned on one elbow, chin in hand, fingering the stiff bristle under his lower lip, letting the sunset print burning orbs on his eyes which blazed into brilliance when he blinked and pressed the lids down. He was about to succumb and beckon over the thigh-flashing viperish-eyed waitress and order brandy, when Laurie quietly came back and sat down facing him, putting the thick green folder on the table.

He might have imagined it, it might just as easily have been a sly cosmetic trick of the ultimate blaze of the sun striking across their table, but he thought there were slight green circles as of exhaustion round her eyes, and tighter lines of shadows about her lips, which showed a mere trace of pinkness; otherwise, she appeared as composed as ever, her beauty as austere, impeccable, almost severe to the point of being glacial, save for the warm quick curiosity that lit her eyes and face whenever a thought or an object or person arrested her attention, and at such times she seemed happy and very willing to put aside all safeguards of composure and poise and be animated by whatever it might be that held her mind.

She wore a simple plain lemon jacket, open at her throat, and matching pleated skirt that showed her smooth knees and marvellously curved legs sheathed in pale coffee-coloured hose. He doubted if ever he would meet a more gracious woman, having a beauty that would deepen and flower more delicately with age. He felt strangely restful in her presence, all the previous unease refined now to a gentle unobtrusive throb of peace.

She smiled as she peeled off her gloves finger by finger and folded them neatly on the table. 'I hope you're not disappointed with my choice of rendezvous?' she said, lifting one hand absently to touch her earring, in the shape of a serpent with an emerald head. 'I've been here once or twice before. Nothing very spectacular, I'll grant, except the view—I thought you might like that.'

'It's very beautiful,' he readily agreed, turning once more to look out.

'I thought it might remind you of Ireland,' she commented, then laughed. 'Was that very foolish of me? After all, there was no mention at all of any sea or coastline or beach in your first book, and there's no earthly reason why you should share my own fixation about the sea—'

'No reason,' he said, 'except that I do. Even in the concrete-and-tar thoroughfares of the city I have my dreams of the sea, hearing it above the traffic, at peace or at war with itself, but never still, never dead, always affirming life.'

'I can see you, when you become a rich and famous author,' said Laurie, 'living in a cottage by the sea, a little fishing village perhaps, full of masts and hulls and sails, going down to the pier to gossip with the local fishermen, having a drink in the pub, which will be an old timber tavern full of cobwebs with stuffed whales and dolphins hanging over the bar, then back to write yet another famous book—preferably by gaslight, though that wouldn't be practical, would it?'

'You paint a pretty picture,' he mused. 'I can even hear old John Masefield in the background telling us how he must go down to the sea again, the lonely sea and the sky.'

She was silent for a few moments. 'What shall we drink to,

Riley?' she asked, studying her folded hands. 'I'd like us to drink to something, together.'

He in turn was silent, then he spotted the imposing-looking waitress hovering nearby, an empty tray under her arm, absently yet suggestively fingering a button on the front of her overloaded tunic blouse.

'If we're going to drink to anything,' he said, feeling oddly and pleasantly masterful, as if firmly precluding any argument, 'let's do it properly.' He looked round at the waitress, holding his head in a consciously commanding way, silently calling her to the table.

'Brandy?' Laurie enquired in a conspiratorial voice.

'Nothing but,' he replied, still telepathically commanding the waitress to spring to attention, who remained obstinately staring in front of her, fingering that tantalising button.

Laurie smiled, seeing his intent. 'You won't catch her eye that way, dear,' she told him with maddening feminine logic. 'Look at her, that look on her face, full of amour, dreaming of one of these terribly Latin olive-skinned waiters, no doubt—'

Just then, as though vindicating his belief in his own silent power of attraction, or more likely merely because she felt she was under discussion, the waitress turned her eyes lazily in his direction, her full lips curling slightly in an ill-disguised scowl as she saw that her services were demanded. She sauntered towards them, tapping the tray rhythmically against her arrogant hip.

'You called, sir?' she said automatically, her voice heavy with Southern sultriness, her eyes flicking to Laurie, surreptitiously measuring her and the supposed clandestine situation up and down, her lip quivering openly now in a greater scowl as she took out pencil and notebook from her hip pocket, wetting the tip of the lead with her fat moist tongue.

Riley, his transitory feeling of mastery now rapidly evaporating before such sheer marvellous effrontery, ordered quickly, covering his confusion by diving at the menu, scanning the liquor list hastily for the most expensive and impressive-sounding choice, ordering a whole bottle, the girl scribbling it down still with the same face on her, and he sighed in audible relief as she swaggered away, the motion of her shoulders and buttocks somehow conveying the same peculiar contempt more eloquently than her look.

Laurie almost clapped her hands together in delight. 'Isn't she terrific!' she said, leaning happily forward. 'Such superb native arrogance! Odd, all the interesting characters one meets purely by chance. I sometimes feel I ought to keep a notebook everywhere I go, just in case, making quick little pen sketches of various people.' She sighed, spreading out her hands in a slight gesture of resignation. 'I guess that comes of being a frustrated writer. You don't need to resort to such amateurish tactics—you just soak them into that brain of yours, like taking pictures with a camera.' She stopped a moment, looking across at him steadily. 'Speaking of cameras—how is Abbie?'

'Very well, the last time I saw her,' he answered evenly, the casual mention of her name bringing a certain constriction in the general region of his chest.

'A sweet girl,' said Laurie, making patterns on the table-cloth with her fork. 'I never really blamed you for falling for her.' She took a deep breath. 'It hurt when you left to stay with her—it hurt more than a bit, but I couldn't really blame you. Randalswood must have seemed pretty dull to you, one large slice of suburbia—it was apt to stick in your throat. The Village must have seemed the ultimate in excitement after it.'

'It wasn't excitement I needed,' he said, after a pause.

The sun had sunk gradually, lying on the horizon like a burning half-crown, lighting the side of her hair turned towards the window with a warm bronzed glow.

'What was it you needed, Riley?' Laurie asked softly. 'I could never quite make out.'

'Probably nothing very important or unusual,' he told her.

'Whatever it was, I hope you found it,' she said, 'though somehow I don't think you did. Maybe it's better that way, since you'll go on looking, and therefore writing. Life is a thing of commas, rather than full stops.' She stopped a second, and then smiled. 'How very profound! I must have culled that from the agony columns of Good Housekeeping.' She passed a hand over her eyes. 'I'm feeling ridiculously sentimental and weepy, the way I used to get when I became pregnant.' She took her hand away and smiled again. 'Alas, I'm not, though Don and I often toyed with the idea—one more for the road, so to speak, but I think we're both too selfish and too securely entrenched in our little suburban niche to risk anything so adventurous.'

She spoke calmly, as though to a friend over afternoon tea, or casually across a garden hedge on a fine afternoon, with light unstressed inflections, yet with a determined, deliberate detachment that moved him more than if she had been quietly crying. She was far from being merely brave, it was nothing as purposeful as that, but something in her voice, in her eyes, in the very way she sat at the table, spoke of a loneliness, a sorrow that until then had been dormant rather than realised, something that she had managed to keep conveniently hidden even from herself, because she had had strength enough until now to guard against it, something that she must now confront and struggle with, almost certainly for the very first time, in earnest. He knew she had a clear understanding of it, an undistorted view of her loneliness, that she was coming upon it with wisdom and without the terrible crushing melodramatic suddenness of the young; he knew too that in such a conflict she would eventually triumph, bringing to it her reserves of truth, tenacity and that prevailing perennial saviour of most human conflicts, common sense. Yet it was precisely that very quality of quiet intelligence that touched him more deeply than that quick hysteria which most usually comes to the rescue of the average woman in times of personal crisis, that merciful escape through the tear-ducts, never touching the more obscure, more enduring anguish of mind, that ultimate approximation of agony that only the truly intelligent, wise and faithful can encounter.

Laurie, more than any other woman he had yet known, had less of the child, less of the girl in her, and would therefore more slowly, more surely, more grievously suffer over a longer desert of time. She would not know that swift volcanic upheaval of pain and lacerated pride that wasted itself out in an orgy of despair, a brief bitter night of unbearable loss followed by the blessed dawn of self-appraisal that would end in welcome acceptance.

He knew he had entered and touched her life deeply, had impregnated her life as she had his own; he had in fact entered into her as surely as though they had known each other in the ultimate physical sense, through all the intimate intricacies of the body, and even as he now wondered at this knowledge he was helpless to understand it or her own wounding because of it. He could only look at her still from the same unyielding middle-distance that he was destined to occupy, could only look on at her hurt, her silent secret wounding, having no last solace to offer her, no tribute save that of eyes, no touch more comforting than that of thought stunted and benighted at its very inception. At the end of everything, there by that soaring window, above the ocean, above the crying of waves, they could only look at each other, like two unhappy strangers who had shared a certain short unscheduled journey together, without anything but the most ordinary words between them.

He felt as poor, as impoverished as any beggar, his mind as empty and bereft of comfort as the hands and pockets of the most destitute beggar under any sun, looking at her on the other side of the table, over the empty plates and the useless unwanted wine, seeing the shadow in her eyes, in her slow wise smile, that long shadow that had fallen on summer, now falling between them once more with the cunning stealth of treachery.

The waitress, returning with the brandy, gave respite to the intolerable sense of impending farewell that hovered almost tangibly between them. The girl set the bottle down with the air of a marathon runner grimly satisfied with having run the course between table and kitchen; he almost expected her to fold her arms in a stance of defiance and vindication, to smack her lips and snort 'Huh!' However, another customer beckoned her away.

As always, the brandy subdued the sharpness of things, softened the glare of the sinking sun, threw a warm veil over his mind, gave him that precious delusion of quiet safety; in his need it was the only enemy he could turn to and be sure of its blessed betrayal lulling him into serenity. Laurie paused, glass in hand.

'Let us drink just one toast, Riley,' she said, an absolute stillness enveloping her. 'Just one. What will it be?'

'You name it.'

Her face was remote, far away, as if listening to the waves far below in their ceaseless assault upon the rocks. She dreamily rubbed the smooth cherubic belly of the glass with her thumb, her eyes clearing with a certain light.

'To another summer, some time,' she said, raising the glass to her lips, 'without any shadow.'

Again, as they drank silently, ceremoniously, he felt more urgently the warm reassurance of the brandy, a hot tongue licking his guts, rather than any definite regretfulness which her words might have evoked in him. She put down her glass and laid her hand on the green folder.

'I'll write, if I may, later and tell you in greater detail what I think,' she said, extracting a thick sheaf of pages, 'but meanwhile let me glance through it. She groped in her hand-bag, found her owl-shaped bookish spectacles, and paused before she put them on. 'What will you do while I'm reading?'

He filled up his glass. 'Enjoy the company of my friend here,' he said, hearing the failed mockery in his voice, fondling the neck of the bottle, 'the happy genie in the bottle. Together we'll watch the sun go down.'

Laurie looked at him for a long moment, grave, uncertain, then she settled the spectacles on the bridge of her nose and started to read.

Abbie, unusually flushed, a daredevil look on her face, already slightly drunk, came back in the noisy meddlesome midst of her friends, who carried her forward into the room like a slight cork upon a swelling wave, spilling into the room, over-flowing into the corners, dismantling the wooden crates, suit-cases, sprawling and straddling on them, the cheap wine flowing, swallowed from the bottle, passed from hand to grasping hand, the midnight beaten like a bronzed gong with voices laughing, arguing, protesting, proclaiming, mangled lines of poetry flung from mouth to moistened mouth, hands waving, thumping the bare boards, gesticulating, a white blur of hands, reaching, clasping, searching, blunt fingers fondling firm feminine denim-clad thighs, a swarm of eyes, rolling, reeling, leering, lost, glazed with drink and tiredness, the sick sweetness of marijuana hanging like a miasma in the air, blur-ring faces, seeping into nostrils, grey scarves of oblivion floating, thinning, thickening, limbs splayed at broken angles, loose-jointed, arms, legs, torsos, faces, heads, disembodied, dislocated, comically dismantled like a doll factory in chaos, the juicy locking of lips in deadlock, the thin clash of teeth, necks waving, drooping like broken stems, brutal fumbling feet crushing her beloved melancholy records into sharp bitter black plastic smithereens.

A man's swarthy face, swimming near to his own, glistening with sweat, nostrils flapping in and out like wings, the breath of stale wine sweeping out of the mouth opening like an obscene orifice: 'You the writing guy, the poet? Abbie's little Wolfe.' A wild hyena hysterical womanly laugh at his own pernicious pun. 'Prisoner in the tower. Ivory, of course.' Again, the inane cackle. 'You gonna shake the world, man, huh? Let me shake the hand that's gonna shake the world.' A fat brown hand, reaching, snakes' heads gleaming on each hairy-jointed finger. 'Let me tell you something, scribe. I hate writers. They should all have their balls cut off. Nothing personal. I like balls myself, except literary ones.' The black gleaming head thrown back, bejewelled hand slapping thigh.

Abbie, looking at him with slain eyes, kneeling over the maimed carnage of her plastic bundle of memories, grinning, a reckless soldier facing the foe, letting her head sway back in avaricious hands, opening her mouth for the blasphemous offering, receding, swamped under a cloud, fading, a lonely echo taking her place.

'Poor Abbie,' A girl's silk-wormy lisp dripping into his captive ear, silver honeyed poison. 'So lost. Always was a sucker for lost causes, stray dogs, hunchbacks and the like.' Eyes with the menace of midnight in them, turning upon him, slim hard fingers digging into his shoulder. 'You the guy with the funny name? Your hand, sir. I am the nymph, Zita.' A high jerky hiccup unsuppressed by hand. 'Some would add maniac to nymph, especially bald men with imagination. I too boast an unusual name. Shake the hand of a brother in this sea of Madison nonentities.' Spiky fingers encircling his hand, pressing, a cold cemetery invitation in them. Zita stooping above, hair tumbling over bare shoulder, showing tips of full bosom crammed into velvet. A serpent gleam of a smile. 'Do writers really only perform between the covers of their books?'

In the boxroom was escape from the heat, the press of bodies, the terrible biting hail of talk, the strangulation of sense, animal mouths emitting screeching parodies of sound, Abbie's wild rebellious young face staring at him over the mashed remnants of her sad blues scattered on the floor, defiant in debasement, grinning ghoulishly, her beauty scarred, clawed at with jarring mouths and hands, hounded and harried into her hole of earth, scrabbling as fierce as any for the flimsy scraps of sustenance thrown her way. Abbie, already gone into yesterday, a lonely echo lingering behind the loud scream that shrouded her.

Abbie now, stumbling into the blank tomb-like room, silhouetted a moment in the yellow glare of the doorway, lurching forward, losing her shoe, falling on the narrow bunk-bed, kneeling, staring at him in the swirling dark, drowned face behind a cloud of hair, musk-rose and stale sweat, beeswax and rancid resin, lavender and leather, gone sour, soiled, used.

She opened her mouth, awkwardly, crookedly, like one fighting for breath or trying to pray. 'Kiddo—' A gurgling noise rose in her smooth white sloping throat. 'Kiddo—' A moment her eyes flared, defying the dark, twin points of flame, burning, out of all the waste that surrounded her, then her shoulders slumped forward, her hands fell, fingers losing their tenacious grip on the sheet, her body making a slight satiny sound as she slipped to the floor.

'Jasmine, baby, in here.'

The voice, silk-wormy, lisping, honey and silver, Zita's broad bare shoulders gleaming in the door, the smaller girl dwarfed beside her, swaying giddily, grabbing at the wide-hipped waist for anchorage. The serpent gleam of a smile flitting down at him huddled on the floor clutching a thick green folder.

'Well, we meet again, poet man.' A hand reaching down, roughly stroking Abbie's fallen head, the voice turning hoarse, coarse, mean. 'Mind if we join in the fun?' The second girl giggled. He looked up into that hard painted face with bright murder in his eyes.

It was hard to distinguish the child from the blaze of green sunlight behind her: Midge, in a little green swimsuit, a cluster of marigolds in her hand, stood under the trees in the front of the house, gravely unsmiling, a look of extreme polite greeting on her face, brown and freckled, her hair quite long now, more golden than he had known it, more than ever an enveloping aureole, casting her face almost in shade. Her strong young colt-like legs were deeply tanned, the shins showing scratches and faint blue bruises. Her bright little body seemed to merge magically into the sunshine that danced around her, her green bathing-suit into the shade of the trees.

'Hi,' she said presently, her intense blue eyes regarding him still with the same solemn stare as he sat on the top step of the porch. The child stood where she was, on the edge of the lawn, her toes tightening on the grass.

'Hello, Midge,' he said, laying aside the book he had not been reading, squinting his eyes down at her.

Very slowly, she came forward and sat on the bottom step, her swim-suit dusty from the walk up from the beach. 'I've been to Grandma's. She lives far away—' Midge looked up at him. 'You ever hear of Virginia?'

He nodded. 'Yes, I've heard of Virginia. Is it nice there?'

She considered for a moment. 'It's hot. Hotter than here. Hot and damp—what do you call it?—'

'Humid, I think,' he gently prompted.

She gave a brief smile of thanks. 'Yes, hot and humid. Daddy drove me and Richard up in one whole day. Richard was sick. He's not very strong,' Midge concluded with a sad shake of her head. 'I am. I'm just as strong as a boy—'

'And much prettier.'

'Yes,' said the child nonchalantly, accepting it more as a fact than a compliment, devoid of thin-skinned grown-up modesty. 'Grandma isn't old, really, not like the Grandmas in my nursery books. She wears pretty dresses, just like Mom, and rides around on a bike. She smells nice, too,' Midge added, no doubt thinking this a considerable grandmotherly asset. 'You weren't here when I got back,' she said next, with the sweet quicksilver turn of thought that belonged uniquely to childhood, sadly forfeited to maturity. She was not accusing, merely again stating a fact.

'No, Midge, I wasn't.' Then, knowing she wanted to know but would not ask if he did not want to tell her, he said; 'I went to stay with a friend for a while.'

'Oh,' she said, shaping her mouth to the sound. Then, again with that disconcerting forthrightness that only children and a very few adults possess, she looked up, shading her eyes with her free hand, and asked; 'Was it that beautiful lady who came here one day and took you away in her car?'

'Yes, Midge, the very lady.'

'She was beautiful, almost as pretty as Mom. Are you going to marry her?' she asked, lifting the flowers to her nose and taking a deep appreciative sniff. 'The beautiful lady?'

'No, Midge, I'm not going to marry anyone,' he said, smiling. 'And I'm much too old to ask you to marry me.'

'Maybe if I grew up in a hurry you might,' Midge speculated, not with any madcap hope or flippancy, but as if it was a distinct if mysterious possibility.

'Oh, then I would, I assure you.'

'Here,' she said suddenly, thrusting the tight little bunch of marigolds towards him. 'These are for you.'

He hesitated. 'Are you sure, Midge?'

'Don't you like them?' she asked, abruptly crestfallen, a tiny cloud passing over her face. 'They're my favourite flowers.'

Unbearably he saw that the precocious, level-headed self-possessed Midge was perilously on the edge of tears.

'I love them, Midge,' he said quickly, 'and because they're your favourites they are mine too. But do I deserve them?'

'Mom says you've finished writing your book,' said Midge, the cloud having passed as swiftly as it came.

'Well, yes, I have—'

'And that you're going back home in a few days?'

'Yes, Midge, I am—very shortly.' They were both silent, looking at one another. Then he reached forward and took the flowers, briefly touching her hot hand. 'Thank you for the marigolds, Midge. I'll put them in my room.' He bent his face to the flowers, feeling their cool delicious texture, their soft cooling flesh, their fresh newness-of-earth scent, and the day grew brighter, the summer more intolerable and intense in its closing.

'You won't be coming back, ever, will you?' the child asked, and he thought she was stating something rather than asking a question.

'I don't know, Midge, but—perhaps not.'

'That is very sad,' Midge said, turning over on her stomach, elbows resting on the step above her, chin cupped in hands, staring up at him.

'Most things are, Midge,' he said, seeing her face through the petals, 'but thank you for the flowers.'

'Yes,' said Midge, heaving quite a large thoughtful sigh, 'and flowers are not sad.'

'No, Midge,' he agreed, shutting his eyes, brushing the marigolds slowly against his face, 'flowers are never sad.'

'We'll be bringing out the book simultaneously,' Martin Ruislip had said, smiling and reaching for another grape, looking at its round succulent surface a moment before continuing, 'on both sides of the Atlantic. Almost certainly next spring.' He looked across at Riley, his face paternal and warm, deep friendly creases round his candid pale blue eyes, the sun glistening on his slightly balding head. 'The Simons and I have absolutely no doubt about this book, old boy, no doubt at all. You must come to London for the big day,' he went on, taking a neat bite of the grape, relishing it as he would a fine line of prose. 'It will be one of the larger events in the history of my firm—the first book launched you, this one will make you.'

They were again sitting on the lawn of the Emerson house, the day was as brilliant as before, if less intensely warm, and again they awaited the arrival of the Simons. The only concession Martin Ruislip would consider giving to the setting and the weather in which he found himself consisted in the absence of just one sartorial item, a tie; his suit was dark and immaculately tailored, his cufflinks gleamed, his trousers showed a sharp severe fold down the shinlengths and his shoes, black patent leather, shone briskly, yet without a tie he looked distinctly undressed, almost reckless, very nearly dishevelled, with his neck-band loose and open, exposing his lean tanned stringy throat, towards which his hand would stray from time to time stealthily, in a guilty, self-conscious manner, as though trying to conceal or at least apologise for something vaguely offensive. Riley smiled inwardly, reflecting on the moral strength it must have taken Martin to abandon his whole appearance; it would be the nearest he would ever approach to casualness in dress; in contrast, Riley felt almost naked in his t-shirt and shorts, which conversely constituted for him the essence of daring, the utmost endeavour to adapt to the ways of the native.

266

Martin, as he spoke, took careful sips of his drink, an iced daiquiri rum, occasionally mopping his face and forehead with a startlingly white handkerchief, match of the ubiquitous one peeping out of his breast pocket like the white snout of a rabbit. There was a glass bowl of many fruits on the garden table between them; grapes, plums, bananas, oranges, pears and apples, a gleaming silver ice-bucket, sliced lemons in another smaller bowl, bottles large and medium of brandy, rum, rye, gin, vodka and some with strange exotic labels which he could neither recognise nor pronounce. From the house came the subdued sound of the stereo system connected to speakers concealed in the branches of trees outside, playing quiet unobtrusive music, inconsequentially unidentifiable to his ears. He did not know the hour of the day, it did not matter; it was pleasant there in the garden, listening to Martin's quietly modulated voice talking so factually about the novel, the brandy spreading its familiar welcome warmth in him, the green shadows of the leaves playing upon the weatherworn timber surface of the table, upon Martin's benevolent countenance, feeling their coolness upon his own skin, a slight breeze from the shore tinged with salt, the languid twitter and wing-rustling of birds in the branches overhead, the sonorous slumbering of old Cricket curled up in a golden ball under a tree, its head resting protectively on one of Midge's toy teddy-bear dolls, ears lazily twitching at unseen gnats.

'I daresay you won't want to even think about writing for another year after this,' Martin remarked, fingers again roving about his throat.

'I don't know yet,' replied Riley. 'I might want to start another book at once when I get home, and it's also possible I won't ever write another one.'

Martin laughed discreetly, waved a deprecating hand. 'I doubt that very much, old boy,' he said, smoothing back his thin sandy shoreline of hair. 'I think you've already got ideas teeming inside you for several books to come, each on one scale or another. I think, for instance, it's inevitable—no, not inevitable, exactly—I don't like that word—let's say I think you will *want* to write about all that you've seen and felt and thought since you came here—New England, the city, the Village—' He coughed slightly behind his hand. 'Er—how did you enjoy your sojourn there, may I ask? I understand you spent something like a month or so there?'

'Yes,' Riley nodded. 'It was interesting.'

Martin hesitated before he again spoke, obviously trying to sound casual. 'You—er—saw quite a lot of—Miss Lang, is it?—while you were there, I believe—'

'We lived together,' Riley acknowledged quietly, picking up his glass.

Martin almost, but not quite, blushed, regaining his aplomb immediately and raising his glass in turn. 'That must have been quite pleasant,' he answered, eyes nearly twinkling. 'Delightful young lady, not at all what one has become conditioned to expect the average young American girl to be—brash, loud, dominant, a sort of walking transistor, blaring forth continuously with perfectly atrocious banalities. I liked her quite a lot —what's this lady's name?—Oh, yes, of course, Abbie. It seems to complement her personality, somehow.' Martin paused, delicately balancing the glass on his knee. 'Life is so full of these quite unexpected encounters. Shall you be seeing her before you leave for home? I don't wish to pry—'

'That's all right, Martin,' said Riley, sitting himself straighter in the chair, turning his face up to the greenness above him in the trees. 'I don't think we'll be seeing each other again.'

'Oh dear,' said Martin, lifting his trousers another inch or so above his ankles. 'That's rather a pity, isn't it? Still,' he added, as if happy to change the subject, 'you know best.' He sounded for a moment like a parent proud of his offspring's wisdom in a difficult matter. He smiled in a way that on another man's face would have been positively roguish, but with him merely signified a measure of self-confidence. 'One is continually gathering copy, isn't one, even when we don't particularly wish to, or when the process is too painful for words. I daresay it will all find itself into a book some day.' And, as if in anticipation of that hypothetical event, Martin raised his drink in an odd ceremonious gesture, dipping it slightly in Riley's direction, and again he seemed to discern in it an absurd tribute to his imagined sagacity in a clouded hour.

He looked at Martin sitting facing him, beginning to be comfortably plump and middle-aged, urbane, genial, fluent, in full possession of himself, satisfied with the past, in control of

268

the present, busily optimistic about the future; he could visualise Martin's life, concise, orderly, uncluttered by mistakes of heart or mind, a long unwinding neatly swept road along which he had sauntered imperturbably, brushing specks of dust from his immaculate sleeve, certain of his allegiances, his trim loyalties, avoiding excesses of whatever kind, a refined epicurean pursuing his measured ambitions with, perhaps, a secret resolve to retire to a country garden and spend all the rest of his afternoons browsing through his life's collection of old soft-leathered vellum volumes, welcoming the undemanding company of others but quite content with his own at all times.

And again he saw Abbie's face, contorted with conflict, oddly haunted, uselessly defiant and fierce, her fresh beauty already tainted, torn, smeared and scarred by a life that should only have been beginning, her eyes asking him a thousand unanswerable questions, bitter, resigned, full of perplexed pain, groping like a blind thing, opening herself up to people, going from one to the other, looking for the key they might hold that would unlock her and set her free to contemplate the uniqueness and wonder of herself.

He resented his friend Martin at that moment, not because he might be complacent and unmindful of the darker possibilities of life, but because for him, and for such as he, these things existed only in the troubled imagination, as if everything led back to that, as if the only authenticity and purpose of pain was that it should all be written down faithfully and put between the pages of a book, as if one lived solely that the past should ceaselessly regurgitate itself, throw up again the experiences, encounters, the long list of lesser dyings through which one had lived, solely to return to the salient point in time when it must all be committed to paper, when every stab of jealousy, every thrust of desire, every earnest prayer and malediction, every raw moment of love and loss must be analysed, dissected, probed at industriously with the scalpel of hindsight, all neatly sewn together and wrapped up in sealing-wax to be delivered to the unheeding world at large. Was it for this that Abbie must suffer, and Laurie bear her obscure pain, and himself go futilely on through the tortuous maze of his life in search of something he could not remotely name? He could not imagine a more profane waste of life, a more odious and contemptible prostitution of living than this merchandise in the dreams and fears that made up the fabric of a single life and set it uniquely aside and singular from any other. He was aware then of a sharp sickness in him that he had allowed himself to commit exactly what he now thought the meanest act of treachery and self-indulgence, a prodigious gesture of conceit.

Martin was regarding him closely, a shrewd look of suspicion on his bland glistening countenance. 'May I put forward the supposition that right now you're thinking that writing is a bloody awful business?' he surmised with his usual delightful, slightly sardonic formality. 'Might I also hazard a guess that right now you're vowing to yourself never to write another damn book?'

Riley studied the drink in his hand. 'I was more or less thinking along these lines, yes.'

Martin chuckled, sipping his drink with curtailed relish. 'Fortunately, that feeling won't last,' he said confidently. 'I may strike you as being pretty much black and white, you may have already put me into my respective slot, and it could possibly be the right one—I'd be the last to deny that I'm pretty stereo-typed. However, I haven't lived all this time without learning one or two things about people, and since writers are usually the sort of people I've dealt with most, they are the people I might claim to understand most.' Martin pushed his wicker chair further into the shade. 'I can't tell you how often writers have told me they'll never write another book—not because they can't, not because they may have dried up and run out of ideas, not because of that, but simply because they basically distrust and resent the very idea of writing—no matter how well they may write, they resent their own compulsion to write, to set everything down on paper, when most of them would much rather be otherwise engaged—exactly as I am now,' again mopping the back of his neck and brow with the hand-kerchief, 'sitting in a charming garden close to the sea, a cool drink in my hand, good food ready to be eaten, and nothing to do except hand out fatuous advice to dissatisfied young authors.' He raised his glass in salute. 'Long may you writhe in the throes of creativity, old chap.'

Riley was again impressed by the perception of the man, his

shrewdness of character, the ease with which he could arrive at deductions that were invariably the correct ones, all this hidden under his bland manners and relaxed smile, his firm polite handshake. Looking over at him, Riley wondered just how wrongly he might have summarised him, how glibly he had rubberstamped the tenor of Martin's existence, thinking it dry, unattached, unruffled by any excess, free of perilous decisions, moving smoothly as a quiet stream on a straight set course. It would be quite an achievement, he thought wryly, to put Martin Ruislip between the covers of a book: it would be tantamount to attempting to put a particularly erudite eel into a minute straitjacket. Martin did not divulge himself to others, not because he was in any way morbid about his privacy; he simply preferred to let other people do the guessing, only occasionally revealing himself behind the bland smile and courteous handshake, showing himself as someone who might know more than most the hidden complexities of life, the toll of living from one day to the next, the price exacted for that privilege.

And yet he could only cling to what he was feeling now, he could only relate to that, to what weighed like a certain conviction upon him, and the thought of spending another long stretch of his life hunched in futile fury over the typewriter, trying to wrench something valid and definite from the inchoate mess of himself, was repugnant to him in the first heady freedom of release from that precise devouring labour. He wanted to know life again without the insane urge to interpret or transpose it, he would bleed if need be and observe the colour of the blood, taste the salt of it between his lips, savour it with a bright bitter intent, without committing the felt moment to paper, without indulging that sad ultimate folly, without yielding to that conceit. He would meet life again with glorious illiteracy, he would let it pamper and pummel his mind and flesh in an excess of total surrender, and not taint it with that slyness of thought which crept over everything with such horrible stealth, ferreting out the stuff of things, nosing its way into the secret places of experience coldly, plucking the warm flesh and fur from the living object, measuring the heart of things, the pulse, rendering it joyless, dry-skinned, brittle, murdering the very moment at which the quality of life should shatter his mind into a thousand brilliant bits.

He would feel grass again, crush it between his fingers, lick it with his tongue, he would walk blind and happy into the rain, let it tear at him, whip his pores into shrill response, he would eat and drink the wind in great gulping mouthfuls, let the sun blister him and the cold numb him utterly, he would be mad again for the taste of smoke and leaves, for the impersonal smoothness of glass, the safe turbulent feel of wood, the many-storied surface of old brocade, he would enter a room again as a child, his heart ready for surprises, ready to be hurt with small unexpected joys, he would reach out his fingers and touch things like a blind man, exulting in the merest touch, the lovely fire of life whipping through him, he would listen in perfect ecstatic stillness to young birds making the morning grow, catch again the ineffable alarm of spring in the opening of a petal, watch a young girl's face in repose lying in the deep canal-side grass, innocently, with no thought other than to watch her dreaming her dreams. . . . All this, and more, infinitely more, he would do, without the scourge to recreate, to model and imitate, without the feverish endeavour to spread-eagle these images upon the typewriter, more imperative than sexuality, more heedless to reason and restraint; all this, and more, he would fill his days with like the blown petals of roses, and he would ask no questions, nor search beneath the known surface of things, nor counterfeit the daily gifts of life with the camouflage and false coinage of written language, the great idleness that had engulfed him for such a long time, that impotence of adventure that kept him captive over a thing of iron when the sun and the rain and the wind were there to be tasted.

Martin was talking, had been talking with an animation rare in him, the rum going eloquently back and forth to his mouth, the sun striking the glass, making bright swathes in the air, but something strange was happening: Riley, staring quite earnestly at his friend, did not hear a word he was saying. He did not hear anything, the garden was utterly still, the birds might all have dropped dead, he saw the branches move in the breeze, noiselessly, silent as the movements of clouds far beyond the capture of sight. Midge came up the path, fresh and shining from the sea, again with the lovely promise of marigolds in her hand, for him, yes, for him, and she spoke kindly, he could tell by her eyes, the deep compassionate kindness in her eyes, but she too had no voice, no sound for his ears. It was a whole green slow-stirring silent world, in which only his mind swayed.

Laurie, too, was saying things, sitting at the table in the cool timber restaurant above the ocean, the heaped typed pages before her, the last page staring nakedly up at him. He watched curiously her face as she spoke, the changing weather in her eyes, the soft expressive movement of her hands pointing again and again down to the manuscript on the table, her fingers forever graceful, intertwining, hands clasping together, spreading themselves out on the manuscript, tapping certain pages, making a point, rummaging in her purse for a biro, scribbling notes in the margins, head bent busily, looking up at him to see if he understood her point, if he approved . . .

He covered his face in his hands, and the only audible thing in the whole deafmute world was the waves far below, singing without hindrance, without the terrible intrusion of a human voice, waving him away from the table of effete etiquette, away from learned dissertation, from white shirtfronts and nautical caps, from the coiffured heads of women delicately removing white gloves, from fat-bellied men in carnival shorts and rum cocktails in bejewelled hands chewing unlit cigars, waving him away from Abbie with her stricken face and eyes deeply haunted in the awful screech of pleasure, away from the sand-pebble world of Midge, egg-shell path and ways of marigold, the bright clean morning that was uniquely Midge and would stay as such in his remembrance whatever portents the waves might hold in their ceaseless eloquence . . .

He was vilely sick in his stomach, trembling violently, as though all the vineyards in the world had poured their brandy down his throat while he lay sleeping; yet there was paradoxically a great healing sense of relief in him, of good will, a welcome feeling of famine. He felt emptied of everything, dispossessed, no longer in need of a star to burn under, no longer needing to strive towards a certain immutable point in his life where a certain ending, a certain conclusion might be attained.

He thought with almost the nervous elation of anticipated love when he could slip into the primordial stillness of himself without explanation, without painful remorse for the puzzled hurt of others, when he could confront the confusion and grotesque contradictions of himself quietly, without raising his voice, without recriminations, return to the priceless sanity of lonely hours watching the antics of sparrows dusting themselves in places where there was a hunger of grass.

He would never again enter a room with a typewriter in it, he would never again endure the self-mortification that passed for literary heat. If he had to have dreams, if he had to speak his dreams, it would not be to any printing machine, it would not be to any brave forgiving woman, no, he would sell his dreams and his nightmares to the mad wind scudding over his scarecrow mind, to the working man's friends, the dogs and sparrows, the horses tethered to the stupid hands of men, the swans who graced the filthy canals with their sad proud loveliness. He would offer his dreams to these gentle people at a cheap price, his nightmares costing slightly more.

Already it was yesterday, the sunlight no longer danced upon the water, a mist was rising over the sea, a familiar mist with soft rain and smelling of green moss and the clean dung of animals, and Laurie still spoke, tapping her manicured forefinger repeatedly on his heaped script, the last page staring nakedly up at him, but she was already belonging to the silence that shrouded everything, and he looked at her face, her austerely beautiful face, and her eyes that held the shadow that had lengthened in the last days.

He looked down, drinking the last amber drops in the glass, seeing the absurdly short word at the bottom of the page, that elusive pygmy of a word that said something only then beginning to grow meaningful.

END

*Also by Christy Brown
available in Minerva*

My Left Foot

The warm, humorous and true story of Christy Brown's supreme courage and triumph over the severest of handicaps.

Christy Brown was born a victim of cerebral palsy. But the helpless, lolling baby concealed the brilliantly imaginative and sensitive mind of a writer who would take his place among the giants of Irish literature.

This is Christy Brown's own story. He recounts his childhood struggle to learn to read, write, paint and finally type, with the toe of his left foot. In this manner he wrote his bestseller *Down All the Days*.

My Left Foot is now a major and critically acclaimed film starring Daniel Day Lewis as Christy Brown.

Down all the Days

The triumphant novel of the slums of Dublin

Pushed around the streets of Dublin by his boisterous brothers, the small crippled occupant of a boxcar is the silent witness of the city's joys and woes. Fully possessed of the thoughts and feelings of his sprawling family, he is the focal figure of the novel which relates his searing childhood and coming of age. At once tormented and relaxed, he is the detached observer of life in the slums of forties and fifties Dublin.

Written with the fearless discipline that Christy Brown had to establish over his own body, *Down all the Days* displays his lyrical gift with language to the full.

'Will surely stand beside Joyce and in front of all the others as Dublin writ large and writ for all times' *Irish Times*

'Deserves the highest critical acclaim, not because it was written with one foot but because it is the work of a real writer who just happens to be handicapped' *Daily Telegraph*

Wild Grow the Lilies

The laughing drains of Dublin

Fond of the girls at Madame Lala's, eloquent reporter Luke Sheridan is fonder still of the sound of his own voice. Bursting with purple prose and ribald repartee, he even dreams of writing *the* Great Irish Novel.

But work comes first – especially when Dublin's evening newspaper is tipped off about the attempted murder of a German count. Going after the scoop of the year, Luke is helplessly and hilariously mixed up in the most wildly flamboyant goose chase that ever crossed the fair city's underbelly.

Wild Grow the Lilies, lively, fluent and derivative . . . is a grossly entertaining novel' *Times Literary Supplement*

'Christy Brown has an extraordinary gift for vivid language and imagery' *The Times*

'Christy's romp is thoroughly enjoyable . . . It is wildly funny, bawdy and vulgar and the writing, whether sonorous or broad Dublin, is a delight' Catherine O Faolain, *Irish Press*

A Promising Career

The fickle world of show biz

Married at seventeen, Art and Janice have more than their love to sustain a partnership – their talent. For both show considerable promise as musicians, as charismatic agent, Simon Sandford, is quick to observe. Under his tutelage, the young couple begin to flourish in the labyrinthine ambit of gigs, tours and recording sessions.

Yet success only seems to accentuate their differences. And Sandford, a seasoned manipulator of this corrupt and exploitative world, has his own wedge to drive . . .

Christy Brown finished *A Promising Career* shortly before his tragic death in 1981. A departure from his astonishing autobiography – and unforgettable film – *My Left Foot*, and also from his native Ireland, it is perhaps his most mature and imaginative novel.

Collected Poems

"Here was a man," as Frank Delaney quite rightly declares, "who had the true writer's gifts." Christy Brown's first collection of poems, *Come Softly to My Wake*, was published to widespread acclaim. He went on to publish two more, *Background Music* and *Of Snails and Skylarks*, before his tragic death in 1981. In paperback for the first time, this *Collected Poems* incorporates all three volumes in a single edition.

'His verse, like his prose, is masculine, direct, unsophisticated and, above all, "a good read"'
Times Literary Supplement

'There is real talent here . . . a freshness of attack, a liveliness, energy and passion that remind one of Dylan Thomas'
Yorkshire Post

'Almost everything Christy Brown has written has the unique appeal of a writer whose primary concern is complete emotional honesty . . . All the time one senses behind the poems a creator whose delight in words is equalled only by his passionate candour of expression'
Sunday Independent

'Vigorous and sensual . . . of his sincerity and passionate commitment to language there is never any doubt'
The Times

A Selected List of Titles Available from Minerva

While every effort is made to keep prices low, it is sometimes necessary to increase prices at short notice. Mandarin Paperbacks reserves the right to show new retail prices on covers which may differ from those previously advertised in the text or elsewhere.

The prices shown below were correct at the time of going to press.

Fiction
☐	7493 9026 3	**I Pass Like Night**	Jonathan Ames	£3.99 BX
☐	7493 9006 9	**The Tidewater Tales**	John Bath	£4.99 BX
☐	7493 9004 2	**A Casual Brutality**	Neil Blessondath	£4.50 BX
☐	7493 9028 2	**Interior**	Justin Cartwright	£3.99 BC
☐	7493 9002 6	**No Telephone to Heaven**	Michelle Cliff	£3.99 BX
☐	7493 9028 X	**Not Not While the Giro**	James Kelman	£4.50 BX
☐	7493 9011 5	**Parable of the Blind**	Gert Hofmann	£3.99 BC
☐	7493 9010 7	**The Inventor**	Jakov Lind	£3.99 BC
☐	7493 9003 4	**Fall of the Imam**	Nawal El Saadewi	£3.99 BC

Non-Fiction
☐	7493 9012 3	**Days in the Life**	Jonathon Green	£4.99 BC
☐	7493 9019 0	**In Search of J D Salinger**	Ian Hamilton	£4.99 BX
☐	7493 9023 9	**Stealing from a Deep Place**	Brian Hall	£3.99 BX
☐	7493 9005 0	**The Orton Diaries**	John Lahr	£5.99 BC
☐	7493 9014 X	**Nora**	Brenda Maddox	£6.99 BC

All these books are available at your bookshop or newsagent, or can be ordered direct from the publisher. Just tick the titles you want and fill in the form below. Available in:
BX: British Commonwealth excluding Canada
BC: British Commonwealth including Canada

Mandarin Paperbacks, Cash Sales Department, PO Box 11, Falmouth, Cornwall TR10 9EN.

Please send cheque or postal order, no currency, for purchase price quoted and allow the following for postage and packing:

UK	80p for the first book, 20p for each additional book ordered to a maximum charge of £2.00.
BFPO	80p for the first book, 20p for each additional book.
Overseas including Eire	£1.50 for the first book, £1.00 for the second and 30p for each additional book thereafter.

NAME (Block letters) ....

ADDRESS ....

....

....